Technology and the Environment in State-Socialist Hungary

Viktor Pál

Technology and the Environment in State-Socialist Hungary

An Economic History

palgrave
macmillan

Viktor Pál
University of Helsinki
Helsinki, Finland

ISBN 978-3-319-63831-7 ISBN 978-3-319-63832-4 (eBook)
DOI 10.1007/978-3-319-63832-4

Library of Congress Control Number: 2017948702

Cover credit: Photo: FORTEPAN/MORVAY KINGA

Printed on acid-free paper

This Palgrave Macmillan imprint is published by Springer Nature
The registered company is Springer International Publishing AG
The registered company address is: Gewerbestrasse 11, 6330 Cham, Switzerland

To Patrícia and Szilvia

Acknowledgements

I am grateful for the many people and institutions who have helped me to carry on and complete this work. Without my supervisors this work could not have been finished. Dr. Petri Juuti, Prof. Pertti Haapala at the University of Tampere and external adviser Prof. Ivan T. Berend at UCLA supported me with constructive criticism and kind generosity. My colleagues at the University of Tampere, UCLA, University of Tallinn, University of Antwerp, WU Vienna University of Economics and Business, New Europe College in Bucharest, and in the Network for the Environmental History of Dictatorships and later in the Interdisciplinary Hub for the Study of the Environment and Authoritarian Regimes supported me with comments and encouragement.

I also wish to thank various institutions and individuals for their moral and financial support. My parents and grandparents. The University of Miskolc and the University of Tampere were outstanding alma maters. The City of Miskolc, the State of Finland, the Center for International Mobility in Finland, the Academy of Finland, the Finnish Academy of Sciences, the Niilo Helander Foundation, the Maa- ja Vesitekniikan Tuki ry, the Department of History at the University of

California Los Angeles, the Rector of the University of Tampere, the Open Society Archives in Budapest and the Visegrad Fund, the City of Helsinki, the Flemish Community of Belgium and the Center for Urban History at the University of Antwerp, the Eesti Institute, the Estonian Institute for the Environment at the University of Tallinn (KAJAK), Professor Ulrike Plath, the staff and students of the Social Anthropology program at the Comenius University in Bratislava, the Republic of Slovakia and its scholarship program, the Scholarship of the Republic of Austria and the New Europe College in Romania all contributed to my dissertation project on which this booked is based. Most importantly I thank my family, Szilvia Szatmári and Patrícia Pál for supporting me while I worked on this book.

Contents

List of Figures

1
Introduction

In 1982 the Hungarian State Television broadcasted District 78 (A 78-as körzet) a six-episode satirical comedy series. Notable actors Ila Schütz and István Sztankay played main roles.[1] The series was filmed and placed in one of the neighborhoods of Rákospalota, a Budapest suburb. District 78 was dominated by turn-of-the-century workers' housing and inhabited by about 300 blue-collar residents. According to the plot, former chair of the district residential committee moves out of town and locals elect Mrs Ilonka Molnár to be the new district chair. Ilonka is an energetic person who believes in communist ideals of social justice, gender equality and environmental protection. In the closing episode of the series "Victory" (Győzelem), locals are confronted with an environmental issue. Due to the construction of an urban section of the M3 freeway party officials order districts along the motorway to be revamped. Houses shall be repainted, worthless tree lines in locals streets shall be replaced with high-quality species. Residents find the plan of central authorities upsetting, especially because officials did not consult residents about the district's real needs, such as low standards of sanitation. When Ilonka is summoned to the council she fears the worst from the local strongman, the council's technocratic chairman. Ilonka

V. Pál, *Technology and the Environment in State-Socialist Hungary*,
DOI 10.1007/978-3-319-63832-4_1

expresses her outrage and fiercefully defends the local old trees. The council chairman reveals that decision has been already made in higher places and a grabber is just about to begin clear-cutting the district's trees. Ilonka rushes back to the district, where residents manage to halt works temporarily by offering the grabber driver a bottle of hard liquor which he consumes with the local drunkard. The council chairman leaves the awkward scene in fury and swears to return with reinforcement to cut all the trees off. Frontlines freeze temporarily and residents organize a 24/7 tree watch to protect their bellowed treelines. They also sabotage felling works in every possible way. Ilonka announces that a world war bomb is found in a nearby lot, hence all works must be halted. The local Catholic church organizes a procession and open air worship on site which prevents the grabber to work. The local school organizes research activities on the history of local trees to raise environmental awareness among residents. Lastly, the village belle manages to persuade the grabber driver to sabotage the works. The council chairman is not willing to swallow the bitter pill, and he organizes a complete brigade for the clearcutting project. Thanks to an informer, residents learn that by 6 am the following morning ten workers will be transported to the district. To stop the felling, locals organize a mass sit-in on the trees. District 78 closes with a hilarious scene when local pensioners and families, the local policeman, and priest sit comfortably in their seats on top of the trees and the council chairman hysterically runs from tree to tree to beg and then blackmail residents to stop exercising their right to protest.

Communism is often viewed as a counterpart of capitalism, a contradictory economic system, and ideology. However, the communism that dominated state socialist countries in East-Central Europe had at least two contradictory faces. First, there was the universal ideology of communism. A human and nature centered ideology that aimed to provide better working conditions, healthy housing, good health care, sufficient leisure time, free or nearly free culture and transport, and finally aesthetic and healthy natural environment for all of its citizens. By providing these facilities and environment, communism would prove its superiority over capitalism. On the level of economic reality, these beautiful ideals matter sometimes little. The one-party systems of Eastern

Europe were equally addicted to economic growth and fossil fuels after World War II than industrialized capitalist countries.

Environmental/economic comparisons between state socialist and capitalist countries did not bring the desired results in my view because authors often compared these systems on the economic-technological level. Very few of these comparisons pointed out the impact of the major ideological difference between communism and capitalism when it came to the environment. Communism took pride to emphasize the protection of worker's interests over capitalists', hence the protection of nature was a bold initiative that was sponsored, supported, and orchestrated by communist governments. Hungary was one of the most extreme cases in this respect. Here, decades-long state orchestrated environmentalism completely changed the society–nature relationship by the 1980s. A large volume of works covered the environmental activism of the 1980s in Eastern Europe. The Danube Circle (Duna Kör) and the mass protests against the Gabčikovo-Nagymaros Barrage System mesmerized journalists and social scientists. Fresh civic energy and environmentalism of the entire society were in stark contradiction with the aging, out-of-touch leadership of the communist party. Also, civic environmentalism seemed to spring up from nowhere. Not having a better answer to the origin of these protests, scholars theorized that the natural environment was a tool in the hands of civic society via the communist establishment could be criticized openly. When civic protests targeted environmental conditions, in reality they protested against the government. Most scholars, with the notable exception of Stephen Brain and Zsuzsa Gille, denounced the communist state's role in the nurture and growth of environmentalism in Eastern Europe. This book is about how the state–nature relationship changed in Hungary during the years of the communist regime, and especially under the post-Stalinist period that is referred in scholarship as the Kádár or state–socialist era between 1956 and 1989. This book investigates the state's attitude toward nature and the state's role in the "pre-history" of environmental movements in Hungary. It also places that state-nature interaction into comparative European context to point out the pivotal role of Western influences, when it comes to society–nature relationships.

This book opens by describing and analyzing the broad economic, technological and environmental context in Europe and the Habsburg Empire prior to World War I. Further on it describes the economic, technological and environmental changes in Europe and in Hungary between the two World Wars. It explains the creation of environmental problems on a general level in Western Europe and in Hungary between 1850 and 1950. Industrialization was already quasi centrally commanded in the second half of the 1930s in Hungary. This was similar to several other East-Central European cases and was influenced by the Italian corporatist and Nazi German examples. On the margin, the Soviet influence is to be traced. Plan economy took a great leap forward parallel with the Sovietization of Hungary. The 1950s were dominated by the extensive Soviet model. This period is well recorded in economic history and the history of technology, however little is known about the environmental impact of extensive development patterns and their consequences.

When analyzing environmental problems in Hungary, I concentrate on the Borsodi Basin industrial area in the Northeastern part of the country. Borsod-Abaúj-Zemplén is water scarce county, home of 820,000 residents in 1980 and the largest concentration of industries in Hungary after Budapest.[2] In 1984, Borsod employed 9.4% of the national industrial workforce, the country's largest industrial district, Budapest, provided work for 29% of the industrial workforce.[3] After World War II Borsod was a model for communist industrial development, often labelled as the Ruhr of Hungary. It rapidly developed the environmental issues scholarship identifies with industrial development and urbanization. Because of its scarce resources, predominantly heavy industrial economy, lack of light industry and services, predominantly proletarian population, and lack of intelligentsia, Borsod provides an excellent laboratory to model the visions, tactics and outcomes of state sponsored environmentalism.

After 1950, a Stalinist industrial development triggered production in East-Central Europe. Industrialization and urbanization came with the universal environmental price tag. In the Borsodi Basin, especially on the Miskolc-Kazincbarcika-Ózd axis. Water supply and water pollution problems grew rapidly and were similar to the environmental issues of any other industrial district in Europe. Similarly, to West Europe, the rise of pollution induced an economic-technological-environmental discourse in East-Central Europe. Environmental problems were noticed and acknowledged promptly by the communist governments. Environmental pollution was unaccepted and not to be tolerated on an ideological level. Based on the ideological motivation of communism, environmental problems had to be and were tackled rapidly. In the world of communist planners and managers, environmental pollution intertwined with a much more important problem of production and profitability. Every cubic meter of water wasted and every ton of coal not efficiently used was a nightmare for communist planners. To reach a higher degree efficiency evolved to be monomania in the planning and industrial organization sector. The Neverland of efficient production and profitability was the ultimate goal, never to be reached. However, every step counted on the way. Economical measures introduced in industrial production indeed had a significant, coincided and positive environmental impact throughout the 1960s in East Central Europe. Without the economical measures during the period of the *economical shift*, environmental pollution and destruction would have been much more disastrous than actually it was. In the period of the *economical shift* in Hungary, roughly the 1960–1970s, the state-socialist regime successfully increased water recycling and decreased energy and material use per production ton. The *economical shift* also relied on new, cleaner fossil fuels. Soviet natural gas and crude oil cheaply acquired enabled East-Central European countries to switch entire industries and cities from the use of coal to the use of natural gas by the end of the 1960s. This *energy shift* unfolded within the framework of the *economical shift* and had pivotal consequence in coal poor and energy hungry Hungary.

After the oil crisis of 1973, Western Europe, despite falling behind globally in innovation, could maintain growth on a moderate level. That modest growth was accompanied with mending environmental performance and a shift to a post-industrial economy. After 1980, environmental quality continuously improved in some of the worst affected regions in Western Europe. Hungary, Yugoslavia and other East-Central European countries aimed to follow international economic trends by restructuring their investments. These projects generally failed, however with notable exceptions, but in general the promise to adjust to new global circumstances decreased every year. By the early 1980s, Hungary and Poland maintained living standards by the help of foreign loans and failed behind in innovation. Both nations joined the International Monetary Fund and the World Bank to access new financial sources.

In the 1970s and early 1980s industry still received priority in investments in East-Central Europe. State-socialist countries first stagnated, later declined in economic output. Worsening economic and technological circumstances had direct negative impact on environmental quality. Pollution problems, which stagnated and decreased in Western Europe, reached new heights in Eastern Europe in the 1980s. Environmental pollution issues of ECE countries that were confined to some of the worst affected areas in the 1960s, became visible nationally in the coming decades. Lacking the necessary basis of innovation and economic/technological tools the state-socialist regime was unable to battle with its self-inflicted environmental degradation.

Worsening environmental conditions were contradictory to the ideological basis and promise of communism, in which nature fulfilled a symbolic and protected role to provide relaxing and healthy environmental conditions for workers. From the end of the 1960s, stricter environmental protection efforts were employed in industrial plants. Such economic-technological measures had a varying degree of success. The state-socialist establishment did not have the required economic sources and level of technological know-how to make the technology fix driven environmental protection successful. When environmental pollution problems grew, something had to be done about it. The one-party state tackled its environmental crisis with the tool it mastered the best: sweeping propaganda. As opposed to the economic-technological solutions, state sponsored environmental protection propaganda grew into a massive success in Hungary in the 1970s and 1980s. Central authorities controlled information flow and had been orchestrating Cold War propaganda for decades. Hence, the instrumentalization of mass environmental protection propaganda did not pose major difficulties for central authorities. The state in Hungary employed a complex set of tools to increase environmental awareness on the industrial level and in the society as a whole. Tens of thousands of newspaper and journal articles, radio programs, TV newscasts and television programs raised environmental awareness in the Hungarian society in the 1970s and 1980s. The extremely high environmental consciousness levels of the residents of District 78 were the televised manifestation of the state initiated and sponsored *environmental shift* in state-socialist Hungary. By the early 1980s, the natural environment meant a great importance to East-Central Europeans. Residents possessed a very high level of environmental consciousness. A significant underlying cause was that they had been continuously targeted with environmentalist propaganda and were encouraged by the state to express their concerns about environmental protection. The imaginary case of District 78 was not a sole standing example in East-Central Europe, thousands of local communities which battled with pollution could tell their stories similar to District 78. The victory of the District 78 residents over the technocrats of the central bureaucracy was in fact communism's symbolic victory over the capitalist mindset. There is nothing more powerful than the voice of the people.

This book argues that the state sponsored *environmental shift* directly fed the ecological turn that unfolded in Hungary in the late 1980s. The nationwide very high environmental consciousness levels was a prerequisite for the ecological turn of the late 1980s. It is argued that environmental consciousness did not grow by itself during the 1960–1980s in societies of East-Central Europe. Rather it was initiated, nurtured and controlled by the systematic and throughout propaganda machine of the state-socialist one party state. This book analyses how the state sponsored *economical shift* and *environmental shift* built up high levels of environmental consciousness and a dense and multilayered environmental discourse by the 1970s and 1980s. It was a cynical backslash of history that the centrally orchestrated and manipulated environmental discourse slipped out of hand of the communists and grew into one of the most important grassroots issues of the opposition movement.

The ecological turn in East Central Europe and the USSR has many interested social scientists and historians. During the 1980s several researchers labeled the environmental policy of communism as exploitative and rapacious.[4] Many of these views were biased and the collapse of the Soviet Union unleashed one-sided scholarly analysis. Victory hymns of capitalism over communism mushroomed in the early 1990s. When it came to environmentalism: communism was a total failure, a disaster, a dead-end-street in history according to several scholars. The liberal capitalism of individual freedom and prosperity triumphed.[5] Environmental history slowly entered the mainstream in the last decade with interest from major academic publishers. Sadly, one sided works are still produced in large numbers. Authors of the 2013 *An Environmental History of Russia* used a meager supply of primary sources and reproduced the black and white, Cold War misconceptions.[6] The case of *An Environmental History of Russia* refers to a wider problem. Systematic archival research and has been painfully lacking in a large volume of works produced on this subject. The ecocide interpretation of the environmental history of communism is understandable in the light of environmental catastrophes, such as the tragedy in Chernobyl and the unacceptable way in which the Soviet Union handled many of its environmental problems. With such skeletons in the closet, it is a challenging task to provide a balanced account on the environmental history of communism.

Alternative views of the prevailing "communism is bad—capitalism is good" picture, however, have existed for a long time. In 1966, the Council of Europe acknowledged the environmental and especially water protection efforts of East-Central European regimes in a policy report published by the Council of Europe on Fresh Water Pollution Control problems.[7] In 1972, Marshall I. Goldman acknowledged the Soviet efforts in the development of water supply and sewage facilities.[8] In 1976 Fred Singleton and Craig ZumBrunnen also acknowledged state socialist environmental efforts: "There are signs that Soviet leaders are aware of the dangers. Laws are passed to regulate environmental misuse, but they are frequently evaded."[9] Mildred Turnbull stated that Soviet journals began to publish environmentally related articles more frequently from the late 1970s.[10] According to György Enyedi and Viktória Szirmai, environmental questions were open to some extent in Hungary under communism, and environmental arguments reached a "limited assertion" in the 1970–1980s in Janos Kádár's regime.[11]

In his 1998 study, Raymond Dominick called for the re-assessment of environmental history under the Cold War. Dominick recalled that in the decades following World War II, economic development received priority in both West and East Germany. Therefore, between 1949 and 1969, both the capitalist West and communist East witnessed continuing environmental deterioration.[12] According to Dominick environmental damage was substantial in both East Germany and West Germany, but it was notably more severe in the West during the 1950s and 1960s. During the following two decades, this trend changed and the West began to tighten environmental policy. In 1999 Douglas Weiner focused on the history of Russian nature protection from Stalin to Gorbachev and concluded that the achievements were notable considering the circumstances.[13] Weiner's work was one of the first scholarly monographs based on extensive archival research and hence his findings were more accurate and balanced than perhaps any scholars prior to his publication. In *Environmental Transformations,* Petr Pavlínek and John Pickles claimed that environmental degradation already became serious in the late 1950s and early 1960s in East-Central European countries. As a reaction to growing environmental pollution, there was a rapid introduction of environmental policies to limit environmental damage caused by industrial and agricultural production. Pavlínek and Pickles stated that despite a common belief and wide array of literature to the opposite, East-Central European governments actually did react to environmental problems with a number of anti-pollution measures and policies from as early as the 1960s. Pavlínek and Pickles assessed that among these policy instruments, some of the measures were "effective and some were not".[14] Pavlínek and Pickles noted that when economic stagnation and later crises hit East-Central Europe in the 1970s and 1980s, "centrally planned economies could not successfully adjust to the new global circumstances" and adopted "supply side" policies that have a negative impact on the environment.[15] In her monograph *From the Cult of Waste to the Trash Heap of History*, published in 2007, Zsuzsa Gille examined waste management practices in Hungary during and after communism by exploring a significant chemical waste disposal site near the village of Garé situated in the southern part of the country.[16] Gille initially was influenced by the negative and schematic presentation of waste management of communism in US media around the time of the collapse of the Soviet bloc. According to Gille, the production of tetra chlorobenzene (TCB) in the nearby chemical works grew out of undelivered state-subsidies and the need to replace them by alternative income sources. She points out that TCB was produced in Hungary to supply an Austrian company, which then produced Agent Orange out of TCB to supply the US Army. After the collapse of communism, a French company was appointed to clean up the waste disposal site in Garé, however, instead of solving the problem, this company proposed building an incinerator, a hazardous and polluting end-of-pipe technology. The incinerator plan was finally abandoned due to the resistance of local people and green politicians. Gille summarizes that on basis of her study, it is impossible to simply see state-socialism as "dirty" and capitalism as "clean" and the savior of environmental problems in East-Central Europe. Stephen Brain's study *The Song of the Forest: Russian Forestry and Stalinist Environmentalism, 1905–1953* has been contested by peer-historians. However, it is one of the few ambitious and innovative reconsiderations of the environmental history of communism. Brain's work is based on extensive archival research in Russia, and in his book, he presents convincing evidence of the influence of German forestry science in Imperial Russia and in the Soviet Union, also during the Stalin era. The brain interprets environmentalism broadly and underlines that environmentalism did exist in Stalin's Soviet Union, even within the state apparatus, but it is crucial to understand that because of the different structure of the state, stakeholders were not identical to the ones we are used to in democratic countries.[17]

Recent scholarship has enriched and altered the previously one sided scientific view on the environmental history of state socialism in East-Central Europe. Today we know that state socialist economic, technological and social changes had negative and positive consequences when It comes to the environment. We also know that environmental policies in state socialism worked to a large extent similarly to Western European policies. But, how and why East-Central European environmental discourses differed from the environmentalism of Western European countries? Even though industrialization and urbanization produced uniform environmental problems regardless of political systems, what answers were found and how and why those environmental issues were tackled?

As we shift our lens from the implementation and impact of economical-efficiency measures and economic policy measures in Hungary's heavy industrial complex and the ecological turn of the late 1980s which today dominate scholarship on the environmental history of East-Central Europe, we need new narratives that reflect state-socialist environmentalism and fill in the loopholes of previous research. New narratives need to come to replace the emotional and political bias many of us carry when it comes to environmentalism in communism. We do not need to apologetically forget the environmental, social and economic destruction of the USSR and her satellites, but we cannot keep repeating the same black and white images when our job is to nurture new generations of critical thinkers. Channeling our supporting personal feelings for liberal democracies where the role of law and freedoms are unquestionably granted, into the environmental history of the USSR and East-Central Europe is counterproductive because it creates one narrative we have kept repeating, with a notable exception of few eminent scholars. We need a competition of narratives in environmental history when it comes to the history of economy, technology and the environment in the Soviet bloc. This is especially true in our time when authoritarian tendencies have strengthened to such degree that several fresh democracies in Eastern Europe have already been overtaken by populist autocrats or are on the way to gradually loose their attributes of being democracies. This book aims to provide one set of possible interpretations to rearrange our understanding of authoritarian regimes in past and present.

Notes

1. District 78 on IMDB: http://www.imdb.com/title/tt2662324/?ref_=nv_sr_1
2. Central Statistical Office Website: http://www.ksh.hu/nepszamlalas/docs/tablak/teruleti/05/05_1_1_1_1.xls
3. Hungarian Statistical Office, *Magyar Statisztikai Zsebkönyv 1984* (*Hungarian Statistical Pocketbook 1984*) (Statisztikai Kiadó Vállalat: Budapest, 1985), 124.
4. For a more extensive version of this bibliography and global relations See: Simo Laakkonen, Viktor Pál, and Richard Tucker. "The Cold War

and environmental history: complementary fields" *Cold War History*, No. 4 (2016): 1–18. Ivan Volgyes edited a volume in 1974 with a telling title: *Environmental deterioration in the Soviet Union and Eastern Europe*. Hilary F. French wrote about "the assault of air pollution and acid deposition" in the Soviet Bloc. In 1992, Murray Feshback and Alfred Friendly Jr. wrote about "water torture" and compared the "ecocide" caused by the Soviet Union to the collapse of the Maya empire. Barbara Jancar, for her part, concluded in her 1987 book on the environmental management of the Soviet Union and Yugoslavia that until the end of the sixties, the Soviet Union and the rest of the socialist bloc dismissed environmental problems entirely. Many social scientists and historians concluded that communism was programmed to cause environmental degradation. Sándor Péter argued that the root of pollution problems in communist countries was to be found in ideology. Ivan Volgyes, ed., *Environmental deterioration in the Soviet Union and Eastern Europe* (New York: Praeger Publications, 1974); Boris Komarov [Ze'ev Wolfson], *The Destruction of Nature in the Soviet Union* (New York: M. E. Sharp Armonk, 1980). French, *Green Revolutions,* 5. Murray Feshback and Alfred Friendly, Jr., *Ecocide in the USSR: Health and Nature Under Siege* (New York: BasicBooks, 1992), 1. Barbara Jancar, *Environmental Management in the Soviet Union and Yugoslavia: Structure and Regulation in Federal Communist* States (Durham: Duke University Press, 1987), 3. People's Republic of China did not escape attention. See, for example, *Judith Shapiro, Mao's War Against Nature: Politics and the Environment in Revolutionary China (Cambridge: Cambridge University Press, 2001).* Sándor Péter, "New Directions in Environmental Management in Hungary," in *Environmental Action in Eastern Europe. Responses to Crisis,* ed. Barbara Jancar-Webster (London: Amonk, 1993), 29–31; See also Charles Ziegler, *Environmental policy in the USSR* (University of Massachusetts Press: Amherst, 1987), 105.

5. For example, Roger Manser's subchapter on state socialist pollution laws in Hungary in his 1993 volume, *Failed Transitions,* does a good job creating a collection of stereotypical claims on the relationship between state socialism and nature. Douglas R. Bori noted that one of the ironies of centrally planned economies was how little they cared about protecting their environments. The myth of triumphant capitalism has prevailed to some extent even up until today. *Environmental Problems of East Central Europe*, edited by F. W. Carter and David

Turnock in 2002, listed only problems and negligence about the environmental history of pollution in state socialism. *Restoring Cursed Earth* published 2004 by Matthew R. Auer was yet another edited volume applying the general image of grey landscapes to the environmental history of the Soviet Bloc. In the historical section of her 2005 assessment on EU enlargement and environmental protection, Barbara Hicks reinforced several misconceptions of social sciences on the environmental history of state socialism. Edward Snajdr in *Nature Protests: The End of Ecology in Slovakia*, published in 2008, blamed communism for causing environmental destruction via misplanned industrialization and urbanization in the Slovakian half of Czechoslovakia.

Roger Manser, *Failed transitions: The Eastern European Economy and Environment Since the Fall of Communism* (New York: The New Press, 1993).

Douglas R. Bori, "Foreword," in *Pollution Abatement Strategies in Central and Eastern Europe*, ed. Michael A. Toman (Washington D.C.: Resources for the Future, 1994), VII.

Alan Dingsdale et al., "Hungary," in: *Environmental Problems in East-Central Europe*, eds. Frank Carter and David Turnock (London: Routledge, 2002), 157–182.

Matthew R. Auer, ed., *Restoring Cursed Earth: Appraising Environmental Policy Reforms in Eastern Europe and Russia* (Lanham, Maryland: Rowman and Littlefield, 2004).

Barbara Hicks, "Setting Agendas and Shaping Activism: EU Influence on Central and Eastern European Environmental Movements," in: *EU Enlargement and the Environment: Institutional Change and Environmental Policy in Central and Eastern Europe*, eds. JoAnn Carmin and Stacy D. VanDeveer (Abingdon and New York: Routledge, 2005), 216–233. Edward Snajdr, *Nature Protests: The End of Ecology in* Slovakia (Seattle: Washington University Press, 2008), 22–48.

6. Paul Josephson et al., *An Environmental History of Russia* (Cambridge: Cambridge University Press, 2013).
7. Council of Europe, *Fresh Water pollution control in Europe* (Council of Europe, 1966), 115.
8. Marshall I. Goldman, *The Spoils of Progress: Environmental Pollution in the Soviet Union* (Cambridge: MIT Press, 1972), 119–120.
9. *Environmental Misuse in the Soviet Union*, ed. Fred Singleton (Westport: Praeger Publishers, 1976), xvi.

10. Mildred Turnbull, *Soviet Environmental Policies and Practices* (Sadbury: Dartmouth, 1991), 1.
11. György Enyedi and Viktória Szirmai, "Environmental Movements and Civil Society in Hungary," in *Environment and Society in Eastern Europe,* ed. Andrew Tickle and Ian Welsh (Harlow: Longman, 1998), 147.
12. Raymond Dominick, "Capitalism, Communism and Environmental protection, Lessons from the Germany experience", *Environmental History* 3:3 (1998): 315. See also: Raymond H. Dominick III, The Environmental Movement in Germany, Prophets and Pioneers, 1871–1971 (Bloomington and Indianapolis: Indiana University Press, 1992).
13. Douglas R. Weiner, *A Little Corner of Freedom: Russian Nature Protection from Stalin to Gorbachev* (University of California Press: Berkeley and London, 1999)
14. Pavlínek and Pickles, *Environmental Transitions, Transformation and ecological defense in Central and Eastern Europe,* 11–12; For a failed solution see Elena Kochetkova, "A history of failed innovation: continuous cooking and the Soviet pulp industry, 1940s–1960s", *History and Technology*, 31, no. 2 (2015): 108–132.
15. Pavlínek and Pickles, *Environmental Transitions,* 13–15.
16. Zsuzsa Gille, *From the Cult of Waste to the Trash Heap of History: The Politics of Waste in Socialist and Postsocialist Hungary.* (Bloomington and Indianapolis: Indiana University Press, 2007), 1–3; See also Viktor Pál, *Crave for Growth: The Environmental History of Water in the Borsod Basin, Hungary, 1945–1980* (Doctoral Dissertation. University of Tampere, 2015).
17. Stephen, Brain, *The Song of the Forest: Russian Forestry and Stalinist Environmentalism, 1905–1953.* (Pittsburgh: University of Pittsburgh Press, 2011) Laurent Coumel, "A Failed Environmental Turn? Khrushchev's Thaw and Nature Protection in Soviet Russia," *The Soviet and Post-Soviet Review,* 40:2 (2013), 167–189.

2

Economy, Technology and the Environment in Europe and in Hungary, 1800–1945

2.1 Industrialization, Urbanization and the Environment in Western Europe, 1800–1945

We label today a series of complex changes which radically transformed human-nature and society—nature relationships as the "Industrial Revolution". Prior to these set of events population in Europe was nearly exclusively engaged in agricultural work and lived in rural areas. Today it is widely accepted what Jan de Vries suggested in his now classic work, *European Urbanization 1500–1800*, that after a long build up process new agricultural techniques were created that enhanced agricultural productivity mostly in the present area of the Netherlands and the United Kingdom. Boosted agricultural output was a great feat compared to earlier periods of human history and enabled a growing number of people to work elsewhere than the land. From a contemporary perspective, this process was very slow, but for observers in the late eighteenth century such changes were radical and dramatic. As a result, the hegemony of the Mediterranean was contested and the center of commerce, industry, and politics shifted to the North Atlantic. This

V. Pál, *Technology and the Environment in State-Socialist Hungary*,
DOI 10.1007/978-3-319-63832-4_2

process reached a threshold in Britain by the nineteenth century from the perspective of society–nature relationship. Here humans began to transform their natural environment so radically and with such speed that has never been seen before in human history. In a nutshell, new environmental changes between the late eighteen and early twentieth century were the consequences of new technologies that spread in manufacturing and transportation and accompanied with the extensive use of fossil energy sources.

England is obsessively labeled by economic historians as "the most well-prepared land in mid-eighteenth century Europe to adapt industrial structural changes". Reasons for that include Britain's easily accessible coal and iron ore deposits, reliable infrastructure and stable government. It is widely accepted in the scientific community that these factors intertwined created the background for business opportunities and enhanced to the role of the private initiative.[1] British economic growth in the first half of the nineteenth century received a new impetus from infrastructure construction. After two brief and bustling periods of railway construction between 1835 and 1837, and again between 1845 and 1847, the core of the present-day railway network of the United Kingdom was constructed. Coal, iron, steel, and railways also meant new markets, and the emergence of new industries to supply these markets. Steel production, for example, was revolutionized by the Bessemer converter, which was a new and enhanced method of steel production. Simultaneously, new technologies revolutionized the chemical industry and gave birth to new industries, such as electro-engineering. Those who could not keep up with the increasing speed of technological change in the nineteenth century soon had to close down their operations. For example, the Cyfarthfa Iron Works in Merthyr Tydfil in Wales was one of the first large iron works in Europe, established in 1765. When the owner refused to convert the factory from iron to steel production, the plant gradually lost its markets and had to close down in 1874. [2]

The industrial change did not only transform the way things were produced, it also radically reshaped how people lived in Britain by the mid-nineteenth century. Then, nine British cities had more than 100,000 inhabitants. For example, Manchester grew from a small-scale town to a bustling metropolis in 70 years. More cities meant more resources consumed. Coal use boomed from 10 million tons of coal in 1800 to 189 million tons by 1914 in the. Dramatic environmental consequences of urbanization and industrialization became inevitable. Although, the industry was an important user of coal and source of smoke pollution, it was domestic coal consumption for heating and cooking that polluted air in large cities such as London, Manchester, and Sheffield. Air pollution problems worsened in the winter months and environmental problems accompanied with health issues.[3] Water pollution had already been well known in Britain before the Industrial Revolution. In London, domestic sewage and industrial activities tainted the Thames. In the long run, the population of salmon and other species of fish depleted in several British rivers. For example, the fish stock loss problems of the Thames, Severn, Avon, and Trent rivers influenced the creation of the 1824 and 1836 parliamentary investigatory committees.[4]

As one would imagine, business interests and pollution control did not go hand in hand. Businesses focused on profitability and output, they perceived that business activities were endangered by the environmental- and public health concerns of local communities. For example, during the parliamentary investigation about the control of industrial smoke pollution of the Dowlais Ironworks in Merthyr Tydfil in Wales, the owner explicitly defended full power steam processes in the works, because in his view they were necessary for production processes. Reducing steam power would have reduced output, and eventually profits. Throughout the nineteenth century, the efficiency of steam engines improved, but their numbers were growing faster and eventually, they produced more pollution. For example, in the Dowlais Ironworks, the number of steam engines nearly tripled from 23 to 63 in less than two decades (1837–1856).[5]

Influenced by wealthy business owners, political actors reacted very slowly to environmental problems of Britain. It took decades of pollution when first effective pollution control laws were finally legislated. The Sanitary Act of 1866 required local authorities to prosecute owners of "smokey" factories. Limits of regulations and measurement were primitive at this stage. The "Paris Smoke Scale" visibly measured the appearance of exhausts from very thick to "faint" smoke. Anti-pollution civil society grew into an important stakeholder by the early twentieth century. The Coal Smoke Abatement Society began monitoring programs and encouraged regular citizens to be active members of their observation groups. Lagging air pollution, water protection legislation improved in Britain. In 1876, the Rivers Prevention Pollution Act required the neutralization of sewage before it was discharged to watercourses. This goal was impossible to meet and sanitary authorities gave regular exemptions to polluters. Hence, this system was soon discredited.[6] New scientific knowledge improved water pollution protection. By the beginning of the twentieth century, a growing number of engineers argued that relying solely on organic compounds was an insufficient method of pollution measurement and the absorption of dissolved oxygen should be included in water quality monitoring.

By World War I, Britain was quickly losing its former importance in economic and political terms, however, it still exported about 30% of the world's industrial products in 1914. Britain's steady decline paralleled the general shrinking of Europe's share in the world market. At the mean, Europe's new rising star: Germany closed the gap and exported nearly as much as Britain by 1914.[7] It is widely known that Germany possessed the advantage of being a "late comer" to industrialization. German industrialists adopted already existing production technologies in the coal, iron, and steel producing sectors and gradually took over Belgian and British firms. Between the 1830s and 1870s, German industries grew from a low starting point but on an enormous rate.[8] Similarly to Britain and Belgium, one of the facilitators of the German industry was the rail network. The construction of the first line in 1833 was followed by rapid expansion, and the rail network reached 6500 km in 1852, 50,000 km in 1873, and 61,000 km by 1910.[9] The German type of industrialization included strong state intervention and therefore was different than the Anglo-Saxon deregulated market of the private initiative.[10] Nevertheless, social and environmental impacts of German industrialization was similar to the British, regardless of different organization methods. Between 1850 and 1910, Berlin grew from a city of 412,000 to a metropolis of over 2 million inhabitants. Hamburg's population was close to 1 million by the end of the same period, and Munich

1774	70,000
1826	455,000
1871	13 million
1913	115 million
1938	130 million
1950	120 million
1996	56 million

Fig. 2.1 Coal production in the Ruhr region, 1774–1996 (Tons/Year). *Source* Cioc, *The Rhine*, 83

surpassed half a million inhabitants.[11] During the same period, Krupp shot out from a manufacturing firm of 60 men to an industrial giant of 16,000 employees. Simultaneously Hoechst, Bayer, and BASF, some of the largest chemical companies globally, were born during this period.[12]

As a result of industrialization and urbanization, contemporaries noticed that pollution caused by Germany's booming industries was becoming overwhelming. Industrial and urban wastewaters took their tolls first in coal mining, iron, and steel manufacturing areas, such as the Ruhr. Here, heavy industrial production skyrocketed, because Europe's largest bituminous coal and lignite fields supplied a ready source of energy, and the Rhine, Western Europe's international transport route, provided easy transportation access for the world (Fig. 2.1).[13]

Industrialists in the Ruhr found themselves in the classic Catch-22 situation of water supply and water pollution by the second half of the nineteenth century. Industries and urban population soared, local slate mountains were not suitable for the storage of groundwater, tributaries of the Rhine had limited capacities, and when industrial plants and towns began to discharge a growing amount of pollution, water supply and water pollution became serious problems simultaneously. To overcome this crippling set of issues, a complex network reservoirs in the Ruhr area was constructed and the Ruhr river became the tap and the Emscher river was designated as the toilet of the Ruhr.[14]

Phenols were the most notorious pollutants in the Ruhr area because they were bound to the coking process. Therefore, phenols remained present in the Rhine until the middle of the twentieth century when oil and natural gas replaced coal as a fuel for the industry.[15] By 1910, half of the Emscher's flow was of municipal and industrial effluent. Over 1.5 million residents, 150 mines, and 100 other industrial plants used the Emscher as a sewer. This river has a low gradient, which meant that during dry seasons, waste-water hardly flowed and caused environmental degradation of the riverbed. Waterborne diseases such as typhoid and cholera ravaged in local communities. The Emscher Association (1899) was meant to handle local environmental issues. Engineers made the Emscher steeper and cemented the riverbed, as a result this river was transformed into a wastewater canal.[16] By the end of the nineteenth century, water shortages were extremely pressing in the Ruhr. Based on experiences in Great Britain and the USA, six large dams were constructed in Rhineland-Westphalia between 1899 and 1965, with a total capacity of 469 million cubic meters of water. Water quality in the river Ruhr and its tributaries was guaranteed by the Ruhr River Association (Ruhrverband), founded in 1913, and water quantity in the Ruhr reservoirs was overseen by the Ruhr Reservoirs Association (Ruhrtalsperrenverein), founded in 1899.[17] Between 1904 and 1958, a total of eight water associations (Genossenschaften) were established in the Ruhr area by special laws (Sondergesetzen). These associations in the Ruhr area carried out extensive planning and construction for waste disposal, water supply, flood damage reduction, and land drainage. These water associations were controlled by their largest and most affluent industrialist members that caused conflict of interests when it came to the contradiction between business and environmental interests.[18] Evident priority was given to industrial needs, however some researchers, e.g. Allen W Kneese and Blair T. Bower defended these associations as "*the only organizations in the world that have designed, built, and operated regional systems for waste disposal and water supply*" until the 1960s.[19]

The Rhine's last stop before flowing into the North Sea carrying its Swiss, French, and German pollution were Dutch cities. The pollution of the Rhine limited access to drinking water in Dutch cities. Water problems were especially pressing in Amsterdam. Following water shortages in dry summers, in 1885 the Dune Water Company was granted a concession to serve Amsterdam with water from the Rhine delta, however this water source was too polluted to be used as drinking water.[20] Rotterdam had similar problems. In 1917, a water quality investigation of the river Elk near Rotterdam found severe organic pollution that was assumed to originate from German paper and pulp factories. In theory, fungi accumulated in the vicinity of German cellulose plants, and in periods of high water, such as Spring floods, fungi was swept downstream.[21] After WWI the quantity of pollutants decreased in Germany. In the Weimar Republic, industrial production began to rise only after 1924 and it surpassed pre-war level.[22]

In the 1920s, the industrial conglomerate of the French-controlled Ruhr area was the major polluter of the Rhine river. Potash was discovered around Mulhouse in 1904 and developed into a major business. In the 1920s and '30s potash was an important ingredient for chemicals, medicines, soaps, matches, glass, paper, aniline dye, bleaching agents, explosives, and fertilizers. In the late 1920s, about 95% of the world's potash production originated from the Rhine area. The Mulhouse potash mining area was concentrated and compact and when in 1931, French authorities granted concessions for potash mines to dump waste salts to the Rhine, it quickly led to dramatic environmental degradation downstream in the Rhine.[23] The Dutch attempted to resolve the issue diplomatically, but eventually the French dismissed Dutch claims as "overreactions" to potash dumping.[24] In 1927, the Dutch Ministry of the Interior and Agriculture established an interdepartmental commission for the "Taste and Smell of River Water" to investigate and analyze the condition of the lower Rhine in the Netherlands. Between 1927 and 1931, monitoring in the Nether Rhine river at the city of Rhenen found very high levels of solid materials, chloride, nitrate, sulfuric acid, ammonium, and alkali metals such as Na^{+}.[25] The Great Depression hit Germany particularly hard. Economic struggles and social issues aided Hitler to gain power with a populist, Nazi agenda in 1933. Once in power, the Nazis began to work to fulfill their election promises, which included the rapid elimination of unemployment. Initially, employment was fueled by the first and second Reinhardt Programs, which facilitated infrastructure construction, especially autobahn (freeway) building. Later, war related industrial production became the key element of Hitler's economic vision of Germany.[26]

2.2 Industry, Technology and the Environment in East-Central Europe, 1800–1914

Maria Theresa and Joseph II were inspired by Western Europe's economic success and facilitated industry in the Habsburg Empire. As a result of this process, Bohemia took a leading position in the modernization amongst the Habsburg lands.[27] In the eighteenth century, Hungary was a dominantly agricultural land. Industry confined to the mountainous regions of Transylvania and the Uplands. In the Borsod Basin that evolved to be Hungary's foremost heavy industrial district by the 1960s, first entrepreneurs were only enticed by Maria Theresa's progressive industrial policies. In 1765 Henrik Fazola, a German-born iron master from Würzburg established a small number of iron manufacturing workshops in the Garadna and Szinva valleys in the vicinity of the city of Miskolc. In the 1820s, forges sought more water power and space, and operations moved a few kilometers downstream in the Garadna Valley. Top annual production of the Fazola works remained under 1,000 tons annually. Despite the financial and administrative support of the Vienna court, the Garadna forges did not prove to be financially stable. Local iron ore was of poor quality and large markets were hard to access from this remote location on unpaved roads.[28]

In the first half of the nineteenth century, industrialization, and urbanization in Western Europe provided further stimulus for East-Central Europe. Between 1800 and 1914 the population of Great Britain quadrupled. Belgium, Holland, Germany's population doubled. In Eastern Europe factories were set up to supply Western Europe's growing population with mostly foodstuff. Export possibilities and growing population attracted foreign investors to East-Central Europe, railroads, mines, and banks were set up by foreign money during the second half of the nineteenth century.[29]

In 1867 Hungarian aristocracy reconciled with the Habsburgs and in the new political climate industry and urban development boomed in Hungary.[30] Between 1867 and 1873, 4100 km of new railroads were constructed. The boom continued between 1882 and 1890 and added 4000 km of new railways to the existing system.[31] Initially, most rails and carriages were imported. However, from the 1880s, a growing number of items of the Hungarian railway infrastructure were supplied by domestic producers. Additional rail infrastructure, for example, bridges also required a great number of domestic products. Simultaneously with the railway boom, major Hungarian river flows were regulated and large areas of agricultural land were reclaimed. Railway construction and river regulation were both part of Hungary's enormous modernization project during the second part of the nineteenth century. As a result of industrialization, the number of factory workers nationally grew from around 660,000 (10% of total workforce) to 862,000 between 1869 and 1890.[32] The center of commerce and industry in Hungary was Budapest. Railroads and commercial and financial ties met there. Budapest became a rising metropolis, home to large commerce warehouses, pig markets, railway head stations, and credit and commercial banks. The city also hosted many large-scale industrial establishments. Grain mills became lucrative business opportunities, and by 1895 they employed about 3600 workers and the total capacity of their machinery was over 15,000 horsepower.[33] The Ganz, Schlick, Láng, Vulkán, MÁVAG and Hunnia companies represented the heavy industry in Budapest. Most of these factories grew large to supply the demands of railway construction and the mechanization of agriculture. After the 1890s electrical engineering, war industries (Weiss Manfréd Works), and the chemical industry grew at a high rate.[34]

During the nineteenth century, and especially after the Compromise of 1867, several provincial towns boomed in Hungary. For example, Miskolc, a formerly sleepy agricultural town emerged as a center for industry and commerce. By the end of the nineteenth century, Miskolc and Diósgyőr, a former royal domain, jointly formed an urban area. A sign of urban growth was that the two main parts of the city were connected by a streetcar in 1897. For the urban areas' growing population, a reliable and safe water supply was needed. Miskolc commissioned József Fodor in 1885, and János Wein in 1890 to conduct research on the urban water supply of the city. Both Fodor and Wein considered two major options for water supply. They researched the limestone cave system of the Bükk Mountains. Here, a significant amount of karst waters were stored in the hollow mountains, which after purification sprung to the surface in a number of locations in close proximity to the town. Another option was water from the river Sajó. However, bank filtration experiments on the Sajó produced unsatisfactory results. Therefore, engineers favoured the abundant karst springs of Tapolca.[35]

The decision to supply Miskolc by the Tapolca springs was followed by lengthy negotiations with the Greek Catholic Bishop of Mohács, the landlord of the area. The city council purchased the property in 1908 and the first version of the city's water supply and wastewater system was built between 1909 and 1913. This first system connected mostly wealthier residents to the water supply system. All together, 840 of the total 4843 houses were on the gird by 1913.[36]

In areas of Hungary where industrial potentials were left unexploited by private entrepreneurs because of the high financial risks involved, the Hungarian state intervened. In 1867, the Ministry of Finance initiated the construction of a state owned rail and rail wheel factory in Diósgyőr. Two civil servants, János Gombosy and Miksa Glanzer, were appointed to manage the construction works. Soon after its launch, The Royal Diósgyőr Iron and Steel Factory received large state orders. The environs of the factory were lower plain of the Szinva Creek, downstream from the previously unsuccessful Fazola Forge, between the provincial towns of Diósgyőr and Miskolc. Within less than a century, these two towns and a handful of other communities grew into an industrial area over 400,000 people called Borsod Basin.

The Diósgyőr factory was donated by the state with a number of coal and iron mines in the immediate surroundings of the factory, and also further away in the Rožňava and Rudabánya area. Local iron deposits around Diósgyőr were insignificant and could only be used as added materials. Therefore, iron ore was chiefly transported to Diósgyőr from the mines of Rudabánya and Telekes. Contrary to iron, local coal deposits in Pereces had substantial potential and were already extracted by the 1880s. In Pereces, a vital mining community had developed and the geographical range of mining had been extended to valleys north of the village by a 2300 m coal and workforce rail tunnel. The upper layer of the Pereces coalfield consisted of poor quality brown coal, but coal from deeper layers was suitable for fueling Diósgyőr's steam engines.[37] Having its own brown coal was an advantage and made Diósgyőr more competitive on the domestic market. Further advantage was taken when the new Rožňava-Miskolc and Miskolc-Diósgyőr rail line was built. By rail, iron ore was easily transported to Diósgyőr, and the factory's steel products were linked to their markets by rail. First, furnaces and rolling plants were installed, but technological setbacks halted production. When production lines were finally running, it was difficult for this state-owned factory to gain a niche in the market dominated by established Western competitors. After years of struggles, the 1873 economic depression hit Diósgyőr especially hard. It took the plant over a decade to recover and it was able to fulfill its annual 11,000-ton rail production capacity for the first time only in the early 1880s.[38] State-facilitated success continued thereafter. The Diósgyőr rose factory was the supplier of the majority of rails during the second wave of the Hungarian railway construction boom in the 1880s. Besides rails, Diósgyőr produced slightly more than 5000 pairs of train wheels a year. The factory also produced steel parts for bridges and the large drill heads for the construction works of the state-initiated, large scale river regulation project called Iron Gate on the Lower Danube. To deal with private competition, Bessemer converters, a Martin furnace, and a new generator plant were introduced. By the late 1880s, Diósgyőr emerged out of mediocracy thanks to its state-ownership and state-sponsorship, and this factory employed 1600 employees.[39] At the end of the 1890s conjuncture was over, without steady state orders Diósgyőr was in crisis and received state orders for steel parts for bridges. Before WWI the growing number of military orders did not counterbalance economic decline, and in 1901, 1000 workers were laid off and hundreds more were forced on holiday. After 1906, war preparations and artillery production orders continued to employ the Diósgyőr plant, and the advance of World War I provided a steady supply of contracts. In pre-WWI Hungary the death or life of industrial plants largely depended on government orders, only few domestic companies expressed export potentials and did not have to seek the favor of national decision makers (Fig. 2.2).

Industrial activity in Diósgyőr had an economic impact in the vicinity of the factory. Coal deposits in the hills around Sajókazinc (later Kazincbarcika) were of limited economic importance before the steel mills began to work. The seams were hard to access, made more

Fig. 2.2 Diósgyőr Iron- and Steel Mills, Rolling Plant, 1909. *Photo* FORTEPAN / MAGYAR FÖLDRAJZI MÚZEUM / ERDÉLYI MÓR CÉGE

difficult by the lack of paved roads or railway transportation in the area. Moreover, waterways in the vicinity such as the Sajó River were not particularly navigable. Ambitious nineteenth century plans influenced by English, Walloon, and German examples intended to make the Sajó River more passable. The Rhine River in Germany and the heavily canalized Sambre and Meuse Rivers in southern Belgium provided excellent transportation routes for local industrial areas. However, the water flow of the Sajó at the time would not have enabled large freight ships to access coal ports in the Borsod Region. It was only after the opening of the first railroad between Miskolc and Gemer (Gömör) County in 1871 that the Sajókazinc coal mines became accessible and potentially profitable.[40] Commercial coal mines were initially small, employing only a small segment of the local population who were primarily engaged with agriculture.[41] The first major private mining firm was the Barcika Coalmine Company (Barcika Kőszénbánya Vállalat). It was established in 1894/95 and sold coal to the steel mills of Ózd, Diósgyőr, and Salgótarján.[42] By World War I, coal mining emerged as a profitable business in Borsod and employed the majority of the adult male population in a handful of villages around Sajókazinc and Berente (Fig. 2.3).

Accelerated industrial activities bought access amount of pollution with them. Before WWI pollution on high levels was unheard in rural Hungary, excluding a few tiny spots of industrial development. In Budapest, however, the situation was different. Large production

Fig. 2.3 Ózd Iron- and Steel Mills, 1926. *Photo* FORTEPAN

capacities concentrated in and around this city, along with a steadily growing population. Act XXVIII of 1885 secured the supremacy of industry over agriculture. This water law expressed that in the case of user disputes over water resources, priority should be given to industrial plants over agricultural users. Field users could access water only on weekends, between 9 pm Saturday and 3 am Monday. Excess water use for agricultural users was only possible if they paid compensation to industrial users.[43] In this 1885 Hungarian law he "polluter pays" principle was also included. Owners of water infrastructures were obliged to pay compensation when "*they (owners of water infrastructures) changed the flow of water and that caused harm*" downstream. The 1885 law forbade any type and quantity of pollution in theory. The law did not establish a system of water pollution fines, rather pollution from "*factories, mines and other companies" were treated on an individual case basis. After the examination of each case "(state) authority decides what measures should be taken.*"[44] For those who did not comply with state measures, polluter fines were set: "*Fines up to 100 forints can be set (on those) (…) who pollute waters with harmful and infectious materials (…).*"[45] The 1885 water law and its remarks on water pollution followed Western European principles over water rights and pollution. Priorities were given to industrial water use over agriculture both in Hungary and in Western Europe. Both Hungarian and Western European law established the "polluter pays" principles in water regulation. To manage flood control, river channelization and the management of water resources, the Engineer Service (Kultúrmérnöki Szolgálat) was established with the leadership of Jenő Kvassay in the Ministry of Agriculture (Földművelésügyi Minisztérium) in 1879. During the second half of the nineteenth century, industrial development and urban expansion multiplied the volume of discharged wastewaters both in Hungary and in Western Europe.

In 1913, Hungarian water laws grew stricter. Tighter regulations reacted to the increased discharge of water pollutants. New regulations complemented the 1885 law and aimed to enforce the protection of public health. The 1885 and 1913 water protection legislation had a favorable impact on water research as well. Gábor Baross, Minister of Communal Works, established a ministerial Department of Hydrography, Hungary's professional government unit for water-related research. In 1952, this department was ordered to be the Institute for Water Management and Research (Vízgazdálkodási Kutató Intézet, VITUKI), and had scientific authority over water supply and wastewater planning issues in Hungary.

2.3 Industry, Technology and the Environment in Hungary, 1920–1945

Hungary was one of the losers in the post-World War I changes. The country was traumatized by the disaster of its assimilation policies and subsequent territorial loss.[46] Extremists thrived in this climate and pogroms and terror attacks against the Jews, the largest minority after the territorial loss were frequent. The nationalist course continued and Jews were removed from public service extensively and universities significantly curtailed study places for Jewish students.[47] Normalization of social and economic conditions was slow compared to Czechoslovakia and Poland.[48] After the World War I, large infrastructural investments lagged behind regional levels and began only after Hungary was able to access considerable foreign loans after 1925. Such loans financed environmental investments, for example, water supply and wastewater system improvements in the city of Miskolc. In 1927, a 400 mm water main was constructed from Tapolca Springs to the city, and in 1937, a water tunnel was constructed under the Avas hill to connect Tapolca Spring and the city center. During the interwar period, the water supply network grew considerably in Miskolc, from 39.4 to 59.8 km, and supplied a growing number of residents.[49]

After 1920, rich coal deposits in Transylvania and the Hungarian Uplands became inaccessible because those territories were shifted to Romania and Czechoslovakia. The importance of previously marginal central Hungarian coal deposits escalated, for example, the coal mines in the Borsod Basin. Coal-based industries, such as the chemical industry and power generation industry also began to exploit the industrial potential of the Sajó Valley. In 1921, Kálmán Kandó a renowned inventor and entrepreneur built an experimental coal-based petrochemical plant in Berente. In 1924, the Borsod Coal Mines Corporation (*Borsod Szénbányák Részvénytársaság*) constructed a small-scale coal-fired power plant that supplied Kandó's chemical plant and local mines with electricity.[50] Kandó's chemical unit was the predecessor of the large Borsod chemical production capacities which were later developed during and after the communist First Five Year Plan (FFYP). Hungary's economy was fragile and just recovering when depression struck in 1929. As a result of the crisis, construction declined by almost 50%, and industrial production fell about 24% by 1933. The decline in iron and steel manufacturing was even more devastating. Iron production decreased from 368,000 to 67,000 tons between 1929 and 1933. Steel production declined from 513,000 to around 180,000 tons during the same period.[51] This trend soon stopped, and after 1933, most industries were growing, and the Hungarian economy reached its pre-World War II peak in 1938. This was followed by a rearmament program, which gave further impetus for the military industry and infrastructure construction.

Industrialization received a new impetus from the mid-1930s when Hungary drifted to the economic and political sphere of influence of Adolf Hitler's Germany. There the environment was increasingly treated as a resource of commodities. Even though the Nazi Germans established over 800 natural protection areas encompassing 3000 square kilometers between 1935 and 1940 by the Reich Nature Protection Law, the economy, and life in Germany became increasingly dominated by the military industry in the second half of the 1930s. The 1936 Four-Year Plan was led by the rearmament program and facilitated coal mining, iron, and steel manufacturing and the chemical industries. Privately- owned heavy industry was important in Germany, but producers, especially in industries crucial for the war effort like the Braunkohlebenzin AG (Brown Coal Gasoline Corp.) in synthetic fuel manufacturing, were often forced to follow state production interests.[52]

The state also established state-owned production plants such as the Reichswerke Herman Göring (Imperial Herman Göring Works). State control and the importance of central plans increased in industrial production as Germany sank into a "total war." German central planning largely depended on the shortage or abundance of raw materials. For example, at the end of the Four-Year Plan in 1940, aluminum, synthetic fiber, and explosives targets were fulfilled. This plan, however, failed to provide desired results in steel, mineral oil, and fat production. Armament policy threatened protected and unprotected lands because war industries were supported by loose environmental and risk protection decrees.[53] For example, from the second half of 1934, the Trading Regulation allowed the secret licensing procedure of arms production plants and related industries. Previously, stricter regulations required producers to obtain licenses from local authorities who evaluated potential fire, public health, and other hazards. The open assessment of the local licensing procedure endangered war efforts, so the evaluation process was made secret, hence more controllable by the state.[54]

This did not necessarily mean, however, that pollution measures were completely abandoned or that war industry was tainting Germany without limits. Frank Uekötter points out, that the war effort and the rapid growth of production, especially in synthetic fibers and armament industries, produced more pollution than before, but the regulation of pollution was not abandoned completely in Nazi Germany even during war times. He argues that complaints against polluters were filled and the assessment of pollution was carried on throughout World War II.[55]

Hungary mimicked the rearmament program of Germany and Italy. The Győr Program of the Darányi Imrédy administrations relocated about 60% of this program's budget for the armament industry. The rest was spent on infrastructure, telecommunications, and transportation. Heavy industrial factories such as the Diósgyőr Iron and Steelworks benefited from the rearmament program and received large state contracts. The Győr Program created a high demand for industrial production, which was unprecedented throughout the interwar era.[56]

By 1941 Hungary was incorporated into the Nazi war machine. At the time, Italy and Germany supplied 79% of Hungary's imports and provided markets for 74% of her exports.[57] Brief heavy-industrial conjuncture was followed by heavy losses during the war. For example, Miskolc's water supply and wastewater treatment system suffered considerable losses. The city's wastewater treatment plant, which was built in 1913, was bombed in an air raid by the allies. The ruins of the Miskolc wastewater site remained untouched until 1984, when the city's new wastewater treatment plant's first mechanical phase was introduced.

Between 1945 and 1984, raw sewage from residential areas in Miskolc and adjacent industrial plants discharged their wastewater into the sewer system of the city.

Notes

1. Eric J. Hobsbawm, *Industry and Empire. An Economic History of Britain since 1750* (London: Weidenfeld and Nicolson, 1989), 14.
2. *Archives Wales, Glamorgan Archives, Cyfarthfa Iron Works records*, http://www.archiveswales.org.uk/anw/get_collection.php?inst_id=33&coll_id=2104&expand= (accessed August 21, 2014).
3. Stephen Mosley, *The Chimney of the World. A history of Smoke Pollution in Victorian and Edwardian* Manchester (London and New York: Routledge, 2008), 2.
4. Ibid., 72.
5. Brian.W. Clapp, *An Environmental History of Britain since the Industrial Revolution* (London-New York: Longman, 1994), 16.
6. Peter Thorsheim, *Inventing Pollution. Coal, Smoke, and Culture in Britain since 1800* (Athens: Ohio University, 2006), 126.
7. 27%. Brian. R. Tomlinson, "The British Economy and the Empire, 1900–1939," in *A Companion to Early Twentieth Century Britain,* ed. Chris Wrigley (Oxford: Blackwell Publishing, 2003), 198.
8. David Blackbourn, *Fontana History of Germany, 1780–1918: the Long Nineteenth Century* (London: Fontana, 1997), 178–180.
9. Ibid., 362–370.
10. Ibid., 185.
11. Volker Berghahn, "Demographic growth, industrialization and social change," in *19th century Germany. Politics, Culture and Society 1780–1918,* ed. John Breuilly (London: Arnold, 2001), 185–186.
12. David Blackbourn, *Fontana History of Germany, 1780–1918: the Long Nineteenth Century* (London: Fontana, 1997), 178–180.
13. David Blackbourn, *The Conquest of Nature, Water, Landscape, and the Making of Modern Germany*, (New York-London: W.W. Norton, 2007), 180.
14. F. W. Renz, "Goals and management of the Ruhr reservoir system since the beginning of our century" (Scientific, Procedures Applied to the Planning, Design and Management of Water, Resources Systems.

Proceedings of the Hamburg Symposium of IAHS, August 1983). IAHSPubi. no. 147., 638–639.

15. „Phenol is both a manufactured chemical and a natural substance. It is a colorless-to-white solid when pure. The commercial product is a liquid. Phenol has a distinct odor that is sickeningly sweet and tarry. You can taste and smell phenol at levels lower than those that are associated with harmful effects. Phenol evaporates more slowly than water, and a moderate amount can form a solution with water. Phenol can catch fire. Phenol is used primarily in the production of phenolic resins and in the manufacture of nylon and other synthetic fibers. It is also used in slimicides (chemicals that kill bacteria and fungi in slimes), as a disinfectant and antiseptic, and in medicinal preparations such as mouthwash and sore throat lozenges." Agency for Toxic Substances and Disease Registry's website, http://www.atsdr.cdc.gov/substances/toxsubstance.asp?toxid=27, (accessed July 14, 2013).
16. Mark Cioc, *The Rhine: an eco-biography, 1815*–2000 (Seattle: University of Washington Press, 2002). 89.
17. Renz, *Goals and management of the Ruhr reservoir system since the beginning of our century*, 639–640.
18. Allen V. Kneese and Blair T. Bower, *Managing Water Quality, Economics, Technology, Institutions*. 2nd paperback ed. (Washington D.C: Resources for the Future and the John Hopkins University Press, 1985). 238.
19. Ibid., 237.
20. Cornelis Disco, "Accepting Father Rhine? Technological Fixes, Vigilance, and Transnational Lobbies as „European" Strategies of Dutch Municipal Water Supplies 1900–1975," *Environment and History* 13, no. 4 (2007): 386.
21. Ibid., 391.
22. Hans-Joachim Braun, The German Economy in the Twentieth Century (London-New York: Routledge, 1990), 48.
23. George S. Rice, John A. Davis, *Potash Mining in Germany and France*, Bulletin 274, Department of Commerce, Bureau of Mines, Washington D.C.: Government Printing Office, 1927, 1–7.
24. Disco, "Accepting Father Rhine? Technological Fixes, Vigilance, and Transnational Lobbies as "European" Strategies of Dutch Municipal Water Supplies 1900–1975," 395.
25. Ibid., 392–394. Figures from the Table on 394.

26. The Fontana Economic History of Europe, Volume 6. Contemporary Economies, Part 1, ed. Carlo M. Cipolla, Collins-Fontana: London. 1976, 200–201.
27. Robert J.W. Evans, *Austria, Hungary and the Habsburgs, Essays on Central Europe, c. 1863–1867* (Oxford: Oxford University Press, 2006), 92.
28. *A Diósgyőri M. Kir. Vas- és Aczélgyár története 1765–1910 (The History of the Royal Hungarian Diósgyőr Iron- and Steel Factory 1765–1910)* (Miskolc, 1910), 2.
29. Andre Armengaud, "Population in Europe 1700–1914," in *The Fontana Economic History of Europe. volume 3. part 1.* ed. Carlo M. Cipolla (London: Fontana/Collins, 1973), 29.
30. László Katus, "A Gazdasági fejlődés politikai feltételei (The Political Preconditions of Economic Development)," in *Magyarország története 1848–1890 (A History of Hungary 1848–1890),* ed. László Katus (Budapest: Akadémiai Kiadó, 1979), 943.
31. Railroad construction provided opportunity for widespread corruption in Hungary. Despite the tumultuous economic and social history of railroad construction in Hungary the presence of an extensive rail network brought economic development to Hungary eventually.
32. Katus, *A Gazdasági fejlődés politikai feltételei (The Political Preconditions of Economic Development)*, Tables 21–2., 1010–1012.
33. Károly Vörös, "Magyarország Gazdasági Központja (An Economic Center of Hungary)," in *Budapest története a Márciusi Forradalomtól az Őszirózsás Forradalomig (A History of Budapest from the Revolution of March (1848) to the Revolution of Roses (1918)),* ed. Károly Vörös (Budapest: Akadémiai Kiadó, 1978), 350.
34. Ibid., 353. A detailed list of factories.
35. Oszkár Vincze, "A miskolci vízmű (Miskolc Waterworks)," *Vízgazdálkodás* 5., no. 5. (1965): 140.
36. Ibid.
37. Antal Péch, *Jelentése a selmeczi és diósgyőri kerületben és Rézbánya vidékén létező állami bányák és kohók állapotáról (Report on the Condition of Mines and Furnaces in the Selmecz-, Diósgyőr-, and Rézbánya Areas)* (Budapest: Magyar Királyi Állami Nyomda, 1873), 70.
38. "d) Súlymértékek: 1 bécsi mázsa annyi mint 56.006: ötvenhat egész, hat ezredrész kilogr.(d) Weight, 1 Wiener Zentner (Viennese Centner) equals to 56.006 kilograms.)" Therefore 200,000 Zentner of iron equals to roughly with 112,000 tons. 1874. évi VIII. törvénycikk a

métermérték behozataláról, (Act VIII/1874 on the Implementation of Metric Standard). Enacted in Budapest, Hungary.

39. *A Diósgyőri M. Kir. Vas- és Aczélgyár története 1765–1910 (The History of the Royal Iron- and Steel Factory in Diósgyőr 1765–1910),* Miskolc, 1910.
40. 1871. évi XXXVII. törvénycikk a gömöri iparvasutak hálózatának kiépitéséről (Act. XXXVII in 1871 on the Construction of the Network of the Gömör Industrial Railways) Enacted in Budapest, Hungary.
41. Péter Tóth, *A Borsod szénbányászat a kapitalizmus korában, 1849–1945 (The History of Borsod Coal Mines in the Capitalist Era, 1849–1945)* (Miskolc: Borsod Szénbányák; (Szolnok) Nagyalföldi Kőolaj- és Földgáztermelő Vállalt, 1986).
42. Sándor Frisnyák Dr., *Kazincbarcika földrajza (Geography of Kazincbarcika)* (Kazincbarcika: Kazincbarcika Város Tanácsa, 1979), 163.
43. 1885. évi XXIII. törvénycikk a vizjogról (Act. XXIII. in 1885 on Water Rights) Enacted in Budapest, Hungary. 30.§ and 31. §.
44. Ibid., B) A hatósági rendelkezés alatt álló vizekről (B) About Waters Controlled by State Authorities), 24. § "A vizeknek ártalmas anyagokkal való megfertőztetése tilos. Hogy mily intézkedések szükségesek arra nézve, hogy gyárakból, bányákból és más vállalatokból hulladékok és megfertőztetett vizek más vizekbe bebocsáthatók legyenek: az iránt a közegészségügy követelményei és a fennálló használatok tekintetbe vételével a hatóság intézkedik."
45. Ibid., VII. Fejezet Büntető határozatok (Chapter VII. Punitive Decisions), 185. § Száz forintig terjedhető pénzbüntetéssel büntetendő: 1. a ki vizeket ártalmas anyagokkal megfertőztet (24. §), a mennyiben az az 1879: XL. tc. 105. §-ba nem ütközik;"
46. Mária Ormos, *Padovától-Trianonig 1918–1920 (From Padua to Trianon 1918–1920)* (Budapest: Kossuth Könyvkiadó, 1983), 6–9.
47. Krisztián Ungváry, *A Horthy-rendszer és Antiszemitizmusának Mérlege. Diszkrimináció és Társadalompolitika Magyarországon 1919–1944 (The Horthy Regime and its Anti-Semitism. Discrimination and Social Policy in Hungary 1919–1944)* (Budapest: Jelenkor, 2016), 110–145 (Chap. 3.)
48. Ivan T. Berend and György Ránki, *The Hungarian Economy in the Twentieth Century* (London: Croom Helm, 1985), 46.
49. Vincze, *A miskolci vízmű (Miskolc Waterworks)*, 141.
50. *BorsodChem Rt. Környezeti állapota. Tényfelmérő és állapotrögzítő tanulmány (BorsodChem Rt State of the Environment. Assessment Study of Facts and Conditions)* (Kazincbarcika: BorsodChem Rt, 1993), 8.

51. Decline was balanced out somewhat by the growth in other production branches, where foreign competition vanished e.g. in textiles, leather, paper, chemical, and electrical energy production.
52. Hans-Joachim Braun, *The German Economy in the Twentieth Century*, 81–82.
53. For detailed information: Thomas M. Lekan, *Imagining the Nation in Nature: Landscape Preservation and Germany Identity, 1885–1945* (Cambridge: Harvard University Press, 2004), 204–251.
54. Frank Uekötter, "Polycentrism in Full Swing, Air Pollution Control in Nazi Germany," in: *How Green were the Nazis?, Nature, Environment and Nation in the Third Reich*, ed. Franz-Joseph Brüggemeiner, Mark Cioc, and Thomas Zeller (Athens: Ohio University Press, 2005), 111.
55. Examples of air pollution problems and the assessment of these issues are to be found in: Ibid., 116–117.
56. Deborah S. Cornelius, *Hungary in World War II. Caught in the Cauldron* (New York: Fordham University Press, 2011), 152–155.
57. Ignác Romsics, *Hungary in the Twentieth century* (Budapest: Corvina-Osiris, 1999), 142.

3

Economy, Technology and the Environment in Europe After World War II

3.1 Economic Growth in Europe After World War II

A second long period of extensive industrial and urban development followed World War II in Europe between 1950 and 1973. This was the period when heavy industrial production reached its climax in Western Europe and various large-scale heavy industries and urban development projects began to dominate East-Central European countries. As a result, pollution skyrocketed both in Western and East-Central Europe during the 1950s and 1960s.

In 1945, it was clear that the economics and international politics of the interwar years could not be continued. Europe was dominated by right-wing, authoritarian regimes between the two-world wars, communism and socialism became popular ideas throughout Europe after World War II. The Left attracted the masses and enticed intellectuals. And the communists formed popular parties not only in the Soviet Union dominated East-Central Europe but throughout the entire continent. In Italy, for example, over two million people joined the Communist Party, which was one of the most radical communist parties

V. Pál, *Technology and the Environment in State-Socialist Hungary*,
DOI 10.1007/978-3-319-63832-4_3

in the West.[1] Also, the socialist idea was very popular in France and in the United Kingdom, which eventually led to a series of nationalizations in both countries. The Christian Democratic movement, which, also saw a large growth after 1945, and the socialists agreed with the rise in state intervention, believing it was necessary to achieve prosperity and economic growth. It was of foremost importance for all major political powers in Europe to avoid the catastrophic spiral of populism and rearmament that lead to the inferno of World War II.

These ideals and a focus on larger state intervention in national economies resulted in the nationalization of key economic sectors throughout Western Europe. Renault, along with several banks, was nationalized in France in 1945. A year later private coal mines and the main electricity and gas providers, Electricite de France and Gaz de France were nationalized. In the United Kingdom after the nationalization of the coal industry in 1946, electricity providers, rails, water transport, and some local gas suppliers were nationalized. In 1951 the state acquired the national iron and steel industry, which later was denationalized by the following conservative government.[2]

Heavy industry was the flagship industry at this time in Europe. The growth of heavy industries was typical in Western Europe between the two world wars and continued briefly after 1945. Heavy industry's share of gross national product was 32% before World War I in Great Britain and it grew to 49.5% in 1938. Similar tendencies were typical in Germany, Sweden, The Netherlands, Norway, and Italy. [3]

Despite the controversial political systems in Western and East-Central European countries, extensive economic growth was more or less sustained without interruption in both the capitalist and communist parts of Europe between 1950 and 1973. As result of capital and technology influx from the United States and a slowly forming the European Union, Western Europe experienced an extremely long period of uninterrupted economic growth between 1950 and 1973. Western European state interventionist industrialization and East-Central European centrally planned economic systems showed a number of similarities in their strengths and weaknesses. According to Barry Eichengreen, economic catch-up in postwar Western Europe was secured by the cooperation of trade unions, employers associations, and growth-minded governments, which mobilized savings to secure investment and full employment. Both in the West and the East "*The problem of getting a set of interdependent industries up and running simultaneously was solved by extra-market mechanisms ranging from government planning agencies, state holding companies, and industrial conglomerates in Western Europe to wholesale nationalization and central direction of the economy in the East.*"[4]

During the golden years, Europe experienced sustained economic growth which was higher than the rest of the world. Derek Aldcroft pointed out that between 1950 and 1970 European gross domestic product grew on average at about 5.5% per annum and 4.4% on per capita basis. These rates were higher than world average rates of 5.0% and 3.0% respectively. Industrial production rose even faster in Europe, at 7.1% a year compared with a world rate of 5.9%.[5]

Rapid growth in Europe was an important change compared to the shrinking economic importance of the Old Continent during the interwar years. Crafts and Toniolo pointed out that the rapid and unprecedented economic growth of the 1950s–1970s was remarkable because in less than a quarter of a century, European GDP nearly tripled. Growth in Western Europe was faster than growth in the USA during these years, and European countries that began to fall increasingly behind the USA between the two world wars caught up after World War II and narrowed the gap of GDP from more than double to 50% in 1973, and then to about third by the mid-2000s. GDP grew between three and 6% per year in most Western European countries between 1950 and 1973. The UK was particularly slow with 2.42%, while West Germany produced 5.02% annual growth.[6]

Annual GDP growth per capita was comparable to the Western European levels in the entire Soviet bloc until 1973. According to data by Crafts and Toniolo, Czechoslovakia produced 3.08% annual growth, Hungary 3.6%, Poland 3.45% and East Germany 4.47% during the postwar extensive period.[7] Even though annual growth rates in the East were comparable to Western European GDP growth per capita rates between 1950 and 1973, the volume of growth in the East did not catch up with the volume of growth in the West, because in the East, the initially lower GDP per capita rates should have grown faster to bridge the gap with Western rates. Data presented by Crafts and Toniolo also shows that labor productivity grew slower in East Germany and in the USSR than in most countries in Western Europe between 1960 and 1970. East Germany produced 2.81% and the USSR had 2.74% labor productivity growth during the 1960s, while more successful Western European countries such as Finland, France, and Germany reached 4.67, 4.93 and 4.36% annual growth in labor productivity, respectively. Considering the fact that labor productivity had been lagging in East-Central Europe compared to Western Europe before 1960, steady growth was maintained with extensive economic developments in East-Central Europe.[8]

Steady economic growth had a positive impact on employment all over Europe. After the war, significantly lower unemployment rates were typical than between the two world wars. In the 1950s, unemployment was only 2.9% in Western Europe, which further dropped to 1.5% in the 1960s. Upward employment trends accompanied large-scale migration. Between 1959 and 1965, 5 million Europeans from the Mediterranean moved and went to work in the more industrialized regions of Western Europe.[9]

After the possibilities in extensive growth were exhausted, Europe should have turned to intensive growth. However, institutions that performed well during the extensive growth period were unsuitable to facilitate intensive growth. This produced a mixture of stagnation and slow-growth in the West, and stagnation and decline in East-Central Europe, where the institutions of the centrally planned economies were too rigid to adapt to changes. According to Eichengreen "*Eastern Europe manifested this problem in its most extreme form. The centrally planned economies were particularly inept at innovation, since new knowledge generally bubbles up from below rather than raining down from above. More than nearly any other activity, innovation responds to incentives, which were in chronic short supply in the command economies.*"[10]

Western technology made its way to East-Central Europe, especially after the economic opening following Stalin's death, but the communist and state socialist economic systems were not able to facilitate invention from below. However, incentives were not in short supply in state socialism; rather the contrary. Still, they could not change the overall growth performance of state socialist East-Central European countries. This was especially true for the years following the 1973 Oil Crisis.

Western European growth, which was 4.5% between 1950 and 1973, decreased to 2.1% between 1973 and 2000. Eastern European GDP grew by 4.7% between 1950 and 1973 and slipped down to –0.2% recession between 1973 and 2000.[11]

In East-Central Europe, where inventions were implemented from above from the state side, much of the technological modernization was funded by an increased influx of loans from OPEC countries and Western capitalist financial institutions between 1973 and 1980. To maintain a high level of investment and domestic consumption, East-Central European regimes slipped into a very high degree of state debt by the early 1980s. Between 1980 and 1982, both Hungary and Poland were on the brink of bankruptcy and Moscow was not able to provide financial help for these countries anymore. As a result, Poland and Hungary turned to the International Monetary Fund and the World Bank to be rescued from financial collapse.[12]

3.2 Postwar Reconstruction in Western and Central Europe and Its Environmental Consequences. The Case of Water Pollution

Economic changes had a significant impact on how the interaction between Europeans and their natural environment changed during the decades of the Golden Age. However, German environmental debate "lagged behind its American counterpart for a number of years" after World War II.[13] This was partly because immediately after the war, feeding an increasing population in Germany caused significant stresses. During the last years of World War II and the postwar years about thirteen million refugees moved to the Western parts of Germany. These Germans fled the Red Army or were brutally expelled from Eastern Europe based on concepts of collective responsibility. They sought stability and safety and settled in the British and American sectors.[14]

The increased population accelerated the use of natural resources and Germans worked with their country's limited raw materials to achieve economic prosperity as rapidly as possible. Extensive growth posed increased demands for environmental resources in postwar West Germany throughout the 1950s. According to Sandra Chaney, West Germany's superior economic growth, accompanied by "an accelerated increase in land, water, and energy use" that threatened nature to a large extent. In such conditions when economic growth overshadowed environmental concerns conservations had little space to navigate and their actions remained ineffective.[15]

During the latter part of the 1940s and throughout the 1950s, industrial pollution in West Germany was often considered the necessary and unavoidable side product of economic growth. In 1951, a medical official in Duisburg concluded that the local population had come "to terms" with industrial air pollution. Similarly to the Duisburg case, the city council of Frankfurt passed a decree in December 1951 that accepted industrial pollution as a nuisance which "must be accepted" in the interest of "industrialization" and "reduction of unemployment."[16]

Similar trends were true for many other Western European countries. The controversy between economic growth and the environment was manifested also in East-Central Europe after the 1950s. Extensive development was the basis of economic policy in communism. During the First Five Year Plan (FFYP) in Hungary, heavy industrial development was prioritized. The communists decided that Budapest was already overdeveloped in industrial terms. Therefore, the regime aimed to industrialize backward rural areas and smaller regional industrial centers. The type of urbanization and industrialization that the Hungarian FFYP initiated was related to an industrialization model which dominated Europe between the 1930s and 1960s. This trend included "government sponsored, central development programs" which were "to create employment" and "facilitate urbanization" to produce "catch-up growth of disadvantaged regions."[17]

As part of these development programs, several new urban areas were developed in Western Europe. For example "new towns" were established in the United Kingdom between 1946 and 1951 and between 1961 and 1966. In Scotland, overpopulation problems of the Clyde Valley, where 36% of the country's population lived and much of the country's industrial production capacity was concentrated, confronted large rural areas with little population and few employment opportunities within Scotland.[18]

It is an easy temptation to blame the communists for inadequate planning and haphazard development that ended up severely rising water needs and eventually pressing water shortages in many industrial areas of East-Central Europe. Similarly to ECE industrial regions, water resources in the Ruhr were also extremely limited. In the Ruhr, industries were located in higher altitudes than the Rhine. Pumping Rhine water to higher areas was not economical. Therefore, a series of dams were constructed on the Ruhr to store as much water as possible.[19] Even though the sources of industrial and urban water supply were secured with the construction of the Ruhr's extensive dam and reservoir network, water pollution and punishing water polluters remained a crucial agenda. As late as 1968, according to Kneese and Bower, *"a large proportion of the wastes discharged from the industrial region into the Rhine* via *the Emscher River now receive comparatively little treatment.*"[20] Similarly to East-Central Europe, pressing industrial water needs surpassed supplies in the United Kingdom after World War II. In 1964, the Imperial Chemical Industries (ICI) decided to construct two of the largest ammonia plants in the world in Northeast England. After the completion of these two new factories, local industrial water needs were projected double. To secure the steady supply of industrial water, planners decided to construct a reservoir. The United Kingdom's Water Resources Board recommended the 770-acre Cow Green area, which was known as the habitat of rare plant species. Conservationists protested, but their claims were dismissed in the Houses of the Parliament and the project was ready to take off in March 1967.[21] A similar issue unfolded in the late 1960s in Northeast England. The rivers in the area were tapped so effectively that the Wear and Tees rivers could not hold additional reservoirs anymore. Suitable locations for reservoirs were found only in the valley of the Tyne River to supply mounting water needs for industrial and residential customers. When, in 1972 a reservoir was planned in the Irthing Valley, public discourse began over the possible location of this new reservoir. This controversial project called the Kielder Water was completed in 1982 and it is the largest artificial lake in the United Kingdom, holding around 200 million cubic meters of water. The Kielder Water also became the part of the United Kingdom's first regional water grid system.[22] Kielder water is the site of the largest hydroelectric plant in the United Kingdom, where a 5.5 MW Kaplan turbine and a 0.5 MW Francis turbine produce around 20,000 Mwh electricity annually.[23]

The British case was unique. Mounting water needs represented a growing challenge in Western Europe between the 1950s and 1970s. The Council of Europe commissioned a report in 1966 on the water resources and their pollution in member countries. The report estimated a steep rise of water needs in Europe. In France, for example, 1900 million m^3 of water were used domestically, 10,000 million m^3 were used by agriculture, and 6500 million m^3 by industry. French industrial requirements were originally 10,400 million m^3, but this was reduced to 6500 million m^3 by effective recycling methods. Moreover, the report estimated that French domestic demand would reach 4000 million m^3, agriculture 15,000 million m^3, and industry a towering 14,000 million m^3 of water by 1970.[24]

The report went on to say that a number of Central European lakes had reached an alarming state of pollution. Monitoring results during the first half of the 1960s found disastrous water quality in the Lakes of Morat, Baldegg, Halwill, and Zug. *Coregonidae,* or freshwater white fish species in these lakes were rare or extinct. Water from these water bodies could barely be permitted for either domestic or industrial purposes. In fact, by 1966 Lake Zurich had reached a state of irreversible biological vacuum and was incapable of sustaining life anymore. Central Europe's largest lake, the *Bodensee* (Lake Constance) had also been severely polluted by the 1960s. As a result, certain fish species disappeared. A similar situation was observed in Lake Geneva, where industrial and urban development had negatively impacted water quality.[25]

The Rhine River evolved to be a symbol of water pollution on a devastating scale. By the 1960s, discharged wastewaters from Swiss, French, German, and Dutch cities, factories and agricultural land resulted in huge amounts of organic pollution building up in the Rhine. The number of germs in Rhine water progressively increased downstream. A research report cited by the Council of Europe found 30–100 germs upstream in the Grisons Canton. This number increased to 2000 where the Rhine entered Lake Constance, and escalated to 24,000 in a 150 km stretch downstream from Lake Constance. Downstream from Basel, the growth of impurities in the Rhine grew exponentially, and the number of germs reached a towering scale totaling more than 200,000. In the French, German, and Dutch sections the Rhine water further deteriorated.[26]

Other Western European rivers suffered similar fates. The River Tees in northeast England sustained a vital commercial fishing community at the beginning of the twentieth century, with an annual salmon catch of 8000 fish. This number shrunk to 3000 by 1920, 2000 by 1930 and to virtually none after 1937. This was not surprising if one takes into account that 55,000 m^3 of domestic, and even more industrial wastewater was discharged into the Tees on a daily basis during the mid-1960s. The Elbe also supported a thriving commercial fishing community which nearly disappeared by the mid-1960s. The Seine contained 15 pathogenic organisms upstream from Paris, which multiplied to an astonishing 1.5 million downstream from Paris in the mid-1960s. Downstream from Rouen, the Seine was barely able to support limited fish life in the 1960s.[27]

The Council of Europe's 1966 report concluded the most important negative side effects of water pollution in Western Europe: These were (1) when polluted water used for irrigation might result in plant die-off, and the buildup of harmful chemical substances in crops; (2) when livestock accessed only polluted drinking water it would be harmfully affected; and (3) when wastewater discharged into rivers such as the Rhine, it endangered the human water supply.[28]

3.3 Environmental Problems and Environmental Laws in Western Europe and the United States After World War II

Water protection bills were first passed in the most industrialized countries. In England and Wales, the *1876 Act on the Prevention of Pollution of Watercourses by Domestic and Industrial Waste* was generally applied until 1951 when a new act came into force. The *1923 Salmon and*

Freshwater Fisheries Act, despite its specific name, was widely applied against water pollution until the mid-1960s. This bill was complemented by the *Rivers Act of 1951* and again in *1961*, both concerned with pollution prevention. The *Rivers Act* of *1951* empowered river boards to make bylaws prescribing local standards when a river should be treated as clean, polluted or noxious. However, these forms of regulation were not effective enough and the bill was strengthened in 1961. The *Clean Rivers Act* (1960) addressed the matter of estuaries and tidal waters, and the *Water Resources Act* (1963) aimed to protect water resources. River boards formed gradually. The *Land Drainage Act* first set up such river boards in 1930. Their network was supplemented in 1948 with the passage of the *River Boards Act*. River boards were replaced by river authorities following the *Water Resources Act* in 1963. All together, 27 such river authorities were established in the UK in 1963.[29]

Wastewater discharge fines were also called effluent taxes and emission taxes. The improvement of such systems proved to be difficult in some of the most advanced industrial countries because of the large number of uncertainties involved in the fine setting process. The cost of pollution should have been determined accordingly, but legal structures often operated inefficiently or counter-productively. Small fines did not fit the objective of discharge fines, while too large amounts may have proved difficult or impossible to collect.

In the United States, the Water *Pollution Control Act* (1948) allotted funds to state and local governments to prevent and manage water pollution control issues. However, the Act focused on the protection of human health rather than the protection of the natural environment. Furthermore, this law proclaimed few nationwide goals or objectives. The years between 1956 and 1966 witnessed increased legislative interest in water pollution in the USA, and Congress passed four laws which "focused on giving additional funding to municipalities for constructing wastewater treatment works."[30]

Such legislative attempts were signs that Americans heavily debated the introduction of a nationwide federal discharge fine system in the 1960s and early 1970s. Unlike West Germany and France, where water pollution was taxed in a unified countrywide system by the early 1970s, water pollution in the US was managed on the local level. Taking into account the massive growth of industrial pollution released into water bodies throughout the twentieth century, a growing number of citizens, NGOs, engineers, and scholars demanded the introduction of a more effective "pollution tax" at the federal level. Pollution tax, however, was a very complicated tool to implement, because each effluent charge system attempts to solve the problem of external diseconomy of water pollution. Economists claim that as long as water is considered a 'free good,' many users will not internalize the cost of their own water use; instead, these costs will be passed along to other users."[31]

Excessive US agricultural, municipal, and industrial water use in the 1960s produced water scarcity issues in the most urbanized northeastern part of the country on a level that could be compared to Western European and ECE nations. According to Morse, "*little understanding of the problems involved in water quality control has existed in the community and courts.*" As a result of growing population and increased water consumption, the "*scarcity of water resources and reducing the quality of water because of misuse and pollution of rivers, lakes and streams*" became widespread prior to the 1960s.[32]

Changing attitudes towards water resources and the environment were signaled in the July 1963 report of the Delaware River Basin Compact; a management area which included the states of Delaware, New Jersey, New York and Pennsylvania. The Delaware River Basin Compact included the largest concentration of urban population and industrial potential in the United States. The report suggested that effluent standards, which were systems of charges based on quantity and quality, should be established to control wastewater discharges effectively and achieve a balance between agricultural, urban, industrial, and recreational water use in the Delaware Basin.[33]

Water scarcity and water pollution problems in California triggered progressive "legislative control of water resources." In 1967, the California State Water Resources Control Board was organized to integrate "water quality and quantity control at the state level." Since wastewater discharges and taxes were still handled locally in the US, there was both a significant statewide and countrywide variation over the effectiveness of such systems.

However, few positive examples existed. The effective wastewater discharge fine system of the San Francisco Bay Area showed that even though the US lagged behind several European countries in introducing a nationwide wastewater discharge program, the operation of effective wastewater discharge systems was already possible at the local level when the will of decision-makers and economic incentives were present.[34]

Between 1962 and 1967 in the San Francisco Bay Area, sewage charges for twelve counties were equal to over half of the total wastewater disposal revenues. Hence, costs of water pollution were "distributed amongst the producers of waste." As a result, local property taxes need not be increased, considerably boosting local public appreciation for this system.[35]

On the federal level, the *Water Quality Act* (1965) further strengthened the position of water protection. The *Water Quality Act* called for incentives to quantify pollutant levels that could be discharged without exceeding the water quality standards. Despite increased spending, however, only half of such standards were developed by 1971. In addition, the enforcement of federal legislation was minimal due to several shortcomings in the legal and institutional framework.[36]

The *Water Quality Act* was the first major legal attempt to control wastewater discharges, but it proved to be weak in enforcing water quality standards. The regulation gave the authority of setting water quality standards to individual states, but failed to name a "concrete authority to force effluent reductions by specific polluters."[37]

During the 1960s, several economists and engineers were in favor of introducing an effluent tax-based system in the US following the example of France, The Netherlands, and Germany. In 1965, the Environmental Pollution Panel of the President's Science Advisory Committee recommended the introduction of a federal effluent charge system. Legislative attempts included proposals from Senator William Proxmire in 1969 and Congressman Lee Hamilton in 1971. These developments indicated that the effluent tax alternative was being seriously considered by the late-1960s. The system, however, was never established. Instead, the *Federal Water Pollution Control Act (FWPCA) of 1972* introduced the National Pollutant Discharge Elimination System (NPDES). In essence, the NPDES was a permit granting program requiring polluters to obtain discharge permits in order to use public resources, e.g. water bodies for waste disposal. The first NPDES permits were issued between 1973 and 1976.[38] As the threat from new industries grew, the 1977 and 1979 amendments to the *Clean Water* Act shifted emphasis from controlling 'conventional' pollutants to controlling toxic discharges. This trend was also observed in Western Europe and ECE. The American system addressed conventional pollutants such as: pH, oil and grease, total suspended solids and five-day bio-chemical oxygen demand (BOD5). Nonconventional pollutants included a long list of toxic pollutants such as phenols, vinyl chloride, and mercury.[39]

After World War II wastewater discharges by industry along the Rhine stagnated for a brief period of time but began to rise again sharply by 1946. The postwar Western European boom, and especially the rapidly increasing West German production concentrated in the Ruhr area, produced an unprecedented amount of wastewater. Both the Dutch and Swiss aimed to engage in discourse over the deteriorating quality of the already polluted Rhine. The International Commission for the Protection of the Rhine against Pollution (ICPR) was established in 1948, embracing all the riparian states. From 1950, the Commission planned extensive water quality examinations along the river. Monitoring took place in 1953–1954, with a research report published in 1956. The outcome of this extensive international survey found heavily depleted water quality in certain segments of the Rhine, especially in the middle and lower stretches.[40] While all riparian countries: Switzerland, France, Germany, Luxembourg, and The Netherlands were motivated to curtail the excessive pollution, individual countries had their own priorities. Switzerland and Germany established the Rhine Waterworks Association (AWR) to restore water quality in the upper- and middle-Rhine. The Swiss and Germans were also concerned about the critical quality of the Bodensee and ratified a treaty in 1960 in conjunction with Austria to improve water quality standards. In 1968, the Lake Constance-Rhine Waterworks Working Group (AWBR) was established to ensure the quality of water supplied from the Bodensee. Meanwhile, Amsterdam and Rotterdam which have been receiving wastewater from upstream communities and industrial areas for centuries established the Rhine Waterworks Commission (RIWA) in 1951.[41]

The Swiss Federal Act on the Protection of Water against Pollution was enacted on March 16, 1955, and prohibited the discharge of any solids likely to cause pollution in water bodies. This law also forbade polluters from discharging any type of wastewater without permission from the water authorities. The French Act on the Prevention of Pollution and the Improvement of Water Resources was enacted on December 16, 1964, and contained a two year period during which further decrees would be legislated to specify technical details, quality standards, monitoring, and enforcement.[42]

Even though the Dutch launched a major cleanup of the Rhine as early as the 1930s, international cleanup efforts did not come into effect until the 1950s. In fact, the Dutch had been very motivated to improve the health of the Rhine because of their own downstream position. Cleanup and international cooperation initiatives, however, remained largely in vain until the 1960s. It was not until concentrated remediation efforts began at the state level in Germany, followed by national and international cleanup efforts, that any headway was made.[43]

Responsibility for water pollution control in West Germany, until the passage of the Federal Control of Pollution Act in 1974, was shared between the federal and individual state governments. The states (*Länder*) had the responsibility for the application of water protection laws and their administration. This situation resulted in fluctuating levels of environmental protection in various German states until the introduction of the federal law. Prior to the overall federal law, state laws complemented the July 27, 1957, Water Management Act.[44]

During the decades of the German *Wirtschaftswunder,* or "economic miracle" stories of environmental destruction were reported throughout urban and industrial areas of West Germany. In 1957, *Die Rheinische Merkur* reported that the air quality in West Germany was so appalling that it was "*no longer bearable.*" In 1959, *Die Frankfurter Rundschau* headlined environmental damage, claiming that the "*Ruhr region is under a gigantic dome of pollution…The air is dangerously polluted.*" In 1961, *Die Augsburger Allgemeine Zeitung* cried out and asked for "*Help! - We are being poisoned. Every year a million tons of industrial dust.*" Even as late as 1970, *Die Kölner Stadt-Anzeiger* predicted that residents of German cities would wear gas masks in the near future.[45]

3.4 Environmental Laws and Environmental Quality in Germany in the 1960s–1970s

Statistical evidence supported anecdotal reporting on the critical levels of air and water pollution in West Germany. For example, sulfur-dioxide and nitric-oxide levels multiplied dramatically in the decades between 1945 and 1972. As a result, lung cancer rates were significantly higher in large urban and industrial zones. During his 1961 election campaign, SPD candidate Willy Brandt made air pollution and pollution remediation in North Rhine-Westphalia a centerpiece of his presidential election. Brandt called for "*blue skies over the Ruhr*" (Blaue himmel über der Ruhr). Even though Brandt's campaign had little immediate impact on national politics, political parties on the state level jointly aimed to achieve effective air pollution control.[46]

A comprehensive air pollution control law was passed in 1962 in Rheinland-Westphalia, including measures against smoke, gases, and noise. Regulations were strengthened in 1964 with legislation against smog. A comprehensive monitoring system was also created. Air protection policy at the federal level followed the example of Rhineland-Westphalia nearly a decade later. The first draft of a comprehensive nationwide environmental protection law was presented in 1968. However, because of the recession, economic incentives were prioritized and environmental goals were neglected. After the recession diminished in 1972, the constitution was amended to give the federal German Government responsibility for environmental matters. However, implementation still remained on the state level.[47]

When federal laws were passed, individual states were obliged to follow them even though they had their own previous existing pieces of legislation covering the same matter. Federal responsibility grew as more environmental legislation was passed and the Environmental Protection Division, as part of the Interior Ministry, was established to manage environmental issues relevant to air, water, and soil. The existence of the Environmental Protection Division was a signal that environmental protection had become prioritized in German politics in the early 1970s. Conjointly with the creation of the Environmental Protection Division, several laws were passed in Germany including; the Act against Noise from Air Traffic in 1971; Leaded Petrol, DDT, and the Waste Removal Act in 1972; and the Federal Emissions Control Act in 1974.[48]

It must be noted that rapid success in the reduction of air pollution was not followed by similar immediate success for water quality. After the immediate postwar production boom and the normalization of life, people throughout West Germany gradually grew more interested in air pollution issues. In particular, public interest in the deteriorating quality of air escalated in the Ruhr. Between 1951 and 1959, media coverage of air pollution in the Ruhrgebiet in the *Frankfurter Allgemeine Zeitung*, Germany's prominent political daily, grew from "less than 100 articles per year to over 400 articles per year."[49]

Water pollution levels were even more alarming. The discharge of urban and industrial wastewater in the Ruhr area had been disquieting since the late nineteenth century. Oxygen content declined by nearly 70% in the lower Rhine between 1954 and 1969. *Der Spiegel* claimed that only 17% of West German households and 43% of West German industrial plants had access to adequate wastewater treatment facilities by 1960. Such an exceedingly low figure was partly the result of delayed construction, and partly the result of wartime destruction. According to Dominick, the wartime damage to sewage treatment facilities and West Germany's rapidly growing population both exercised stress on the country's crumbling environmental protection system in the 1950s.[50]

As a result of *Wirtschaftswunder*, water resources which had so far been spared from industrial effluents became polluted. Lake Constance, a large alpine lake shared by Switzerland, Austria, and Germany which previously had clean water, underwent a dramatic transition and became severely polluted by the 1950s–1960s. At first, water pollution issues received less public interest, therefore they were also more difficult to tackle. After the postwar boom, German water associations considered introducing more indirect methods to reduce wastewater discharges. These changes in production processes complemented end-of-pipe technologies. By the end of the 1960s, the Emscher Association's phenol remover plants removed around 65% of waste phenols. The Ruhr's iron and steel industry was also encouraged to recover iron sulfate and sulfuric acid. Normally, recovery was a process that did not produce financial profit but was still cheaper than neutralization. In order to encourage plants to maximize recovery, the Ruhrverband used effluent charges, economic arguments, and technological fixes. For example, a German association encouraged a Dortmund plant to reduce its water intake. According to their argument, this action would decrease water intake costs and effluent charges. As a result, the Dortmund plant in question introduced water recirculation, internal treatment and material reuse processes to "virtually eliminate effluent from the plant." According to Kneese and Bower, several Ruhr facilities reduced their water intake and waste generation at the end of the 1960s.[51]

Despite attempts to regulate water pollution, oxygen concentration in the Rhine continuously decreased between 1945 and the end of the 1960s. Oxygen concentration dropped in the Rhine to under 5 mg/l in 1952, and the downward trend continued. Oxygen content went to under 4 mg/l in 1956 and 3 mg/l in 1961. Water quality reached a negative record between 1968 and 1972 when the oxygen content in the Rhine was hardly above 2 mg/l. The negative trend reversed only after 1973. Oxygen content finally climbed up, with intermittent slippages, to 7 mg/l by 1990. Throughout the 1950s, 1960s and early 1970s Rhine water quality incessantly deteriorated. A positive upswing was only visible after the Oil Crisis.[52]

Air pollution was a different story. Beginning from the end of the 1960s, German authorities successfully reduced air pollutants. The sulfur-dioxide concentration that topped 200 $\mu g/m^3$ in 1964 was reduced to less than 150 $\mu g/m^3$ by the end of the decade. Rapid initial success was followed by the fluctuation of sulfur-dioxide concentration at relatively high levels throughout the 1970s but then plummeted to under 100 $\mu g/m^3$ in 1980 before decreasing yet further to below 50 $\mu g/m^3$ in 1988. Similar trends were observed for suspended particulates (SPM) and lead concentration in ambient air in the Rhine-Ruhr area. SPM levels in the Ruhr at the end of the 1960s topped 200 $\mu g/m^3$. These emissions were halved by 1974 and decreased even further from 1978 until they reached a steady low level of 60 $\mu g/m^3$ between 1988 and 1992. A decline in lead concentrations was recorded from 1974, in which year lead concentration reached around 1.1 $\mu g/m^3$. Lead concentration declined to beneath 0.4 $\mu g/m^3$ by the early 1980s followed by a further decline after 1985 until it approached 0.1 $\mu g/m^3$.[53]

At the local level, the tendency in Western European countries in the 1950s–1960s was to organize local and regional authorities according to geographical boundaries and drainage basins. In the UK, drainage basins provided a possibility for the organization of river boards, and later river authorities. In Germany, river co-operatives, such as the *Emscher Genossenschaft* fulfilled such geographical water management duties. In Hungary, similar geographical distribution of regional water authorities were established, such as the Northern Hungarian Water Directorate.[54]

Funding models of industrial water protection also varied by country. In Belgium, Denmark, France, and Sweden government aid and tax concessions were not granted to industrial plants in the 1960s. In Austria, companies could apply for low-interest, six-year loans, which could cover a maximum of three-quarters of proposed wastewater treatment costs. In Italy, such grants were only available to the poorest regions of the country, for example in the south, and in Sicily and Sardinia. In West Germany, financial support was available for wastewater treatment equipment for up to half of the estimated costs, and for up to a third of the costs to the treatment facilities. Between 1949 and 1966, 975 million DM was granted to German industrial plants to cofinance wastewater treatment investments.[55]

Notes

1. Similar tendencies were true for both France and the United Kingdom, where the French Communist Party and the British Labour Party attracted a large share of the population.
2. See more on contemporary debates of nationalization in Western Europe at: Mario Einaudi, Nationalization of Industry in Western Europe: Recent Literature and Debates, *The American Political Science Review*, 44, no. 1 (1950). 177–191.
3. Iván Berend T., *Gazdaságpolitika az első ötéves terv megindításakor 1948–1950 (Economic Policy during the First Three Year Plan 1948–1950*) (Budapest: Közgazdasági és Jogi Könyvkiadó, 1964), 13.
4. Eichengreen, *The European Economy Since 1945*, 3–4.
5. Derek Aldcroft, *The European Economy 1914–2000* (London, New York: Routledge, 2001), 128.

6. Based on Table 12.1. Levels and growth rates of real GDP per capita: Western Europe and United States ($ 1990 GK and % per year) Western Europe in 1950: 4582, 1973: 11,431, 2005: 20,589 and United States in 1950: 9561, 1973: 16,689 and 2005: 30,519. 299 Based on Maddison.
7. Broadberry and O'Rourke, *The Cambridge Economic History of Modern Europe*, 301–302.
8. Ibid., 306.
9. Eichengreen, *The European Economy Since 1945*, 132–133.
10. Ibid., 3–4., 7. On problems with extensive and intensive growth in Europe Ibid., 5–8.
11. Ibid., 16. Table 2.1.
12. More on state debt and IMF membership Attila Mong, *Kádár hitele. A Magyar Államadósság Története 1956–1990 (Kádár's Credit. The History of Hungary's State Debt 1956–1990* (Budapest: Libri, 2012) 171–221 (Chap. 5).
13. Frank Uekötter, *The Age of Smoke, Environmental Policy in Germany and the United States, 1880–1970* (Pittsburgh: University of Pittsburgh Press, 2009), 132.
14. Sandra Chaney, *Nature of the Miracle Years. Conservation in West Germany, 1945–1975* (New York, Oxford: Berghahn Books, 2012), 46.
15. Ibid., 48.
16. Frank Uekötter, *The Age of Smoke,* 133.
17. "1945 után Európa keleti és nyugati felé egyaránt kormányzatok által menedzselt központi fejlesztési programok kezdődtek, amelyek egyszerre kívántak munkahelyeket teremteni, az urbanizáció terjedését segíteni (…) és az elmaradott régiókat felzárkóztatni." Pál Germuska, *Indusztria bűvöletében (Mesmerized by Industry)* (Budapest: 1956-os intézet, 2004), 89.
18. Ibid., 40.
19. Kneese and Bower, *Managing Water Quality, Economics, Technology, Institutions*. 238.
20. Ibid., 240.
21. Sheail, An environmental history of twentieth-century Britain, 79–81.
22. Ibid.
23. *Kielder Hydro Site website at RWE website*, http://www.rwe.com/web/cms/en/312572/rwe-innogy/sites/hydroelectric-power-station/united-kingdom/sites-in-operation/kielder/ (Accessed July 8, 2013).

24. Council of Europe, *Fresh Water pollution control in Europe* (Council of Europe, 1966), 18.
25. Ibid., 32–33.
26. Ibid., 33.
27. Ibid., 34.
28. Ibid., 35–37.
29. Ibid.
30. "Water Permitting 101", *Office of Waste Water Management, Environmental Protection Agency (EPA) Website,* http://www.epa.gov/npdes/pubs/101pape.pdf (accessed on June 16, 2013).
31. Anita L. Morse, "The Cost of Purity: Use of the Effluent Charge in Water Quality control and Management," *Valparaiso University Law Review* 7, No. 2 (Winter 1973): 170–171.
32. Morse, "The Cost of Purity: Use of the Effluent Charge in Water Quality control and Management," 176–177.
33. Ibid.
34. Ibid., 175.
35. Ibid., 175–176.
36. "Water Permitting 101", *Office of Waste Water Management, Environmental Protection Agency (EPA) Website,* http://www.epa.gov/npdes/pubs/101pape.pdf (accessed on June 16, 2013), 1–2.
37. James Boyd, *Water Pollution Taxes: A Good Idea Doomed to Failure? Discussion Paper 03–20* (Washington D.C.: Resources for the Future, 2003), 4.
38. "Water Permitting 101", *Office of Waste Water Management, Environmental Protection Agency (EPA) Website,* http://www.epa.gov/npdes/pubs/101pape.pdf (accessed on June 16, 2013). 3–4.
39. A comprehensive list of pollutants is available at *Cornell University Law School, Legal Information Institute website,* http://www.law.cornell.edu/cfr/text/40/401.15 (accessed on June 19, 2013).
40. Disco, "Accepting Father Rhine? Technological Fixes, Vigilance, and Transnational Lobbies as "European" Strategies of Dutch Municipal Water Supplies 1900–1975," 398–399.
41. Ibid., 398–400.
42. Council of Europe, *Fresh Water pollution control in Europe* (Council of Europe, 1966), 65–72.
43. Disco, "Accepting Father Rhine? Technological Fixes, Vigilance, and Transnational Lobbies as "European" Strategies of Dutch Municipal Water Supplies 1900–1975," 398–400.

44. Ibid.
45. Raymond Dominick, "Capitalism, Communism, and Environmental Protection, Lessons from the Germany Experience," *Environmetal History* 3, No. 3 (1998): 316.
46. Franz-Josef Brüggemeier and Thomas Rommelspacher, *Blauer Himmel über der Ruhr. Geschichte der Umwelt im Ruhrgebiet 1840–1990* (Essen: Klartext, 1992), 66.
47. Disco, "Accepting Father Rhine? Technological Fixes, Vigilance, and Transnational Lobbies as "European" Strategies of Dutch Municipal Water Supplies 1900–1975," 398–400.
48. Miranda A. Schreurs, *Environmental Politics in Japan, Germany, and the United States* (Cambrdige: Cambridge University Press, 2003), 51–58.
49. Ibid., 50–51.
50. Dominick, "Capitalism, Communism, and Environmental Protection, Lessons from the Germany Experience," 316.
51. Kneese and Bower, *Managing Water Quality, Economics, Technology, Institutions*. 252.
52. Karl-Ulrich Rudolp and Thomas Block, *The German Water Sector, Policies and Experiences* (Bonn: Federal Ministry for the Environment, Nature Conservation and Nuclear Safety, 2001), 6.
53. Manfred Pütz, "Monitoring Industrial Emissions: A successful instrument for environmental enforcement," *Third International Conference on Environmental Enforcement: Proceedings Volume 1, 1994 Oaxaca, Mexico at the National Service Center for Environmental Publications (NSCEP) Website* http://nepis.epa.gov/Exe/ZyNET.exe/300R94002.HTM?ZyActionD=ZyDocument&Client=EPA&Index=1995%20Thru%201999%7C1976%20Thru%201980%7C2006%20Thru%202010%7C1991%20Thru%201994%7CHardcopy%20Publications%7C2000%20Thru%202005%7C1986%20Thru%201990%7C2011%20Thru%202015%7C1981%20Thru%201985%7CPrior%20to%201976&Docs=&Query=Oaxaca%20&Time=&EndTime=&SearchMethod=2&TocRestrict=n&Toc=&TocEntry=&QField=&QFieldYear=&QFieldMonth=&QFieldDay=&UseQField=&IntQFieldOp=0&ExtQFieldOp=0&XmlQuery=&File=D%3A%5CZYFILES%5CINDEX%20Dat.%5CNSCEP%5CELECTRONIC%5C00000002%5C300R94002.HTM&User=ANONYMOUS&Password=anonymous&SortMethod=-%7Ch&MaximumDocuments=15&FuzzyDegree=0&ImageQuality=r85g16/r85g16/

x150y150g16/i500&Display=hpfr&DefSeekPage=x&SearchBack=ZyActionL&Back=ZyActionS&BackDesc=Results%20page&MaximumPages=1&ZyEntry=1&SeekPage=x (accessed July 22, 2014) 231–232.

54. Council of Europe, *Fresh Water pollution control in Europe* (Council of Europe, 1966), 72–78.
55. Ibid., 83.

4

Stalinist Vision for Economy and Environment in Hungary in the 1950s

4.1 Postwar Reconstruction and Communist Takeovers in East-Central Europe

In 1945, it was clear that the economics and international politics of the interwar years could not be continued. Europe was dominated by right-wing, authoritarian regimes between the two-world wars, communism and socialism became popular ideas throughout Europe after World War II. The Left attracted the masses and enticed intellectuals. And the communists formed popular parties not only in the Soviet Union dominated East-Central Europe but throughout the entire continent. In Italy, for example, over two million people joined the Communist Party, which was one of the most radical communist parties in the West.[1] Also, the socialist idea was very popular in France and in the United Kingdom, which eventually led to a series of nationalizations in both countries. The Christian Democratic movement, which, also saw a large growth after 1945, and the socialists agreed with the rise in state intervention, believing it was necessary to achieve prosperity and economic growth. It was of foremost importance for all major political powers in Europe to avoid the catastrophic spiral of populism and rearmament that lead to the inferno of World War II.

V. Pál, *Technology and the Environment in State-Socialist Hungary*,
DOI 10.1007/978-3-319-63832-4_4

While the socialist idea was popular in Western Europe after the war, communism would provide a hope of prosperity for backward East-Central Europe. A relative popularity of the communist ideology in ECE was backed by the military presence and political pressure of the Soviet Union. Even without the massive political weight of the USSR after the World War II, communist ideology was enticing for many. This was because, in theory, communism was believed to create more favorable preconditions for economies, and would provide better production results than capitalism. It would eliminate the anarchy of the market and fluctuations in supply and demand. Workers would be freed from exploitation and would work more enthusiastically. Communism was believed by many of its followers to be a purer and nobler system than capitalism. According to them, communism would ensure social justice and equality.[2]

In reality, communism arrived brutally to East-Central Europe. After the war, Moscow-backed communists seized power in most East-Central European countries. In Poland, the script of establishing a dictatorial regime was similar to Hungary and the German Democratic Republic. The Moscow-backed Polish Workers' Party (Polska Partia Robortnicza, PPR) eliminated political opponents gradually. Geopolitical factors also facilitated central planning in postwar Poland. After 1945, borders were restructured, and the country's territory shrunk by 20%, and "shifted" to the West. Her new 110,000-square-kilometer Western territory was rich in coal and iron deposits and had advanced infrastructure that fitted well for Stalinist-type industrialization.

In Czechoslovakia, the communist party operated legally between the two world wars. Therefore, in 1945, the KSČ (Komunistická strana Československa) had a strong basis of support. The party was established already in 1921, and within four years it acquired 350,000 members, with 41 parliamentary deputies and 13.3% of the votes in the state election.[3] During the war, both Czechs and Slovaks had important communist underground movements, which identified themselves with national liberation. After the war, the Czechoslovak Communist Party produced the fastest growth in the region among communists and had more than 1,000,000 party members by 1947. Without much support from Moscow, the Czechoslovak communists gained 38% of votes at the country's first postwar election in March 1946. The communist candidate, Klement Gottwald, was named Prime Minister (1946–1948). Gottwald slowly changed his initial tactic of political cooperation and coalition government, and by February 1948, communists forced all noncommunist ministers to resign.[4]

In Hungary, Allied air raids destroyed significant production capacities all around the country. During the war, hundreds of thousands of Hungarian soldiers and civilians died, and over half a million Jewish Hungarians were deported and murdered by the Hungarian police and German occupational forces.[5] In November 1945, the Smallholders' Party won the election with 57% of the vote, while the communists and the social democrats received 17% of votes.[6] Between 1945 and 1948, Hungarian Muscovites eliminated their rivals aggressively by slicing them up one by one.[7] The final cut of the salami was in 1947–1948 when several important political figures, including Prime Minister Ferenc Nagy, were charged with conspiracy. During the plot, Nagy was on holiday in Switzerland and decided not to return to face charges.[8]

Western and East-Central European countries developed controversial political systems after World War II, however the economic foundation of both the capitalist and communist modes of production were the same: growth. Because of both the capitalist and communist system was clinging on economic growth, and without growth they stagnate and decline environmental destruction has been inseparable from both capitalism and communism.

The period between 1950 and 1973 was characterized on the one hand by a long period of uninterrupted economic growth, on the other hand unprecedented environmental pollution that tainted every larger area on both sides of the Iron Curtain.

According to Barry Eichengreen western European state interventionist industrialization, and East-Central European centrally planned economic systems showed a number of similarities in their strengths and weaknesses. Eventually, they were both excelling in economic catch-up, at least initially. Bridging the large gap between Western Europe and the USA in the postwar era was aided by the cooperation of trade unions, employers' associations, and growth-minded governments. These groups of decision makers conjointly mobilized savings to secure investment and full employment. Full employment was especially crucial in Western

Germany in the late 1940s and in the 1950s, where the memories of mass unemployment and hyperinflation were well remembered.

Postwar reconstruction was followed by a period of extensive growth in both the Western and East-Central parts of the continent that worsened environmental conditions in the West and introduced industrial and urban environmental pollution on an unprecedented scale in countries of East-Central Europe. Here, especially in rural areas, such levels of pollution had been unknown until the introduction of communist central plans.

During the 1950s and to a lesser extent in the 1960s, the major goals of industrial development in Western and East-Central Europe were similar. During the same period of time, the management of environmental resources resembled each other in both the Western and East-Central parts of the European continent.

4.2 Stalinist Economic Policies in East-Central Europe in the Early 1950s

Czechoslovakia (especially Bohemia and Moravia) and East Germany have already witnessed notable degree of industrialization before the implementation of the extensive Stalinist growth. Therefore the relevance of primitive accumulation was even less in these countries than in Hungary. This was because initial accumulation in Stalinist state-socialist states was mostly the result of the increased workforce and the most intensive production of already existing production units. Most of the new and reconstructed plants took years to build in ideal circumstances. However notable delays were commonplace throughout the region. Developers did not yet have the experience for such largescale production units, substantial materials were often lacked because of the shortage or because they were hard to obtain from the West. Because new industrial plants were about to begin their operations later, and the initial ambitious targets of industrialization were further increased several times in the plan period it was impossible to reach the required targets. Despite the economic reform attempts, Stalinist investments were carried on and build up with substantial delays. The abandonment of key projects could have harmed the regime even more.

In Czechoslovakia, the law to nationalize key industries was passed on October 24, 1945, and large firms, banks, and insurance companies that employed more than 50% of the industrial workforce became state-owned. During the Czechoslovak FFYP (1949–1953), agriculture was neglected and foreign trade was redirected to the socialist bloc. Exports grew to socialist countries from 40 to 78% between 1948 and 1953.[9] Similar to Hungary and other East-Central European countries, energy needs soared in Czechoslovakia. In the 1950s, energy consumption per capita in Czechoslovakia was comparable to the United Kingdom and was approximately two times larger than in Poland and Hungary.[10]

Czechoslovakia was soon integrated to the socialist bloc and its industries were developed to supply heavy industrial outputs. Agriculture was neglected even more in the revision of the Czechoslovakia First Five-Year plan (1949–1953) in 1951 than initially planned. Czechoslovakia's foreign trade was redirected to the socialist bloc and her exports grew to socialist countries from 40% in 1948 to 78% to 1953.[11] As a result of the new forced structure of industry, Czechoslovakia shifted from exporting mostly consumer goods and some raw materials such as coal to the export of machinery and also raw materials. Between 1948 and 1953 the export of machinery grew from about 20% of the total exports to 42%, while the export of consumption goods decreased from 30% to 12%. The 1951 version of the plan targeted even more unrealistic outputs the original 1949 version. Some of the main products such as iron ore, cement, motor vehicles, meat had to be more than doubled by the end of the plan period. Coal, steel, fabrics had to reach a" mere" 40–70% growth in the five-year period. This plan failed in Czechoslovakia. Shortage was commonplace in all major raw materials and work force as well. Industry used to be already an important sector in Czechoslovakia the number of workers increased from about 1.5 million to over 2 million between 1948 and 1958. Industry was rather developed and also energy wasting, and as a result, Czechoslovakia had one of the highest energy consumption per capita in the world by the second half of the 1950s, approximately on the level

Fig. 4.1 Political assembly in Miskolc at AFIT, No. XVI. Car-repair Company. Zsolcai kapu 9–11, 1952. *Photo* FORTEPAN / UVATERV

of the United Kingdom and approximately double of other ECE states such as Poland and Hungary (Fig. 4.1).[12]

Poland, similarly to Hungary, was less industrialized in general than the Czech lands and Eastern Germany. After the already initially ambitious First Six-Year Plan targets, plan revisions were made in 1951–1952. The total output was increased by almost 17%. Most of the new targets were relocated for the favor of the war industries. As a result, between 1949 and 1955 the output of the metal-working industries almost tripled. There was an over 130% growth in chemical production and construction materials as well. Only 23% of the total output came from new enterprises, that was because most investments were not operational by the end of the 1950s. Similarly to other ECE countries during the early planning period, economic policy and its main institutions have changed a number of times. This made construction and planning even harder. The main reason for changes was often the search for effective organizational structure. Therefore most of the production growth was initiated by working old plants more intensively and with more workers.[13] In this first period of industrialization, productivity was still lagging behind prewar levels. These tendencies were similar to what was happening in Hungary and to some extend Czechoslovakia and East Germany. Unemployment was targeted to be ended, and women were encouraged to take full-time jobs. This put dual pressure on women under the 'cover' of gender equality because now they had to fulfill expectations both at home and in work. In addition, political prisoners, students, and pupils were also involved in the production process. In Poland, the number of workers dramatically grew. Between 1948 and 1953 it went up from 308,000 to 771,000 in construction, and from 220,000 to 515,000 in machine building. Most new workers moved to growing cities where construction could not keep up with the demand. Overcrowded and deteriorated housing conditions were commonplace. Poland's half-war economy was not dissolved after the death of Stalin. Compared to Hungary, where Imre Nagy, Chairman of the Council of Ministers relaxed oppression and began a new course of somewhat more livable communism, in Poland the Stalinist regime was not shaken until the Polish October. The plan changed somewhat however, the Ninth Plenum of the Central Committee of the United Workers' Party in September 1953 scaled down the total plan budget, but only took a few half-finished plants off the list for an unspecific period of time, and decided to finish most of the investments with a few or more years of delay. One of the flagship investments of the era was the steel plant and city of Nowa Huta. Here a steel plant and workers' housing units were initially planned to be constructed by the Reyn Engineering Company based in Chicago before the Second World War. In the new Communist era, 'Nowa Huta' was destined to be the seat for Poland's new metallurgical combine. It has been discussed to be built on the meeting of the Central United Metallurgical Industry in 1945. The Central Administration for Metallurgical Industry formed on May 17, 1947, and the government decreed the construction of the works and the housing estates on January 26, 1948. Work on Nowa Huta began simultaneously to other gigantic investments in ECE in mid-1949. It took five years to put the first stage of the plant into operation and it was opened in 1954.[14]

In Poland, the results of central planning were similarly disastrous. There, key industries were nationalized in the coalition era and the FTYP was implemented between 1947 and 1949. Soon after, the Central Planning Office (Centralny Urząd Planowania) began to prepare the Stalinist-type First Six-Year Plan that was based on the massive development of heavy industries. The Polish First Six-Year Plan (FSYP) was ambitious, but in 1951–1952 it was redesigned to aspire to even greater output. Most of the new targets were relocated in favor of the war industries. As a result, between 1949 and 1955, the output of the metalworking industries nearly tripled in Poland. There was also an over 130% growth in chemical production. Most of the production growth came from old plants worked more intensively and only 23% of the total output came from new enterprises. This was typical throughout ECE and most FFYP and FSYP investments were not operational until the end of the 1950s. Constant structural reorganizations and changing economic policy measures prevented developers from finishing most new projects on time.[15]

Central planning was introduced in East Germany during the second half of 1948, which was followed by the First Two-Year Plan (1949–1950) and the First Five-Year Plan (1951–1955). Similarly to Hungary key sectors of the industry were nationalized. By 1950, 68% of industrial production came from the public sector and agriculture was not yet collectivized.[16] Parallel to the First Two-Year Plan, a Soviet-style Stakhanovite movement was introduced in East Germany in 1948. Adolf Hennecke, who was a symbolic figure of this production enhancement movement increased his daily output of coal by 380% and was pledged by the SED (Socialist Unity Party of Germany) as the hero of labor.[17] During the implementation of the planning system, fundamental changes took place in the East German flow of trade. Whereas in 1947 75% of trade was with West Germany and only 7% was with other socialist countries, next year trade with socialist countries (44%) already suppressed West German trade slightly (43%). This trend continued and by 1951, 76% of GDR's trade was with socialist countries, and West German trade shrank to a mere 7%.[18]

International tensions in Korea, Yugoslavia and especially with West Germany drove military spending up. On July 1, 1952 the People's Police in Barracks, *Kasernierte Volkspolizei, KVP* was created and plans were laid out to increase the total number of KVP troops up to 200,000 in a short period of time. This force was the basis for the East German People's Army.[19] Soviet-type industrialization and a growing pressure for larger armed forces played a major role in the outline of the First Five-Year plan in 1950. As a result, 1.8 million tons of iron ore, over 210 million tons of various types of coal were to be produced with a new merchant fleet of 22 ocean-going vessels during the five-year planning period.[20] During the planning period, outstanding achievements were recorded. Steel production for example, rose from 999,000 tonnes in 1950 to 1,517,000 tonnes in 1955 and similar success was reported in coal mining and the chemical industry. These successes, similarly to Hungary were achieved at the expense of light industry and living standards. Most consumer goods were in short supply and butter, meat, and sugar were still rationed. Wages hardly rose and the collectivization of agriculture discriminated many of the private farmers. Prices were escalating, and the government decided to control its growing deficit by raising production norms. More and more decided to leave the country. According to the statistics, 165,648 fled the GDR in 1951, a year later this figure grew to 182,393. The year of the death of Stalin holds the record with 331,390 leaving the GDR due to growing hardships of the economy.[21]

In East Germany, by 1950, 68% of industrial production came from state-owned plants.[22] East German steel production rose from around 1 million tonnes to over 1.5 million tonnes between 1950 and 1955. Similar trends were typical in coal mining and the chemical industry. In the mean time, most consumer goods were in short supply and butter, meat, and sugar were still rationed.[23] Social tensions escalated in East Germany and on June 17, 1953, over 500,000 workers were involved in an uprising that was crushed by the Soviet army. As a result, the East German government altered the FFYP and gave some priority to consumer goods and food rationing in 1954.

Dissatisfaction with Stalinist industrial policies grew throughout East-Central Europe during the first half of the 1950 and led to widespread resistance and a handful of armed conflicts, such as the Hungarian Revolution of 1956. Growing tensions finally escalated into the June 17 uprising in which over 500,000 workers were involved and which was ruthlessly crushed by the Soviet army. All together over 200 people were executed after the uprising and about 1400 people received life sentences. As a result, the East German government was forced to alter the plan as a result of the June 1953 demonstrations following Stalin's death and gave higher priority to consumer goods and food rationing in 1954.

After the death of Stalin possibilities of economic reforms were investigated throughout ECE. Already planned and constructed production units were not shut down but were extended and amended in the coming period. Soon the acceleration of industrialization and urbanization led to similar environmental issues that had been witnessed in Great Britain and Germany earlier in the nineteenth and twentieth centuries. Stalinist development in East-Central European countries showed similar signs of crisis and inadequate planning. Industrial growth was produced with large externalities and accompanied with environmental destruction. Construction of wastewater treatment facilities was neglected both in old and newly built units. Increased pollution levels emerged first in the old plants that produced more intensively. Old air cleaning and wastewater treatment facilities, which had been in operation since the first half of the twentieth century, did not cope with the increased volume of by-products. By the late 1950s, pollution from new FFYP plants also appeared. As a result of increased water pollution from both old and new industrial sites, the level of water pollution escalated in East-Central Europe from the mid-1950s. This critical situation, however, was typical only for a brief period of Stalinist-type development in East-Central Europe, roughly between 1949 and 1953/1956. After the total fiasco of Stalinist-type economic policy in East-Central Europe, governments tackled both economic production and environmental destruction issues surprisingly rapidly.

4.3 Stalinist Economic Policies in Hungary in the Early 1950s

During the FFYP in Hungary, heavy industrial development gained absolute priority. The communists saw that Budapest was already overdeveloped in industrial terms, meanwhile the rest of the country remained agricultural. Therefore, the regime aimed to industrialize backward rural areas and smaller regional industrial centers. The type of urbanization and industrialization that the Hungarian FFYP initiated was not only related to Soviet Stalinism, it also followed the industrialization model which dominated Europe between the 1930s and 1960s. This trend included "*government sponsored, central development programs (...) which aimed to create employment, facilitated urbanization (...), and helped the catch-up growth of disadvantaged regions.*"[24] The regional differences Hungary faced were similar to challenges in several European countries. In 1946, 9 million lived in Hungary and over 1.5 million resided in and around the fairly developed Budapest. Communists aimed to improve the economy in areas inhabited by the rest of the 7.5 million (Fig. 4.2).

After the National Plan Office (Országos Tervhivatal, OT), and other important infrastructural bodies were established during the First Three-Year Plan (FTYP), central planners aimed to tackle large regional economic differences.[25] In 1948, the Area Management Institute of Hungary (Területrendezési Intézet, TERINT) that researched regional planning and urban issues received a contract from the OT to prepare a plan to develop new industrial areas. One would have been constructed south of Budapest along the Danube River, another would have been developed in the northeastern part of the country around Miskolc. The latter was envisioned as a "counter center" to Budapest with over 300,000 people living in Miskolc and an additional 200,000 living in the other towns of the Borsod industrial area. Miskolc and Ózd, the two primary towns of Borsod, were planned to be developed further. As part of the plan, two new chemical and power generating centers would be built in Kazincbarcika and Leninváros (Tiszaújváros). Mines and factories would be extended and opened in several smaller

Fig. 4.2 Kazincbarcika, In front of Egressy Béni (Lenin) út No. 21., 1958. *Photo* FORTEPAN / LECHNER NONPROFIT KFT. DOKUMENTÁCIÓS KÖZPONT / VÁTI

towns and villages, for example in Berente, Rudabánya, Sajószentpéter, Sajókeresztúr, Sajóbábony, Alsózsolca, Nyékládháza, and Tiszapalkonya. Settlements in the Borsod Basin were planned to be transformed from partly agricultural settlements to towns of an industrial belt.[26] During the FFYP, communists in Hungary contemplated and changed their development plans haphazardly, according to Germuska. Despite changes throughout the design process, the pivotal role of Borsod remained in plans. The valley of the Sajó was far from dangerous border areas in the West and South, hence seemed to be a suitable location to develop Hungary's largest rural industrial center. This decision, however, did not calculate with the lack of adequate resources available in the area (Fig. 4.3).[27]

On November 10, 1949, the Political Committee of the Hungarian Workers' Party discussed the draft of the FFYP and precisely a month later the Hungarian Parliament formally enacted "Act XXV" of the FFYP (1950–1954). The country was "ready" for full-fledged command

Year	Pig iron production (tons)	Steel production (tons)	Tractor production (units)	Motorcycle production (units)
1949	428,000	890,000	2,300	12,000
1954	960,000 (224%)	1,600,000 (179%)	4,600 (200%)	23,000 (191%)

Fig. 4.3 Selected annual production targets of the First Five Year Plan for the Iron, Steel, and Machine Industry, 1949–1954. *Source* 1949. évi XXV. törvény A Magyar Népköztársaság els ötéves népgazdasági tervér I, az 1950. január 1-t I az 1954. december 31 -ig terjed id szakra. (Act XXV/1949 on the First Five Year Plan of the People"s Republic of Hungary from January 1, 1950 to December 31, 1954.) Enacted in Budapest, Hungary. II. Fejezet: Termelés és beruházások terve. A, Ipar, (Chapter II. Plan of Production and Investment, A) Industry) Enacted on December 10, 1949, Budapest, Hungary

economy as the communists self-confidently proclaimed: "Three years ago factories, mines and metallurgy were almost solely owned by capitalists, today 92 per cent of them are owned by the state. The banking system was almost solely owned by capitalists, today it is owned by the state. Our foreign trade was almost solely owned by capitalists, now foreign trade is wholly owned by the state. Our wholesale trade was almost solely owned by capitalists, now whole sale trade is completely state owned." [28]

In the FFYP light industry, agriculture, transportation, trade, and living standards played only supporting roles. Therefore, the FFYP invested from its total 50.9 billion Forint budget, 36% into energy intensive heavy industries. The light industry received little less than 6%, while agriculture—the main branch of national economy at the time—received less than 16% of the total funding. 18.3 billion (36%) went to energy intensive and highly polluter heavy industries. The light industry received only 3 billion Forints (5.9%). Agriculture itself—the main branch of national economy at the time—received 8 billion Forints (15.7%) of funding. Agriculture and agriculturally related industrial, infrastructural, educational, and medical expenses absorbed in fact 12.5 billion Forints, about 24.5%. Infrastructural expenses cost 7.5 billion Forints (14.7%), and expenses related to living standards such as housing, urban development, medical and social care, and cultural life were funded with 7.4 billion Forints (14.5%).[29]

The FFYP aimed to reduce the supremacy of Budapest and strengthen regional industrial areas. It envisioned two new complex industrial districts outside of Budapest. Both of which would be based on local coal deposits as a primary source of energy and raw material. One of these new industrial areas was situated around the city of Pécs, close to the coal deposits of the Mecsek Mountains of Southwestern Hungary. The other area was the Borsod Basin, in the Sajó Valley between the towns of Miskolc and Ózd, where brown coal mines, and iron- and steel factories represented the backbone of industry until the 1960s when chemical production emerged around Kazincbarcika and later in Lenintown. This plan's flagship new town project was Sztálinváros (Dunaújváros) and adjacent steel mills (Dunapentele, Sztálinváros, 1951–1961), 60 km south of Budapest. Other important new town projects included: Kazincbarcika (Sajókazinc, Kazincbarcika, 1948–), and Leninváros (Tiszaszederkény, until 1970, Leninváros, 1970–1990) in the Borsod Basin. In addition, former industrial center was developed during the plan period, such as Greater Miskolc (Nagy-Miskolc), Ózd in the Borsodi Basin and Salgótarján, Tatabánya, and Dorog (Fig. 4.4).[30]

In reality, the outcome of the Hungarian FFYP was disastrous. This was because efforts were concentrated in a handful of randomly chosen centers, while the plan abandoned large rural areas in the Great Plains (Alföld) and light industrial and service segments of the economy. Even essential facilities, such as adequate housing, were neglected.[31] Parallel with the immense growth of industrial production and the construction of new towns, electricity, and water use soared in Hungary. The FFYP ordered electricity production to be doubled from 2200 to 4270 million kWh within 5 years. The increased demand for electricity would be supplied from coal-fueled power plants in Kazincbarcika, Várpalota, and Mohács, and the Lovászi natural gas and Tiszalök hydropower plant.[32] Planning was inadequate, and the rapid need for large quantities of electricity surprised planners. Domestic mines struggled to meet soaring the coal needs of the rapidly extended industry. Simultaneously, low quality domestic brown coal was inadequate for coking. Therefore coke,

Fig. 4.4 View of the Diósgyőr Iron- and Steel Mills, 1959. *Photo* FORTEPAN / BAUER SÁNDOR

an essential component of enlarged iron and steel production capacities, was in short supply and had to be imported from Czechoslovakia (Fig. 4.5).[33]

Along with the centralization of industry, water management bodies were also centralized in East-Central Europe. In 1952, Stalinist purges reached professional water managers in Hungary. After the devastating flood on the upper Tisza River, several water officials and managers were charged with sabotage and were prosecuted. Politically reliable water professionals were forced into new peak water administrative body, the National Water Management Office (Országos Vízgazdálkodási Hivatal, OVH). VITUKI, the formerly independent research institute, became part of the OVH. Between 1953 and 1968, the OVH was converted to the National Water Directorate (Országos Vízügyi Főigazgatóság, OVF).[34]

Fig. 4.5 Tiszalök Hydropower Plant, 1955. *Photo* FORTEPAN / UVATERV

In 1954, the OVF organized twelve regional Water Superintendents. One of these, the North Hungarian Water Superintendency (Észak-Magyarországi Vízügyi Igazgatóság, ÉVÍZIG), supervised the area of the Borsod Basin. After 1961, the ÉVÍZIG was responsible for the protection of waters and for monitoring and fine setting procedures. Therefore, the OVF facilitated the establishment of regional waterworks and regional water supply networks (Víz-, és Csatornamű Vállalatok, Regionális Vízmű Vállalatok). Hungarian regional waterworks resembled the functions and operational goals of German associations. However, Hungarian regional water networks were solely state-owned, and Germany water associations were partly private and partly state-owned.[35]

The water lobby was a relatively strong state-owned body in Hungary during the state socialist period. It employed 77,000 workers in the 1970s in a country of around 10 million residents. Also, the control of water resources underwent significant development in Hungary between 1945 and 1989. The number of surface water quality monitoring stations grew from 207 in 1938 to 1221 in 1986. Between 1970 and 1985, water use skyrocketed from 2.9 billion cubic meters to 5.5 billion cubic meters. Parallel with growing water demands, storage capacity improved radically from 50 million cubic meters to 730 million cubic meters between 1945 and 1975. The importance of water infrastructures, including wastewater treatment plants, continually rose after 1945 in Hungarian central development budgets. In 1950, 11.7 billion Ft (0.8% of the annual state budget) was spent on water infrastructures, whereas 101.3 billion Ft (3.9% of the state budget) was spent in 1970, and 239.6 billion Ft (5.9% of the annual state budget) was spent in 1985.[36]

4.4 The First Five Year Plan and Its Economic and Environmental Impact in the Valley of the Sajó River

Accelerated industrialization posed an increased stress of resources and the natural environment in East-Central Europe. Water for industrial and municipal use was one of the first resources that experienced scarcity on a level that planners had to take into account. Prior to the FFYP, water quantity problems were uncommon in Miskolc. When public water supply services began in Miskolc in 1913, water was supplied only in wealthy and central neighborhoods of the town. In poorer neighborhoods, groundwater wells were used. The water supply system was extended in the 1920s and 1930s, but large residential areas, especially in less well-to-do areas, remained without water supplies or wastewater networks. In 1945, much of the drinking water in the city of Miskolc was supplied by the Miskolc-Tapolca springs. There, three pumps produced a maximum of 14,000 cubic meters of water a day. This amount was nearly 80% of the total 18,000 cubic meters a day water production in the city. In the pre-World War II period, Miskolc spared diseases because of its relatively safe water supply source: the limestone karst springs. Karst water springs in and around Miskolc were supplied from the limestone cave systems, in which water traveled from the plateau of the Bükk Mountains. Karst water springs and their output were very vulnerable to weather changes and precipitation. In the case of unusual weather conditions, the water production dynamics of these springs changed rapidly. Erratic fluctuation in water supply added further stress to the system soon after the kick of industrial drive in the late 1930s and under World War II. Water supply did not face supply problems immediately after World War II. During the coalition years between 1946 and 1948, the price of water was the main concern for residents, many of whom struggled to make ends meet in the postwar era. The quantitative water supply perspective and the Stalinist "exploitation of water sources" philosophy was established by the FTYP. This soon escalated to the percentage-obsessed, Soviet-type "water production" in 1949.[37]

After communist urbanization and industrialization triggered water use and cheap water was made available, it was difficult to keep up with demand for the city waterworks.[38] Water was imperative for the communists. Industrial water supply was essential to maintain economic growth and proved that communism was a better economic and social system than capitalism. Urban water supply, besides being a public necessity, was an important social message for the communists. A large number of contaminated private wells remained in use in many districts of Miskolc until the 1950s, and communists aimed to bring free or cheap water to all residents, including poor neighborhoods. Providing clean water abundantly was an integral part of the communist propaganda.[39] As a result, several water fountains were installed in the city's peripheral neighborhoods to provide clean and safe drinking water for free in the first half of the 1950s. The number of households connected to the network was also extended, as was the amount of water used per household. In newly built multistory housing units, every resident used approximately 250 L of water each day. This, if we take into account the growth of the population in Miskolc, resulted in a rapid rise in demand for water. As a result, municipal water use grew rapidly. This paralleled the staggering growth of industrial production and industrial water use.[40]

In Miskolc, pressing water needs turned into periods of water shortage as early as 1951–1952 and it was marked by *"regular water service shortcomings, regularly dysfunctional taps in upper floors (of buildings) and lines of women (waiting for water) by the inadequately functioning public well in Pereces, (a higher altitude mining neighborhood), before dawn.*"[41] Officials feared that if residents in uphill neighborhoods were unable to access safe and clean drinking water from the city water network, they would use the old and contaminated ground water wells. On April 25, 1954, an article by Ilona Adamovics in *Észak-Magyarország*, a local daily, described the dramatic water supply situation in Miskolc, the country's chief communist production center in detail: "*water moves in the waterpipes like – mercury. Sometimes it (the water) fills it (the water pipe), sometimes it the water) disappears without trace.*"[42] In 1951–1952, the maximum water need in Miskolc was around 50,000 cubic meters a day and was growing. Water needs were especially soaring during dry summer months when the karst springs produced close to their minimum. This controversy between water needs and supply added further stress to the water supply system. In addition, reservoir capacity was meager; hence, winter and spring surplus water could not be stored for dry summers.[43] As a result of multiple factors, the water shortage problem became apparent for the public and decision-makers in Miskolc between 1951 and 1956. Immediate action needed to be taken to avoid the deterioration of the situation (Fig. 4.6).

First, water shortage was tackled by pumping more water into the system from the existing network of karst springs. From 1951, the extra

Year	Annual consumption of water cubic meter
1913	400,000
1935	2,400,000
1945	3,800,000
1954	7,000,000
1956	11,000,000

Fig. 4.6 Water consumption in Miskolc, 1913–1954. *Source* Ilona Adamovics, "Miskolc Vízellátása (Water Supply in Miskolc)," Észak-Magyarország, 25 April 1954.

water needs in Miskolc were satisfied from additional karst resources in the Bükk Mountains in the localities of Lillafüred and Tapolca. The system was also extended. In 1953–1954, the Tapolca waterworks were extended and new wells and pumps supplied the city with an additional 15,000 cubic meters of water daily. To store more water, a new 3000 cubic meter underground water tank was constructed between 1952 and 1954. A further 5000 cubic meters of storing capacity was added to the system later in 1962. These improvements were vital but were not enough and the Tapolca springs grew to be so heavily utilized in the 1950s that they reached their maximum output by the early 1960s. In 1958, water was supplied to Miskolc from six karst water springs which were situated around the city to the west and southwest. One of the smallest sources, the Galya spring, supplied the Baross-Pálinkás mines and six residential units in Pereces with 230 cubic meter/day. The "Felsőforrás" spring supplied the mining community of Pereces with 470 cubic meters/day and had a 60–70 cubic meter/day surplus, which could be used to supply the peripheral Lyukóbánya mining settlement and mine. The Anna cave spring in Lillafüred delivered 5000 cubic meters/day, which was enough to supply most residential areas in Diósgyőr and Újdiósgyőr including the newly built Kilián housing estates and the Győri kapu neighborhood. Surplus from the Anna cave spring was stored in the Görögszőlő-hegyi water tank. The Szinva spring supplied 300 cubic meters/day for Lillafüred and the Palota Hotel. The Tavi spring in Diósgyőr supplied 5000 cubic meters/day and was used in the Lenin Metallurgical Plants and in the surrounding workers' colony. The above-mentioned five springs contributed together an average of 11,000 cubic meters/day to the water supply system of the city. For the city of Miskolc, the most important sources of water were the Tapolca springs. These series of karst springs supplied 35,000 cubic meters/day. Springs in Tapolca and around Diósgyőr produced a maximum of 46,000 cubic meters a day combined.

Extensions were trailing booming industrial and urban water needs. The growth of the city and its industries accelerated, and it was becoming very difficult to satisfy that excess water need of Miskolc from the city's traditional karst resources.[44] Finding and tapping more water was a war against natural forces to run a communist industry with success.

New springs were vital resources for the planners. Extending the water supply system was a heroic fight for the makers of propaganda: "battle for more water" and the "conquer of new springs", thus they raised the attention of regular workers. Heroes of the Battle for Water were the brigades of the Miskolc Waterworks Company. These brigades participated in compulsory work competition meanwhile conquering new springs and those performing well earned the "Socialist Brigade" (Szocialista Brigád) title and economic privileges. Heroes of the Battle for Water were pivotal for industrialist propaganda: they would show a good example of communist work ethics, morale, and creativity to improve production. For example, the Sereg (Army) Socialist Brigade was one of the sources of Brigade pride at Miskolc Waterworks. Members of this brigade submitted six new innovation ideas (újítás) and carried out all the designated projects by given deadlines. According to company reports, members of the Sereg Brigade achieved outstanding results at the Szent György spring, at Szabadság (Freedom) and Diósgyőr Baths, and they repaired Pump No. 3 at the Tapolca Springs well before the given deadline time. Sereg Brigade's "Socialist path" was followed by the young and ambitious János Répássy, who formed the August 20 Brigade with other overly enthusiastic young workers on August 1, 1967. Only five months later, the August 20 Brigade was already praised in the company annual report. These young lads were setting an example. They did not have unjustified absences from work or work accidents. In addition, they were very active socially and organized social and, more importantly, political events. It was not only construction and repairmen that aimed for better results at the Miskolc Waterworks. Truck drivers formed the Olejnyik (Olejnik) Brigade that aimed to reduce fuel consumption and minimize needs for vehicle repair. Competitions among local brigades were complemented with regional work competitions, where brigades from Szeged and Debrecen took part. In addition to brigade competitions, the Innovation Movement (Újítómozgalom) produced innovations. In 1967 four of these new innovations were patented, and innovators received 1200 Ft in compensation each for their patents. One of these patents received an 80,000 Ft compensation from the state-owned Investment Bank (Beruházási Bank) and that sum was dispersed among innovators.[45]

Extensive growth in water production did pump more water into the water supply network but it did not solve the structural problems of that supply network. When extra water was pumped into the system from new springs, the overload of existing pipes became critical. Two old mains between Tapolca and Miskolc—a 425 mm diameter from 1913, and a 400 mm from 1928—delivered water to the city with 9.5 atmospheric bar pressure in 1957. Overloading threatened the system with regular malfunctions due to high water pressure in the pipes.[46] That is why a 12 km-long 800 mm-diameter water main was constructed between 1957 and 1958. This new main connected Tapolca with the city's new 4500 cubic meter underground water tank in Tetemvár Hill, directly north–northwest of the center of Miskolc.[47]

The water shortage in Miskolc was also tackled on the user side. During the first years of the water shortage, thrifty water use slogans advertised water recycling and economical water use. Such campaigns were similar to the Gazda movement, which was a recycling campaign of metals in the 1950s.[48] Local waterworks estimated in 1957 that malfunctioning taps and water closets in Miskolc wasted about 430,000 cubic meters of water a month (!), an amount that could have covered around third of the municipal water need in the city (Fig. 4.7).[49]

Extensive growth of water production and supply required the extensive growth of fossil fuels to produce energy to pump more water to industrial plants and residential blocks. During the 1950s, to make things more complicated not only water was in scare supply in Borsod but also the energy. Apart from the dry periods, when there was enough water from the karst springs to supply Miskolc coal supply and engines hardly could keep the pace with supply needs. In spring and autumn, when rains created water surplus to be pumped into the water supply network, coal in inadequate supply and engines struggled. But during these months, the Miskolc Waterworks struggled to acquire enough coal to run water pumps effectively. In 1958, in Miskolc, 85% of supplied water was pumped to the system by coal-generated electricity and only 15% arrived from higher altitude springs through gravity. Between 1951 and 1958, the coal supply was erratic in Hungary, even in Miskolc, the capital of the Borsod coal mining region. Coal supply was so meager that the city baths were often closed for long periods of

Fig. 4.7 Rail car dumpers at the Coal Sorting Facility in Kazincbarcika, 1955. *Photo* FORTEPAN / UVATERV

time to save on heating coal. Instead of heating up the baths, local coal was used to run water pumps to supply residential consumers. In 1957, workers in Miskolc complained because many of them were unable to clean themselves. These workers did not have access to tap water and cleaning facilities at home, nor at their workplace, and their only choice was one of the public baths in Miskolc. When these baths were closed, workers lacked regular means of personal hygiene. The coal scarcity and its implication on public hygiene were taken seriously by the Miskolc Waterworks. In 1957, László Szilléry, Chief Engineer of the waterworks, told *Észak-Magyarország*: "*The most pressing problem of Miskolc's city baths is coal supply (...) mines are unable to supply coal continuously, therefore bathing possibilities are very restricted: baths are open by fits and starts. This situation cannot be tolerated because of public hygiene reasons, and because it gives a bad reputation to the capital city of the Borsod coal mining region: Miskolc.*"[50]

The revolution of 1956 not only halted the utilization of additional karst springs for a brief period of time but after the consolidation period in 1957, modified the technological-environmental philosophy behind water infrastructure projects. Shifting ideology of human–nature relationships was gradual, and Stalinist policies continued well into the reform period of the late 1950s and 1960s. Immediately after the dramatic events of October–November 1956, Hungarian planners aimed to stabilize erratic coal supplies and to minimize human and economic damage over the long and cold, coal-poor winter. The planner was particularly concerned about the rationalization of heating and heating costs. New alternatives were sought to replace hard to get coal. As early as 1957–1958, natural gas was introduced as a cheaper and more reliable alternative to poor quality and quantity domestic coal and expensive Czechoslovak coal in Miskolc. In line with the government's target to secure domestic heating supply after the disruptive coal shortages of the early 1950s, Miskolc purchased the first natural gas-based gas extractor in Hungary in 1960 from Czechoslovakia. This machine would also mark the beginning of a decade-long shift from coal to natural gas in the Hungarian heavy and energy-generating industries. Between 1958 and 1960, a natural gas storage station and a 10 km natural gas pipeline were constructed from Miskolc to Tiszapalkonya, where the Miskolc pipeline connected to the national natural gas grid.[51]

The development of the domestic chemical industry was one of the most important segments of Hungary's shift from coal to natural gas and crude oil. During the FFYP, the development of the chemical industry was relatively important but it still came second to the development of the iron and steel industries. Under the FFYP natural gas and crude oil played little importance, rather Stalinist ideals dominated development. The FFYP concentrated on fertilizer production plants and aimed for the mechanization of agriculture. The chemical industry was obliged to reach a 138% growth within the given five-year period. Its primary products were ordered to be coke, nitrogen and phosphorous fertilizers, and sodium hydroxide. On the margin, new products appeared such as super-phosphate, aniline, plastics, and pharmaceutical products (Fig. 4.8).[52]

Fig. 4.8 View of the Borsod Chemical Combine in Kazincbarcika under construction, 1954. *Photo* FORTEPAN / KOTNYEK ANTAL

During the FFYP, all Kazincbarcika investments were centrally commanded by the National Planning Office (*Országos Tervhivatal*; OT). The OT managed Barcika projects as parts of the Borsod Cooperation (*Borsod Koóperáció*, BK) industrial conglomerate.[53] Immediately following the launch of the FFYP, BK coal mines were extended because a new power plant and a nitrogen fertilizer factory had to be fueled.[54] The 194 MW Borsod Power Plant (*Borsod Hőerőmű*) was the largest of its kind in Hungary. The power plant was built between 1951 and 1957 and it supplied about 20% of domestic electricity production. The construction of the power plant was burdened with planning issues and delays. Hungarian planners lacked required experience for large-scale power plant construction projects. Adequate machinery could not be purchased from domestic sources and construction materials were often delivered sporadically and late. It was only after years of delays when generators and other key components were delivered from renowned East German power plant specialist firm EKM Bergmann-Borsig, that the plant could complete construction.[55]

The OT also ordered the construction of a fertilizer plant on June 15, 1950. The Barcika Fertilizer Factory was built to produce 110 tons of 20.5% nitrogen content fertilizer a day.[56] The Barcika Plant was one among a series of new fertilizer plants which were to supply Hungary's industrialized agriculture.

Delays were typical during the planning and construction phases. Confusion in economic planning was manifested even in the legal status of the Barcika Factory. In 1949, the Kazincbarcika chemical plant was erected as the Borsod National Nitrogen Works (*Borsod Nitrogénművek Nemzeti Vállalat*), supervised by the Chemical Works Investment Company (*Vegyiművek Beruházási Vállalat*). In March 1952, the plant was still under construction and the People's Economic Committee (*Népgazdasági Tanács*) re-named the plant as the Sajó Chemical Plant (*Sajómenti Vegyiművek*).[57] Only a few months later, the Borsod Industrial Trust (*Borsod Ipari Tröszt*) was created by the government to replace the Borsod Cooperation. The nitrogen fertilizer factory became a subdivision of this new trust.[58] The plant was not even finished when the Council of Ministers, (*Minisztertanács*) decided to increase the plant's capacity by another 50% in July 1954.[59] Test runs began in July 1956 when the factory was again renamed. Between 1956 and 1991, the company operated under the name of Borsod Chemical Plants (*Borsod Vegyi Művek*, BVK). Full capacity production came on line in 1958, long after the initial deadline had passed. Shortly after production began, it was halted because of dysfunctional domestically-produced compressors installed during the FFYP. These components were abruptly replaced with imported Soviet machinery (Fig. 4.9).[60]

The company's first manufactured good was "Agronit," a product identical to the "péti só" (Salt of Pét) brand.[61] Péti Só was a type of nitrogen fertilizer and had been invented and produced at the

Fig. 4.9 Pét Nitrogen Fertilizer PLC, "Péti só" storage facility, 1940. *Photo* FORTEPAN / VESZPRÉM MEGYEI LEVÉLTÁR / KOZELKA TIVADAR / A PHOTOGRAPH OF TIVADAR KOZELKA

Péti Chemical Works since 1931.[62] One of the main components of péti só was ammonia, a toxic agent that depleted water quality when discharged. Ammonia should have been produced on-site in Kazincbarcika, but the local coking plant project was left half-completed in 1953.[63] After 1956, BVK, like its counterparts LKM and ÓKÜ imported coke from Czechoslovakia. The import of Czechoslovakian coke increased production costs, but the use of coke was later abandoned upon the introduction of new production methods.[64] The use of coke and the production of ammonia immediately began to generate substantial amounts of wastewater in Kazincbarcika.

Notes

1. Similar tendencies were true for both France and the United Kingdom, where the French Communist Party and the British Labour Party attracted a large share of the population.
2. Janos Kornai, *The State Socialist System, The Political Economy of Communism* (Princeton: Princeton University Press, 1992), 49–54.
3. Joseph Held, *Dictionary of East European History since 1945*. (London: Mansell, 1994), 138 ("Communist Party of Czechoslovakia").
4. Jaroslav Krejčí and Pavel Machonin, *Czechoslovakia, 1918–92. A laboratory for Social Change* (London: Macmillan, 1996), 78.
5. About 90 per cent of industrial plants were damaged, 40% of the rail network and 70% of rolling stock were lost. Iván T. Berend, *A szocialista gazdaság fejlődése Magyarországon (The development of socialist economy in Hungary)* (Budapest: Akadémiai Kiadó, 1974), 10–11.
6. Charles Gati, "From Liberation to Revolution, 1945–1956," in: *A history of Hungary*, eds. Peter F. Sugar, Péter Hanák, Tibor Frank, (Bloomington, Indiana University Press, 1990), 370.
7. Peter Kenez, *Hungary from the Nazis to the Soviets. The Establishment of the communist Regime in Hungary, 1944–1948* (Cambridge: Cambridge University Press, 2006), 133.
8. Ibid., 262–263.
9. Matin Myant, *The Czechoslovak Economy in 1948–1988, The battle for economic reform* (Cambridge: Cambridge University Press, 1989), 17.
10. Jan M. Michal, *Central Planning in Czechoslovakia, Organization for Growth in a Mature Economy* (Stanford: Stanford University Press, 1960), 28. Table 2.1.
11. Matin Myant, *The Czechoslovak Economy in 1948–1988, The battle for economic reform* (Cambridge: Cambridge University Press, 1989), 17.

12. Jan M. Michal, *Central Planning in Czechoslovakia, Organization for Growth in a Mature Economy* (Stanford: Stanford University Press, 1960), Based on Table 2.1, p. 28.
13. John Michael Montias, *Central Planning in Poland* (New Haven: Yale University Press, 1974), 62.
14. Henryk Makarewicz and Wiktor Pental, *802 procent normy*, Pierwsze (Kraków: Lata Now: Without publication year), Description of photo 114 in Appendix, without page number.
15. John Michael Montias, *Central Planning in Poland* (New Haven: Yale University Press, 1974), 62.
16. Adrian Webb, The Longman Companion to Germany since 1945, Longman: New York, 1998. 222.
17. Mike Dennis, *The Rise and Fall of the German Democratic Republic 1945–1990* (New York: Longman, 2000), 42.
18. Martin McCauley, *The German Democratic Republic since 1945. Studies in Russia and East Europe*, (Basingstroke: Macmillan, 1983), 55.
19. Dennis 2000. 57.
20. Adrian Webb, *The Longman Companion to Germany since 1945* (New York: Longman, 1998), 223.
21. Dennis, Mike, *The Rise and Fall of the German Democratic Republic 1945–1990* (London-New York: Longman, 2000), 63.
22. Adrian Webb, *The Longman Companion to Germany since 1945* (New York: Longman, 1998), 222.
23. Dennis 2000. 63.
24. "1945 után Európa keleti és nyugati felé egyaránt kormányzatok által menedzselt központi fejlesztési programok kezdődtek, amelyek egyszerre kívántak munkahelyeket teremteni, az urbanizáció terjedését segíteni (…) és az elmaradott régiókat felzárkóztatni." Pál Germuska, *Indusztria bűvöletében (Mesmerized by Industry)* (Budapest: 1956-os intézet, 2004), 89.
25. Penal law was also modified by the FTYP, and based on the new law authorities could „immediately prosecute" those who would not follow regulations of the National Plan Office and the Council of Plan Economy. Unlike the FTYP, that had ideological ties to the Keynesian plans of the West, Act XXV aimed to remodel the structure of the Hungarian economy as a whole, with stress on the development of mining- and heavy industries.
26. Germuska, *Indusztria bűvöletében (Mesmerized by Industry)*, 96–97.

27. Ibid., 100–104.
28. 1949. évi XXV. törvény A Magyar Népköztársaság első ötéves népgazdasági tervéről, az 1950. január 1-től az 1954. december 31-ig terjedő időszakra. (Act XXV/1949 on the First Five Year Plan of the People"s Republic of Hungary from January 1, 1950 to December 31, 1954.) Enacted on December 10, 1949, Budapest, Hungary.
29. Ibid.
30. Strategically speaking, the FFYP envisioned two new complex industrial districts outside of Budapest. Both of which would be based on local coal deposits as primary source of energy and raw material. One of these new industrial areas was situated around the city of Pécs, close to the coal deposits of the Mecsek Mountains of South-Western Hungary. The other area was the Borsod Basin, in the Sajó Valley between the towns of Miskolc and Ózd, where brown coal mines, and iron- and steel factories represented the backbone of industry until the 1960s, when chemical production emerged around Kazincbarcika and later in Lenintown. 24. § (...) (4) (...) A nagybudapesti ipari központok mellett két új, nagy nehézipari gócot kell kialakítani: a Borsodt és a pécs-mohácsit. Az ötéves terv megváltoztatja az egész ország társadalomgazdasági térképét, felszámolja Magyarország évszázados ipari elmaradottságát. "(...) Besides the industrial centers in Budapest, two new, large heavy industrial centers have to be created in the Borsod- and the Pécs-Mohács area. The (First) Five Year Plan will change completely the social-economic map of the country and will eliminate hundreds of years of economic backwardness in Hungary." Ibid.
31. Germuska, *Indusztria bűvöletében (Mesmerized by Industry)*, 131 and 135.
32. 10. § (...) (2) „A villamos energia termelés növelésére 3.285 millió forint értékű beruházást kell megvalósítani. Várpalotán, Barcikán és Mohácson csekély fűtőértékű szén- és lignit-készleteket hasznosító erőművet, Lovásziban földgáz felhasználására alapított erőművet, Tiszalökön vízi energiát hasznosító erőművet kell építeni, továbbá más, kisebb erőművek létesítésével és a meglévők bővítésével kell a termelési előirányzat teljesítését biztosítani. Az energia gazdaságos elosztására és szállítására új 100 kV. elosztó állomásokat és 850 km hosszú új 100 kV. távvezetéket kell építeni." ("3285 million Forint investments has to be realized to enhance electric power production. In Várpalota, Barcika and Mohács power plants have to be set up, based on the low calorie

coal and lignite deposits, a power plants has to be built in Lovászi based on a natural gas resources, a power plant has to be built in Tiszalök based on hydropower, in addition further small scale plants have to be constructed and the existing ones have to be enlarged to fulfill the projected production plan. New, 100 kV distribution stations and a new 850 km long 100 kV transmission line has to be constructed to provide economical transportation and distribution solution for electricity.") 1949. évi XXV. törvény A Magyar Népköztársaság első ötéves népgazdasági tervéről, az 1950. január 1-től az 1954. december 31-ig terjedő időszakra. (Act XXV/1949 on the First Five Year Plan of the People"s Republic of Hungary from January 1, 1950 to December 31, 1954.) Enacted on December 10, 1949, Budapest, Hungary.

33. Germuska, *Indusztria bűvöletében (Mesmerized by Industry)*, 108–109 and 116.
34. 1060/53 (IX. 30) Kormány Határozat (1060/53 (IX. 30) Order of the Council of Ministers), 30 September, 1953, Budapest, Hungary.
35. Germuska, *Indusztria bűvöletében (Mesmerized by Industry)*, 10–11.
36. Ibid., 2–3 and 11.
37. "200 százalékra teljesítik a hároméves tervet a miskolci Vízgazdálkodási Hivatal dolgozói (The Three Year Plan has been Completed on 200 per cent by Workers of the Miskolc Water Management Authority)," *Észak-Magyarország*, 2 October 1949, 4.
38. "Miért olyan drága a víz (Why Water is so Expensive)," *Felvidéki Népszava*, 3 January 1946, 3.
39. In 1949 a growing number of hydrants were installed in Miskolc. These locations previously had lacked urban water supply: Thököly utca, Csalgány utca, Sánc utca, and Üteg utca. Hydrants were installed with a 100,000 Ft investment budget. At the mean time the construction works on the Soltész Nagy Kálmán utca water supply main pipeline began with a 350,000 Ft investment, and the Diósgyőr waste water supply main construction works began with a 750,000 Ft investment budget."Jelentékenyen bővül Miskolc vízvezetékhálózata (Miskolc's Water Network has been Considerably Extended)," *Észak-Magyarország*, 16 July 1949, 2.
40. "Több figyelmet kell fordítani Miskolc ivóvízhálózatának fejlesztésére (More Attention Should be Given to the Development of the Water Supply System of Miskolc)," *Észak-Magyarország*, 2 November 1958, 5.

41. "Mindnyájan emlékszünk még az 1951–52-es évek nyári csúcsfogyasztása idején rendszeresen jelentkező vízhiányokra, a felsőbb emeletek csak ritkán használható vízcsapjaira és a percesei asszonyok hajnali sorakozására egy-egy gyéren folyó közkút mellett."László Szilléry, "Néhány szó a Miskolci Vízművek és Fürdők Vállalat dolgozóinak eredményes munkájáról (A Few Words on the Successful Work of the Employees of the Miskolci Waterworks and Baths Company)," *Észak*-Magyarország, 27 January 1957, 6.
42. "Éppen ilyen magától érthető az is, hogy a falba helyezett csapból bő sugárban ömlik a pohárba a kristálytiszta hideg víz – akár a negyedik emeleten is. Ez már minden városban így van, kivéve Miskolcot. Itt a víz úgy jár a vezetékben – mint a higany. Hol megtölti azt, hol nyomtalanul eltűnik. Pereces lakói sokat tudnának beszélni arról, hogyan figyelik hajnalban, sőt éjszaka is a csapnál: jön-e a víz." Ilona Adamovics, "Miskolc Vízellátása (Water Supply in Miskolc)," *Észak-Magyarország*, 25 April 1954.
43. Sándor Borbély, "Nagy-Miskolc vízellátása (Water Supply of Greater-Miskolc)," in Borsodi Földrajzi Évkönyv I., eds. Győző Peja and Sándor Frisnyák (Miskolc: TIT B.-A.-Z. Megyei Szervezete, 1958), 35–38.
44. Oszkár Vincze, „A miskolci vízmű (Miskolc Waterworks)," *Vízgazdálkodás* 5, no. 5 (1965): 142.
45. "Miskolci vízművek, Fürdők és Csatornázási Vállalat 1967. éves Szöveges mérlegbeszámoló (Miskolc Waterworks, Baths and Drains Company 1967 Annual Textual Balance Report)." 26–28. Borsod-Abaúj-Zemplén Megyei Levéltár, Mezőcsát Fióklevéltár (Borsod-Abaúj-Zemplén County Archives Mezőcsát Branch Archives) XXIX. 113. Miskolci Vízművek Iratai. 34 box.
46. "Bővül Miskolc vízellátása. Véget ért az egynapos vízkorlátozás (The Water Supply Network in Miskolc is Extended. The One-day Water Restriction is Over)," *Észak-Magyarország*, 30 March 1958, 2.
47. "Új, 12 kilométeres csővezeték Miskolc vízellátásának biztosítására (A New, 12 km Long Water Pipe to Supply Miskolc)," *Észak-Magyarország*, 4 September 1957.
48. Gille, From the Cult of Waste to the Trash Heap of History.
49. "Óvatos számítások szerint Miskolcon 10 ezer rossz-szelepű ülőkagyló van. Ez tízezer liter, azaz 10 köbméter víz. Összegezve: egy hónap alatt 430 ezer körméter víz vész kárba." Daily municipal water use in Miskolc was 40,000 cubic meters in 1957. "According to conservative estimations there are ten thousand malfunctioning water closets in

Miskolc. This is ten thousand liters of water (per minute!). Conclusively 430 thousand cubic meters of water are wasted in a month."

50. "A miskolc fürdők legégetőbb problémája a szénkérdés. (...) bányáink a folyamatos szénellátást nem tudták biztosítani, így a fürdési lehetőségek is meglehetősen korlátozottak: a fürdő hol kinyit, hol bezár. Ez természetesen már egészségügyi szempontból sem engedhető meg, de különben is rossz fényt vet a borsodi bányavidék központjára: magára Miskolc Városra is." Szilléry, "Néhány szó a Miskolci Vízművek és Fürdők Vállalat dolgozóinak eredményes munkájáról (A Few Words on the Successful Work of the Employees of the Miskolci Waterworks and Baths Company)," 6.
51. "Tervek Miskolc ivó- és iparvíz ellátásának javítására – a csapadék- és a szennyvíz elvezetés megoldására. Megkezdődött az energia és közmű ankét (Plans to Improve (Residential)-, and Industrial Water Supply in Miskolc – and (to Improve) Storm Water-, and Waste Water Discharge. The Energy-, and Public Works Conference has begun)," *Észak-Magyarország*, 24 April 1959, 2. "Az energia- és közmű ankét második napja. Értékes javaslatok az energiahálózat bővítésére, - a miskolci szénbányászat fejlesztésére és a távfűtés lehetőségeire (The Second Day of the Energy-, and Public Works Conference. Interesting Proposals to Enlarge the Energy Supply Network – and to Develop Coal Mining and District Heating)," *Észak-Magyarország*, 25 April 1959, 3.
52. "A vegyipar termelésének 1954-ben el kell érnie a 4.843 millió forint értéket, ami 1949-hez képest 138%-os emelkedést jelent. (...) (2) A vegyiparban a termelés emelésére 1.934 millió forint értéket kell beruházni. E beruházás keretében új szuperfoszfát gyárat, új nitrogénműtrágyát, marónátront előállító üzemet, új anilinfestékgyárat, gyógyszergyárat, műanyaggyárat kell létesíteni. (The value of chemical production has to reach 4843 million Forint value by 1954, which is 138% growth compared to 1949. (...) (2) 1934 million Forints have to be invested in the chemical industry. New superphosphate-, nitrogen fertilizer-, caustic soda-, anilin paint-, pharmatics and plastic factories have to be installed.)" 1949. évi XXV. törvénycikk a Magyar Népköztársaság első ötéves népgazdasági tervéről, az 1950. január 1-től az 1954. december 31-ig terjedő időszakra (Act. XXV in 1949 on the First Five Year Plan of the People's Republic of Hungary for the period between 1 January 1950 and 31 December 1954) Enacted in Budapest, Hungary.

53. The Borsod Cooperation was managed by the Borsod Cooperation Committee and consisted the following factories: Coal Separator and Central Machine Shop of the Borsod Mines Corporation (Borsod Szénbányák Vállalat Központi Osztályozó és Gépjavító üzeme); Berente and Herbolya Pits of the Bükkalja Mines (Bükkaljai Bányaüzem berentei és herbolyai aknája); Borsod Power Plan Corporation (Borsod Hőerőmű Vállalat); Mine Shatfing Corporation (Bányászati Aknamélyítő Vállalat); Borsod County State Construction Corporation (Borsodmegyei Állami Építőipari Vállalat); Light Weight Concrete Factory—Plant No. 2 of the Light Concrete- and Iron Works (Könnyűbetongyár, Beton- és Vasművek 2. sz. Üzeme); Plant No. 3 of the Logistical Corporation of the Construction Industry (Építőipari Szállítási Vállalat 3. sz. Üzeme); Milanese Knitwear Factory (Habselyem Kötöttárúgyár).
54. The *Országos Tervhivatal* ordered construction works of the fertilizer plant on June 15, 1950.
55. Other foreign equipment were supplied by the *VEB Brücken- und Stahlbau* in Leipzig in the German Democratic RepublicFrisnyák, *Kazincbarcika földrajza*, 192.
56. Ibid., 213.
57. Magyar Dolgozók Pártja, Gazdasági Bizottság (Hungarian Workers' Party, Economic Committee), 126/1952 Határozat, 1952.03.20. (Decision No. 126/1952 on March 20, 1952).
58. Magyar Dolgozók Pártja, Gazdasági Bizottság (Hungarian Workers' Party, Economic Committee), 319/1952 Határozat, 1952.08.07. (Decision No. 319/1952 on August 7, 1952).
59. Magyar Dolgozók Pártja, Gazdasági Bizottság (Hungarian Workers' Party, Economic Committee), 540703/2/1952 Határozat, 1954.07.09. (Decision No. 540703/2/1952 on July 9, 1952).
60. Frisnyák, *Kazincbarcika földrajza*, 210–214.
61. $NH_4NO_3 + CaMg(CO_3)_2$
62. The fertilizer plant began test operations on August 19, 1955.
63. Some domestic coke was also used in Kazincbarcika until 1964 produced at the Óbuda Gas Factory (Óbudai Gázgyár).
64. Generator gas was produced from coke firstly, which was filtered and distilled to get rid of from its sulfur content. This purified product was turned into ammonia under in special 'NEC'-type converter under quite heavy—300 BAR—pressure. Frisnyák, *Kazincbarcika földrajza*, 214.

5

Economic Reforms and Environmental Protection in Hungary the 1960s

5.1 Economic Reform Ideas in Hungary in the 1950s

During the brief Stalinist period in ECE from 1949–1956, industrial capacity focused on iron and steel manufacturing, and to some extent on chemical production. After Stalin's death, the need for political reform swept through Eastern Europe. Political reform was also manifested in new forms of industrial production, for example, the rapid rise of the chemical industry. After Khrushchev seized power in the USSR, he worked towards a ceasefire in Korea and abandoned the anti-Tito campaign against Yugoslavia. Khrushchev's idea was the "co-existence" of the capitalist and the communist economic and political systems. He also eased strict Stalinist agricultural policies. As a result, investment in Soviet agriculture increased by 55% between 1950 and 1960.[1] Living conditions also improved in the USSR. For example, infant mortality was sharply dropping and the level of education was rising rapidly during the 1950s. Fear and centrally orchestrated terror loosened, and the gulag system released over 80% of its inmates by the end of the 1950s. The Soviet economy also altered. Between 1950 and 1965, foreign trade

V. Pál, *Technology and the Environment in State-Socialist Hungary*,
DOI 10.1007/978-3-319-63832-4_5

grew with other communist countries.[2] But much of the generated income came from the gigantic armament industry. Trade with partners in advanced economies remained minor, and the flow of incoming new and competitive technologies was not sufficient. Resources in Eastern Europe were exhausted by the 1970s. By that time, the Soviet Empire and its satellites should have built up considerable centers of innovation for further development and growth. However, they failed to do so. The state socialist economy was suitable to produce extensive growth, and state socialist countries were able to build up large and inter-connected industrial infrastructures. However, Comecon countries were unable to adapt to the rapidly changing international economic and technological environment, especially after the Oil Crisis of 1973. When the speed of technological change accelerated, the industrial structure and economic performance in the USSR and in other state socialist countries became outdated.

Stalinism in Hungary produced a social and economic crisis as early as 1951–1952. In 1953, the Hungarian Stalinist leader Mátyás Rákosi was summoned to Moscow and forced to resign. His successor, the reform-minded communist Imre Nagy exercised economic policy corrections and relaxed the Stalinist terror. Thanks to Nagy state investment budget was decreased from 16.8 to 11.8 billion Forints between 1953 and 1954 to ease pressure on Hungary's economy. The industrial budget of the First Five Year Plan (FFYP) was decreased from 47 to 41.5%, therefore the share of heavy industry in the FFYP was lowered, from 43 to 36.5%. Hence, investing in agriculture nearly doubled and its share rose from 13 to 24%. Due to dramatic housing conditions state housing budget was to rise from 6 to 11%. As a result of economic corrections, pressure on industrialization was eased somewhat, and agriculture, Hungary's traditional source of income was facilitated and the government aimed to provide better housing conditions for the rapidly urbanizing country. Nagy followed public will to sacrifice less on enforced industrialization, and balance the plan out. Despite vital economic corrections in 1953 to avoid public unrest, the overall structure and future direction of industry did not change dramatically.[3]

After 1953, economic reform discourse surfaced publicly on the pages of the *Economic Review* (*Közgazdasági Szemle*), a professional journal for theoretic economics. This was a new symptom that signaled, economic decisions are not solely made anymore by copying the Soviet pattern without adopting the economic program to Hungarian circumstances. Participatory changes empowered actors, and a large number of economists in Hungary engaged in the emerging reform debate. They agreed that Stalinist planning had to be altered immediately.[4] György Péter, head of the National Statistical Office, pointed out in the *Economic Review* that rigidly planned production goals were the reason behind issues such as low-quality products. György Péter argued that companies should be interested, not only in the qualitative fulfillment of main indicators in the plan, but companies should have a "financial interest" in the production process. Péter's radical reform ideas proposed that socialist companies should actually operate in an environment with real prices and in quasi-market conditions. Péter believed that a reform economic environment would facilitate "economical management" and "profitability," which he saw as key components for economic success under state-socialism. Less radical visions of economic reforms, for example, an "Imre Nagy-backed special committee report," was assessed by the end of November 1954. This document was less critical, but also called for "prices to reflect true costs." The young János Kornai's ideas on economic reform were very formative during the reform process of the late 1950s and 1960s. Kornai defended his doctoral dissertation just before the revolution in September 1956. Therefore, scientific debate on his work was postponed by the outbreak of armed resistance. Discussions were halted during the 1956 Revolution, but after hostilities stopped, economic debate was renewed.

After November 1956, the leadership of János Kádár and his new Hungarian Socialist Workers' Party (Magyar Szocialista Munkáspárt, MSZMP) sought legitimization and consolidation following a period of terror. Kádár broke away from Stalinism and understood the need for economic reforms. However, he dismissed radical approaches to avoid a second revolution and to secure wide support for his course. As a result, the Hungarian planned economy did not strategically change after 1957. In theory, Stalinism was proclaimed to be a stigma and an approach of the past. Economic incentives in the early Kádár-era focused on economical planning, "thriftiness", and the production of profitable products which required limited energy and raw material input. New economic plans aimed to enhance productivity and to reduce production costs. In theory economic ideas of the post-1956 Kádár course were following global trends and promoted energy efficiency, shift from coal to natural gas and crude oil, the abandonment of heavy industry and the shift to light industry and highly finished products. In reality, correction was less radical and partially successful. This had a direct impact on the human–nature relationship of the Kádár regime.

Kádár and his new communist party supported István Friss' study that was conducted for the Department of Economic Policy of the Hungarian Socialist Workers' Party at 30 state owned companies in 1957. Friss called for moderate reforms and "minor corrections of the mechanism". Kádár's Second Three-Year Plan (1958–1960) criticized "*the pursuit of quantitative development (which) became predominant (in earlier years). Meanwhile, thriftiness, quality improvement, production cost reduction and international cooperation were pushed into the background.*"[5] Theoretically, the new economic policy under Kádár acknowledged that Hungary was poor in raw materials and energy resources. The Second Three-Year Plan emphasized the development of competitive, export-oriented, and profitable industries. In line with modernization goals, the regime started a diesel engine program, but that proved to be a fiasco. Communication engineering projects were run at the Csepel Iron and Metalworks (Csepel Vas-és Fémművek) with very limited success. In reality, the Second Three-Year Plan and ambitiously envisioned new technologies did not challenge the dominating position of the iron and steel industry in the 1950s. The development of large, heavy industrial capacities remained pivotal in Hungary in the 1960s and to some extent in the 1970s.

Partial modernization efforts of heavy industry provided some successes. In the iron and steel industry, priority was given to investments which aimed to increase production efficiency.[6] For example, a modernized coke manufacturing plant was added to the Danube Ironworks (Dunai Vasmű, 1956–) in Dunaújváros in 1961.[7] In the Ózd Metallurgical Factory's (Ózdi Kohászati Üzemek) furnaces were modernized. The construction of a nationwide natural gas supply grid provided more environment-friendly fuel for industrial energy generation and opened the door to more energy-efficient technologies in the heavy industry.

The natural gas project was also a success and was ahead of its time by Western European standards. By the end of the 1960s, a large number of industrial plants in Hungary shifted from the use of coal to natural gas. The introduction of natural gas-based energy generation reduced production costs and significantly enhanced energy efficiency. When heavy industrial plants shifted their source of energy from coal to natural gas, phenols, some of the most dangerous metalworking industrial pollutants, disappeared from industrial wastewater.

5.2 Extensive Development and Environmental Pollution in Hungary in the Late 1950s and Early 1960s

In Hungary, only 22% of the population had access to local sewage systems in 1958. Regional variations were huge. For example, 53% of the total 3373 km long national wastewater grid were operated in Budapest, the capital. Fifty-six percent of the nation's users connected to waste water systems lived in Budapest. The capacity of the Budapest waste water pipes was also disproportionate, they carried 83% of discharged wastewater nationally![8] Further regional variation among non-metropolitan counties was also significant. In 1958, in some of most rural parts of Hungary, such as Békés, Tolna, and Szolnok Counties, the share of the population serviced by sewage pipes was as low as 1–5%. The situation was somewhat better in the centrally located Pest County where coverage was 5–10%. Hungary's industrial counties performed only slightly better than Pest, with 15–20% in Borsod, Komárom and Veszprém Counties and 20–25% in Baranya, Győr, and Fejér Counties.[9] Wastewater systems almost exclusively covered urban settlements in 1958. In villages where 5.9 million Hungarians or nearly 60% of the population lived, sewage systems were virtually nonexistent, serving only 1.5% of the rural population.[10]

According to László Szitkey, a water engineer specializing in wastewater treatment, in 1958 the threat posed by untreated and discharged wastewater very dangerous: "*Discharged wastewater is causing at least as large a public health problem as the absence of sewage networks.*"[11] Szitkey highlighted the fact that among major Hungarian towns, only very few were situated close enough to a large river into which sewage could be discharged and adequately diluted.[12] Szitkey condemned the quality of existing wastewater treatment plants in 1958: "*Most wastewater pipe networks lacked wastewater treatment systems. On the one hand, existing wastewater treatment plants do not provide adequate cleaning results. On the other hand, they are overloaded and operate with low efficiency or without any results.*"[13] According to Szitkey, this situation was worrisome because industrial water pollution and the discharge of tar and phenols rapidly grew in Hungary between 1940 and 1958.[14] Szitkey did not see how the lagging construction of wastewater treatment facilities could be sped up in the 1960s because the sluggish construction of wastewater treatment plants was largely due to their "high costs." Conversely, Szitkey believed that the construction pace of sewage and wastewater treatment capacity had to match water supply systems as soon as possible to "*prevent an outbreak of pandemic(s) more serious than in previous times*".[15]

The treatment of industrial waste waters was especially pressing. During and soon after the FFYP several industrial units were enlarged and constructed. Most of these developments lacked environmental investments entirely since extensive production received priority in Stalinist plans. Earlier environmental protection systems remained in place, however, these decade old environmental protection systems could not function effectively under the boosted production regime. The environmental impact of enforced industrialization was dramatic nationally.

In 1953, the Diósgyőr Steel Mills were renamed as the Lenin Metallurgical Factories (Lenin Kohászati Művek, LKM, 1953–1989) and emerged as one of the symbols of Hungarian heavy industry. LKM was a dominant landmark that operated in front of the eyes of hundreds of thousands in the center of the metropolitan area of Miskolc. Following the introduction of the FFYP at LKM, preexisting air and wastewater cleaning facilities were victims of an unprecedented production boom that intensified the release of various by-products and eventually led to the overuse and serious deterioration of treatment facilities. LKM did not have a central wastewater treatment unit until the early 1970s. Therefore, several individual wastewater cleaning technologies were installed at the factory in the 1950s. Sources of water pollution from iron and steel mills were numerous, but these were dwarfed by the volume and spectrum of pollutants discharged by heavy chemical plants. At LKM, Siemens–Martin smelters were one of the major sources of air and water pollution. These so-called, "Great Smelters" (*Nagy olvasztók*) had capacities ranging between 300–1000 cubic meters of material and had been in operation since the 1870s. Manufacturing iron required numerous layers of coke and iron ore to be piled on top of one another. Meanwhile, pressurized air was introduced to accelerate smelting. When the ore reached the extremely hot 1200 °C operational temperature, iron ore melted and flowed down to the bottom where it was gathered. These gigantic smelters in Diósgyőr were in continuous operation for 5–10 years. Having little remaining evidence of industrial pollution in Diósgyőr from the mid-twentieth century, it is hard to estimate the amount of contaminants released into the air. Based on data collected by the Public Health and Epidemiological Station (Közegészségügyi és Járványügyi Állomás, KÖJÁL) in Miskolc between 1956 and 1960, it is possible to estimate that approximately 90–95 tons of SPMs were emitted into the air from the LKM daily (Fig. 5.1).[16]

Smoke and dust from iron smelters were relatively abundant. Prior to the FFYP, it was in a manufacturer's financial interest to capture and recycle ore dust. For that purpose, LKM used water sediment filters produced by Elex AG in Switzerland. Unfortunately, sources do not state the exact age and type of these filters. Elex AG was established in 1934, therefore it is surmised that the filters were built sometime between 1934 and 1948. The technology consisted of large water sediment tanks that absorbed smoke directly from the smelters. In these water tanks, solid particulates from smelting smoke and dust would sink to the bottom and slowly form a layer of iron ore-rich sludge. The top water layer, poorer in solid particulates, was released into the Szinva Creek after sedimentation. It should be noted that Elex filters were employed because of

Fig. 5.1 Lenin Metallurgical Plan, Miskolc, 1978. *Photo* FORTEPAN / URBÁN TAMÁS

economic reasons, but did eventually also reduce the level of the factory's air pollution. In fact, these filters converted air pollution into less harmful water pollution when they discharged sediment-laden waters into the Szinva. Iron ore pollution flowing via the filters into the Szinva was eliminated after 1970 when, as a part of production modernization effort, vacuum scrubbers replaced the Elex filters.[17]

Iron production pollution was a mere nuisance compared to grease and especially phenols discharged by LKM into the creek. The management of the factory, citizens of Miskolc, and after 1961, ÉVÍZIG's environmental unit were all concerned about the emitted fats and phenols. Grease was primarily used at the Cold or Hot Rolling Units, where pig iron and steel were rolled.[18] Before iron and steel arrived at rolling facilities, their oxidized surface was cleaned in brine. After the brine treatment, metal nodules left on the surface were rinsed off with hot and cold water, resulting in a substantial amount of wastewater.[19] Rolling itself, especially cold rolling, required large amounts of lubricants because oils cooled down rolls and made them run smoothly. In Diósgyőr, a mixture of fish oil, spindle oil, and various oil acids were applied. Further types of grease, e.g. tallow and cottonseed oil were used in the Deep Pressing Unit. After rolling and deep pressing, lubricants were washed off with hot water and then discharged. Regrettably, sources do not clearly reveal what exactly happened to oily waters after being rinsed off. What is known is that in the 1950s some of this wastewater was treated in "Dorr-type" sedimentation tanks. The actual effectiveness of these Dorr facilities is vague. The quantity of treated oily wastewater has not been established either. Sources only acknowledge that the Dorr unit at the rolling plants employed "old equipment." Therefore, the apparatus was probably installed during the first decades of the 1900s.[20] Moreover, it can be established from a 1962 environmental agency site visit report that even though there were several Dorr units in operation at LKM, acid, tallow, lubricants, and metal salts were regularly discharged from the Cold Rolling, Deep Pressing, and Smith Plants into the Szinva. The out-of-date Dorr units simply could not cope with the extensive volume of production after 1949. Grease was deliberately released throughout the 1950s, and the regional environmental agency found substantial amounts of oils in the Szinva downstream from LKM throughout the 1960s.[21]

In the case of LKM, large amounts of discharged oils might be perceived as a minor threat compared to pungent and poisonous phenols. Still, phenols were bound globally to the iron and steel industry in the 1950s. They were released during coal-based coking processes and coal-fueled energy generation. In addition, the removal of phenols was difficult and costly. It was mentioned in Chap. 2.1. In this dissertation that phenols had caused significant environmental problems in Germany from the late nineteenth century onward. German rivers, especially the Emscher, was polluted with phenol-laden wastewaters discharged by the steel industry along the Ruhr.

Coking in Borsod was a minor issue because, with few exceptions, LKM imported coked coal from Czechoslovakia. LKM generated coal gas during the energy generation process. Large quantities of discharged phenols were immediately noticed because of their distinguishing odor. The stench of phenols was particularly noticeable along the stretch of the Szinva running nearly 7 km through several neighborhoods and the center of Miskolc from the discharge locations to the confluence of the Szinva and the Sajó River. Residents in this growing industrial town could literary smell the reeking phenol-laden waters at many locations around the city. Most likely this is why LKM's phenol discharges emerged as a debated "public health hazard" issue well prior to state sponsored industrial water pollution monitoring being introduced in 1962.[22]

From the mid-1950s, a network of KÖJÁL laboratories supported claims against the phenol threat. From 1954 to 1955, the KÖJÁL laboratory in Miskolc administered public health-related water quality monitoring and focused on the surveillance of the quality of drinking water and public health issues. Phenols that were released from LKM and subsequently flowing through Miskolc were considered by KÖJÁL as a major public health threat. Markedly, KÖJÁL was only concerned with public health issues and did not investigate environmental harm. Later, the phenol question emerged as one of the few common concerns of both KÖJÁL and the Northern Hungarian Water Superintendence Water Monitoring Group (Észak-Magyarországi Vízügyi Igazgatóság, ÉVÍZIG, Vízminőségvizsgáló Csoport). Problems with oily and phenol-loaded wastewater at LKM were stereotypical for Hungarian heavy industry in the 1950s.[23]

The Ózd Metallurgical Plants (Ózdi Kohászati Üzemek), another flagship of the Hungarian iron and steel industry in Borsod and situated 35 km northwest from LKM, used similar production methods and struggled with similar pollution problems as Diósgyőr. In Ózd, industrial effluent was produced in the furnaces, rolling plants, Smith plants, and the coal-fueled gas generation facility. Sedimentation tanks and Dorr pools were in operation in Ózd as well. Similar to the situation at LKM, Dorr pools were in operation at various locations around the Ózd factory, with some of these pools concentrated in close proximity to the furnaces. The one big difference between the wastewater management at Diósgyőr and Ózd was that Ózd operated a large central settling pond where most of its wastewater was "treated" in a large settling pond called the "Big Lake" (*Nagy-tó*). It is unknown how effective this Big Lake was, however, it had to be large enough to manage both the factory's sewage and industrial wastewater on a daily basis.[24] The settling pond operated along a technological idea akin to the Dorr pools.

Solid particulates heavier than water sank to the bottom of the pool. In addition to mechanical treatment, a mild degree of biological treatment was also introduced. Bacteria in this pool ate certain pollutants. Even though little information is available, it is assumed that a certain degree of mechanical and biological treatment was exercised. Cleaned wastewater was then discharged into the Ózd Creek, a tributary of the Sajó (Fig. 5.2).[25]

Neither is there much information available relevant to how acids, fats, and oils were treated in the Cold and the Hot Rolling plants in Ózd. Sources suggest that similarly to LKM, there might have been a mechanical treatment facility equipped with fat and oil traps. The oil remover at LKM was several decades old and quite laxly maintained; suggesting perhaps that the grease treatment situation could not have been much different in Ózd than in Diósgyőr. Phenols were also discharged in Ózd to the Ózd Creek. However, phenols at ÓKŰ remained out of public sight and therefore out of mind. In the 1950s in Ózd, phenols were produced at coal-fueled electricity generators built in 1903–1904. Sources convey that the coal-fueled facility in Ózd was

Fig. 5.2 Lenin Metallurgical Plant, Sinter Plant, Miskolc, 1977. *Photo* FORTEPAN / BALÁZS LAJOS

equipped with an unidentifiable type of tar remover. This may seem to be an advantage compared to the circumstances at LKM, but environmental agency reports from 1962 reveal that the equipment was "out of date" and operated at "low efficiency." Annual pollution monitoring data from the 1960s confirms that most of the phenols and tar produced in Ózd were discharged into the Ózd Creek throughout the 1950s and 1960s. In the end, Ózd shifted from coal-fueled energy generation to natural gas in 1967. After this technological switch, phenols were no longer discharged from ÓKŰ.[26]

Dramatic events in 1964 changed the attitude of the government over Miskolc's water problems, and central resources were allocated for the planning and constructions costs of the new Miskolc Waterworks. From 1965, the Water Planning Company (Vízügyi Tervező Vállalat, VIZITERV[27]) was delivering plans for the first stage of the Eastern Peak Waterworks (Keleti Csúcsvízmű, KCS). The KCS was built on the Hernádnémeti gravel basin between the Sajó and Hernád rivers east of Miskolc. These works consisted of two stages and were designed to produce 30–35,000 cubic meters/day of water, combined. In the first stage, 30 wells were planned to be constructed on the banks of the Sajó River. Wells were dug in the flood zone 40 meters from the river. Their location was between the contaminated river flow and its formerly regulated and cut off backwater. The total budget for the two stages of the KCS gravel basin development was estimated around 130 million Ft in 1966 and the first stage was planned to be put into operation by 1968.

During the planning process, several concerns arose over the KCS and it was contested in a lively scientific and social debate in Borsod. Actors in the debate agreed that steps needed to be taken as soon as possible to meet Miskolc's pressing municipal and industrial water supply needs. However, many expressed concerns over the proposed KCS plan, which would use water from one of the nation's most polluted rivers, the Sajó.

In 1966, Lajos Király, an independent water engineer based in Miskolc, expressed his concerns over the KCS in an opinion piece in *Észak-Magyarország*. Király pointed out in his article that the KCS would be built in a groundwater area where the change of pollution levels in ground waters was unpredictable. He reminded readers that the source of water at the KCS was "*highly problematic,*" because it was "*heavily polluted by both Czechoslovak and Hungarian plants upstream.*" Király stressed that not only did the Sajó River endangered water quality in the gravel basin, but the quality of the Hernád River was also unpredictable because the Košice Steel Mills (Východoslovenské železiarne, VSŽ Košice) discharged wastewaters to the Hernád River. Even though the wastewaters of the VSŽ Košice rarely produced critical pollution in the Hernád, Király assumed that in the event of a malfunction at the VSŽ Košice, little could be done to stop pollution entering the Hernád. In his opinion, such an event would jeopardize the water quality at the KCS and water supply for Miskolc. Király believed that it was a good decision when in 1913 the city of Miskolc decided against building its waterworks on the Sajó River and decided to use karst springs to supply the city with drinking water instead. Király also recalled successful Yugoslav experiments with underground karst reservoirs and he recommended developing such water storing capacities inside the Bükk Mountains around Miskolc.[28]

Others proposed a variant of Király's plan. They recommended using the excellent quality waters of the karst springs but dismissed experiments such as the Yugoslav underground karst reservoirs because they considered these projects too risky. Engineers recommended the extension of the existing Hámor dam and the construction of a new dam in Felsővölgy, a neighboring valley to Hámor. Engineers estimated that if those two reservoirs were connected with an underground pipeline, combined they could store enough water to secure the water supply of Miskolc. Both Király's and the latter plan were abandoned in 1965 and the OVH and VIZITERV made the decision to supply the city's water needs from the gravel basin between the Sajó and the Hernád rivers.[29]

The first proposal for the location of KCS wells, the so-called "Arnót variant," was researched in June 1965. The Arnót location was quickly abandoned because the water there was too polluted and contained a high risk of further pollution. A new location for the KCS was researched and found later in 1967. Negotiations among the Miskolc Waterworks, OVH, and KÖJÁL over the new site ended on June 2, 1968, when local decision makers of the Miskolc Waterworks, OVH, and KÖJÁL agreed on the future location of new KCS wells. The decision was made but the exact source of funding remained unclear. In 1968, Oszkár Vincze, an engineer at ÉVÍZIG, claimed in one of his published writings in *Borsod Szemle*, a regional magazine published for the technological intelligentsia in Borsod, that the OVH did everything possible to secure the construction funds for the future waterworks. Vincze recalled that the OVH had already sponsored the planning phase of KCS with a million forints and allocated another 6 million forints, matching a fund from 1969 for construction works. The estimated 130–140 million forint total budget, however, was out of the scope of the OVH.

Due to the high costs of construction and scant financial resources available, Vincze and the ÉVÍZIG recommended constructing only the first phase of KCS and postponing the second phase for an uncertain period of time. With such a decision, the need for funding would be reduced from 130–140 million forints to 60 million. Vincze assumed that if the OVH supplied 6 million forints, about 10% of construction costs for Phase 1, the other 90% could be allocated by the Miskolc City Committee. According to Vincze, the city of Miskolc would have benefited most from the construction of the KCS. Therefore, he wrote: "*For that purpose the OVH initiated a meeting with local council officials in Miskolc on August 9, 1968. (…) It is the local committee that needs to prioritize water supply. It would be right, if they were considerate and learned the lessons of this year's drought.*"[30]

In 1966, KCS was planned to be operational by the end of the 1960s. In 1969, completion was postponed to 1972. To cover the gap between promises and the slowly proceeding reality, a large number of propaganda articles were published at the end of the 1960s in Miskolc to remind citizens that the construction was actually proceeding and that water shortages would soon be eliminated in the city. Propaganda accounts included titles such as "*Water scarcity will cease in Miskolc*," "*We will get water from Felsőzsolca*," and "*Actions to mend water supply*," suggested that drinking water would be secured in the near future for Miskolc. The 1969 article entitled "*Water scarcity will cease in Miskolc*" promised the installation of KCS Phase 1 by the end of 1971. According to this coverage, much of the water supply pipeline between the new waterworks and the Tetemvár reservoir had been built by 1969.[31]

Because KCS construction was lagging behind schedule and water needs continued to be pressing, two immediate solutions were implemented in Miskolc. In 1970, a pipeline was built to connect the city of Miskolc with the Borsod Regional Waterworks at Sajóecseg Industrial Waterworks (Sajóecsegi Ipari Vízmű). The new 500 mm diameter pipe was able to add a maximum of 12,000 cubic meters of water to the system per day. An additional 6000–8000 cubic meter/day arrived at the city from Alsózsolca. There, clean gravel layer water resources had been found during the construction of a prefabricated house factory. The accidentally discovered Alsozsolca water layer promised higher water quality, and lower iron and manganese content than the prioritized KCS.

Simultaneously with the success of alternative solutions for water supply, the KCS lost importance. When KCS Phase 1 came into operation in 1974, the water supply problems for the city of Miskolc had somewhat eased up, thanks to the Sajóecseg and Alsózsolca extensions. Also, the growth of Miskolc and her industrial producers had slowed down after the Oil Crisis of 1973.[32]

Eventually, as opponents anticipated, the quality of water produced at the KCS site was unsatisfactory because it contained manganese over 2 mg/l and iron between 0.5–0.8 mg/l. The manganese and iron content had to be reduced to make KCS water suitable for drinking purposes. This was a costly, ineffective, and eventually this centrally backed megaproject was a failure.[33]

Miskolc was not alone in Borsod with water supply problems. From the early 1950s, water scarcity had become a typical problem for the entire Borsod region and it jeopardized water supply for residents and industrial plants. Ózd, Kazincbarcika, and smaller industrial settlements such as Ormosbánya, Rudabánya, and Sajókaza struggled to secure municipal and industrial water supplies because their straightforward source of water, the Sajó River, was heavily polluted. In small industrial towns and villages, minor local waterworks supplied drinking and industrial water before the FFYP. Sporadic industrial water needs and low-scale resident water demands did not pose major problems until the mid-twentieth century. It was first wartime capacity building rather than the large-scale industrialization or urbanization projects of the FFYP which raised water demands that exceeded existing capacity. Many of these local water sources had been the subject of health concerns, and after 1950 KÖJÁL lobbied for the establishment of new water supply systems that could distribute water that was safe to use.

After 1950, growing pressure on limited water sources produced escalating water supply issues in nearly every developed settlement in water-scarce Borsod. When, in 1950, new investments began in and around Tiszaújváros, Kazincbarcika and Sajóbábony, the water supply for residential and industrial needs were developed from scratch. In Tiszaújváros, the Tisza River provided relatively clean and abundant water for residential and industrial use. The situation in Kazincbarcika was more complicated. There, the problems resembled those of Miskolc. The local Tardona creek and a temporary well supplied some water during the construction of the first housing blocks of the new socialist city. This capacity was too meager to satisfy the needs of the growing factories in Kazincbarcika. In 1953, the so-called "II/a" Waterworks produced water from the gravel layer along the Sajó River. But "II/a" was more a small-scale waterworks than a large-scale water production plant. The first stage of the larger Kazincbarcika waterworks was "Borsodszirák I," and it was put into operation in 1955 in Borsodszirák, a neighboring community to Kazincbarcika on the opposite bank of the Sajó River. The Borsodszirák plant was built on the gravel layer of the Bódva River that received limited pollution upstream. Therefore, this plant was extended on several occasions to a supply of 15,000 cubic meter water/day for Kazincbarcika's residents and industry.[34]

Research work conducted by OVF, FVT and MÉLYÉPTERV on the gravel layer water sources indicated that an adequate amount and quality of water was rarely available at the sites of planned and existing industrial plants in the Borsod Basin. This was the reason why the OVF began a discourse over an interconnected network of regional water supply systems that could solve the painful water shortages in industry-rich, but clean water-poor Borsod. The regional water supply system was a complex water engineering undertaking and was similar in principle to those in the Ruhr. In the 1980s the North-Hungarian Regional

Waterworks (Észak-Magyarországi Regionális Vízművek, ÉRV) included 14 large-capacity reservoirs and water tanks, which supplied 43 towns and villages in Borsod after completion.[35]

The plans of the Borsod Water Supply System (Borsod Vízellátási Rendszer, BVR), the first regional water supply system of its kind in Hungary (which was also the predecessor of ÉRV), were drawn by the Waterwork Plan Office (Vízügyi Tervező Iroda).[36] Central authorities backed that plan because it was necessary to secure production. Since financial sources were abundant, the plan was implemented relatively smoothly. The Council of Ministers authorized the Borsod Regional Water Supply System and allocated funds in 1955.[37]

Work began during the same year. The first phase of construction included a local waterworks to supply Kazincbarcika with 3500 cubic meters of daily capacity. A few pumping stations and several wells were added to supply local villages with individual waterworks locally. Finally, an iron and manganese remover plant was added to the "Borsodszirák I" plant of Kazincbarcika to prevent health dangers that may have been posed by contaminated water. When the BVR I was put into operation on 6 July 1958, it served 8000 residents in and around Kazincbarcika with 3000 cubic meters of water and 15 km of water supply pipes. The BRV I was dwarfed compared to the length and capacity of new Miskolc Waterworks, but it was extended between 1958 and 1962. Then, a second phase of the BRV was constructed with a 62.6 million Ft budget.[38]

Its major investment was the 5.7 million cubic meter Rakaca Valley Reservoir (Rakaca-völgyi felszíni tározó) and adjacent dam infrastructure. In the ÉRV system, water from the Rakaca Valley Reservoir was combined with supplies from the Sajóecseg Industrial Waterworks and further supply came from the Borsodszirák I Waterworks on the Bódva River.[39]

The third phase of ÉRV was carried out between 1962 and 1968, when an extension concentrated on the Borsodszirák I plant. Phase four, between 1966 and 1971, invested 252 million forints, and its major undertaking was the 6.2 million cubic meter Lázbérc Reservoir and adjacent infrastructure. Lázbérc was capable of supplying 20,000 cubic meters of water daily, which was ill needed in the ÉRV grid. The reservoirs of Lázbérc and Rakaca eased industrial and urban water supply issues in Kazincbarcika and Ózd plants.[40]

Initially, the BRV was operated by the Vízügyi Beruházási Vállalat (Waterworks Investment Company). Later, the OVF established the Sajómenti Vízművek (Sajó Area Waterworks), which took over ownership and management on January 1, 1962. The Sajó Area Waterworks company was extended in 1970–1971, when the Northern Nógrád Regional Water Works (Észak-nógrádi Regionális Vízüzemek) were added to the company and it was renamed to the "Northern Hungarian Regional Water Works and Water Management Company (Északmagyarországi Regionális Vízmű és Vízgazdálkodási Vállalat. ÉRV)." In 1978–1979, the ÉRV was also given control over the KCS, which had been under the management of the Miskolc Waterworks. After ÉRV was given both the Nógrád and Miskolc Waterworks, ÉRV controlled most of the water supply systems throughout the Northern Hungarian industrial area, spanning from Salgótarján to Ózd in the north and Leninváros in the east.[41]

By the end of the 1970s, grand plans to extend the KCS were abandoned by ÉRV. That was because the KCS was not able to supply adequate quality of water. Instead, the ÉRV decided to extend the Sajóecseg Industrial Waterworks. From Sajóecseg, the ÉRV built a second large, 1000 mm diameter water supply pipeline to supply the city of Miskolc. In Salgótarján, industrial plants and residents suffered as much under inadequate supplies of water as they were burdened in Borsod. ÉRV was equipped with adequate financial tools and intervened in Nógrád. There, ÉRV began the construction of the Mihálygerge Waterworks that was planned to supply 5000 cubic meter/day. The second phase of ÉRV's construction program included a 4.2 million cubic meter reservoir in the Komra Valley. Komra supplied 7000 cubic meters daily to the northern Nógrád water supply network. In 1978, a 2 million cubic meter reservoir was constructed in Hasznos, in Central Nógrád County, west of the Mátra Hills. From Hasznos, 10,000 cubic meters of water were pumped to Salgótarján daily.[42]

Dissatisfaction with Stalinist industrial policies grew throughout East-Central Europe during the first half of the 1950 and led to widespread resistance and a handful of armed conflicts, such as the Hungarian Revolution of 1956.

Stalinist development in East-Central European countries showed similar signs of crisis and inadequate planning. Industrial growth was produced with large externalities and accompanied with environmental destruction. Construction of wastewater treatment facilities was neglected both in old and newly built units. Increased pollution levels emerged first in the old plants that produced more intensively. Old air cleaning and wastewater treatment facilities, which had been in operation since the first half of the twentieth century, did not cope with the increased volume of by-products. By the late 1950s, pollution from new FFYP plants also appeared. As a result of increased water pollution from both old and new industrial sites, the level of water pollution escalated in East-Central Europe from the mid-1950s. This critical situation, however, was typical only for a brief period of Stalinist-type development in East-Central Europe, roughly between 1949 and 1953/1956. After the total fiasco of Stalinist-type economic policy in East-Central Europe, governments tackled both economic production and environmental destruction issues surprisingly rapidly.

Simultaneously, professional and public discussions about the future of the water supply in Miskolc continued. Between 1954 and 1964, experts considered the gravel basin of the Sajó and Hernád rivers one of the safest and most adequate options to establish bank filtration plants. The project was on a grand scale and had to fit into the modest financial means of the Kádár regime. Also, it should have been completed in a realistic time span, according to the officials of Miskolc Waterworks.[43] In reality, construction works did not begin until 1964.

It was easy to see serious water supply disruptions coming because the water supply situation in Miskolc was worsening from the early 1950s. The water supply system in Miskolc was vulnerable to sudden changes of weather, and when the city experienced a series of dry periods, extreme weather induced one of the most severe service disruptions in water supply during the summer of 1964.[44] The shortage of water in 1964 was epic: "*Our largest spring in Tapolca provided so little water, that according to our records this has been unprecedented since the beginning of service in 1913,*" noted company correspondence.[45] Several newspaper articles documented the drought of 1964. *Észak-Magyarország* recalled the dramatic events of 1964 two years later: "*We remember the summer of 1964, when residents in new housing blocks walked stairs from upper floors to ground floor (to access drinking) water.*"

The dramatic account continued in the latter part of this article: "*In many streets disinfected street-wash-trucks distributed drinking water. Some of the District Chief Medical Officers worried about epidemics, because residents began to drink water from old, contaminated wells as (their) last resort.*" The escalation of water shortage triggered professional and public discourse over water supply issues: "*(Many) Conferences and meetings followed one after another. Opinions of hundreds of experts were interviewed on how (water) problems of the city (of Miskolc) should be resolved. Opinions agreed that no matter how much it would cost, the so-called Eastern peak (central)-water work of the city has to be built immediately.*"[46] Water shortage was accompanied with excess use of water pumps that caused significantly higher electricity consumption for the waterworks and reduced the life expectancy of water pumps by around 5 or 6 years.[47]

The excess energy consumption in water supply and water pumping emerged as a financial and economic issue at the Miskolc Waterworks, but it had a direct environmental impact as well. Water pumps with high energy demand were to be replaced to reduce company energy use and to fulfill central plan directives for economical energy use. For example, Pump No. 4 was replaced in the Tapolca pumping station by a more effective pump in 1965. This change reduced energy use, provided more economical pump operation, and had a favorable environmental impact.[48]

Normal weather conditions returned to Miskolc in 1965 and water supply increased by over 15.5% (2.5 million cubic meters) between 1964 and 1965. However, this was due to favorable weather conditions. In general, the water supply in Miskolc was still very vulnerable to weather conditions.[49] In 1966, the Szinva spring was connected to the city's water supply system, and the amount of water supplied by the Miskolc Waterworks grew by 600,000 cubic meters (6.5%).[50] In October 1966, the Szent György spring was connected to the city water grid that added over 1.2 million cubic meters (7.4% growth) of water supplied annually.[51] In 1967, 18.3 million cubic meters of water was supplied to Miskolc annually. Most of it was still coming from the Tapolca springs, which were the backbones of the Miskolc water supply and provided an average of 27,000 cubic meters of water a day, while additional small springs supplied 12,700 cubic meters a day. The Szinva spring stood out from these additional springs with a considerable 10,300 cubic meter water supply a day.[52]

Brigade competitions and innovation movements could mobilize the Miskolc Waterworks to some extent, but they could not solve the company's most pressing water problems. External funds, especially direct government funds, were essential to carry out large-scale water supply and waste water treatment projects, such as the Eastern Peak Waterworks (Keleti Csúcsvízmű), the city's new Eastern water and wastewater mains, and the central wastewater treatment plant. The Miskolc Waterworks was not able to manage these large and pressing projects. In the state socialist economy, company correspondence often showed that companies felt very competent in smaller issues, but when they faced large projects, state-owned companies would often act as victims and helpless actors. The feeling of powerlessness also dominated the Miskolc Waterworks when company leadership talked about the Eastern Peak Waterworks: "*Generally it has to be stated, that our company investment fund (Miskolc Waterworks) and contribution from supervisory bodies and other contributions are totaled at 22-25 million Ft annually. This sum is enough to carry out projects of smaller importance, but it is inappropriate to realize large-scale investments (such as) water production, wastewater production, wastewater drainage and treatment, also the reconstruction of* baths."[53]

State-owned companies were also at the end of the state socialist food chain of taxes. Their activities were heavily taxed and it endangered their normal activities when economic growth slowed down in Hungary. However, the state would bail out endangered companies to secure their activities. Extensive growth in water supply externalized economic and environmental problems at the Miskolc Waterworks. New infrastructural projects increased energy consumption and company taxes to be paid. As a result, production costs increased and company profit decreased. The company report for the first half of 1971 predicted that profit may turn to loss in a few years' time if negative trends continued. This report suggested that either tax should be decreased or higher sale prices should be allowed to cover higher operational costs.[54] Gloomy company budget predictions were supported by a loss in the first quarter of 1971 when high taxes produced negative financial results. Taxes and fees rose from 4.96 to 7.81 million forints between the first quarter of 1970 and the first quarter of 1971. Eventually, taxes and fees eroded the profit of the Miskolc Waterworks in 1971 (Fig. 5.3).

What challenged the Miskolc Waterworks the most was the extensive growth that the company underwent during the 1960s and 1970s. New water supply and wastewater treatment investments resulted in excess energy consumption growth and extra workforce needs at the Miskolc Waterworks. For example, Miskolc's traditional water intake plant, the Tapolca springs, employed 11 workers in 1971; the new "Eastern Peak Waterworks" was planned to employ at least 40 persons when operational in the 1970s. It was not the aim of the Miskolc

	1970 first quarter (million Ft)	1971 first quarter (million Ft)
Sales: water supply	8.95	9.68
Sales: waste water discharge	4.84	5.050
Total sales	16.71	16.70
Material costs	2.45	2.78
Salaries	1.71	1.96
Various taxes (közteher, illetményadó, eszközlekötési jutalék, OVH költség különbözet vízellátás és szennyvízelvezetés)	4.956	7.813
Company result after all costs and taxes	1.67	-0.74

Fig. 5.3 Economic data of Miskolc Waterworks during the first quarter of 1970 and the first quarter of 1971. *Source* "Miskolci vízművek, Fürdők és Csatornázási Vállalat IV. 5 Éves Terv Szöveges Indoklása (Miskolc Waterworks, Baths and Drains Company 4th Five Year Plan Textual Reasoning) June 21, 1971". 1. Borsod-Abaúj-Zemplén Megyei Levéltár, Mezőcsát Fióklevéltár (Borsod-Abaúj-Zemplén County Archives Mezőcsát Branch Archives) XXIX. 113. Miskolci Vízművek Iratai. 36 box

Waterworks to put more men to work; rather the contrary, the company aimed to replace human labor force with more productive and cheaper machinery. "*We have aimed to enhance productivity with better and more machines so far, and in the future we aim to mechanize physical work to a greater extent in services, construction works, and maintenance.*"[55]

Despite modernization efforts, the workforce at the Miskolc Waterworks grew from 412 to 439 employees in just one year, between 1970 and 1971. Total salaries grew from 8.2 million forints to 8.94 million forints annually, while the average income grew modestly from 21,299 forints to 21,996 forints between 1970 and 1971.[56] The growth of the labor force was both quantitative and qualitative. New positions, such as operational engineer, chemical engineer, and call center attendant were created where specialized water and energy-related knowledge was demanded.[57] By the early 1970s, the Miskolc Waterworks struggled to find workers for meagerly paying blue-collar and part-time/seasonal jobs: "*workers, laborers, earthwork laborers are missing, we can maintain bath services only with student and pensioner (employees).*"[58]

After major water supply disruptions in the summer of 1964, economic measures in industrial plants slowed down the growth of water demand in Miskolc. Water thirst was further eased by the growth of the tapped karst spring network in the Bükk Mountains. Water shortages disappeared briefly during the latter half of the 1960s and reappeared in 1970–1971.

Even though the growth of industrial and residential water needs had slowed down, they were still growing. By the late-1960s, water supply sources from the Bükk were becoming over-extracted and the capacity of the water supply system in Miskolc was brought close to its limits by the early 1970s. The situation was so severe that unfavorable variation in seasonal precipitation could have paralyzed the whole water supply system within a few months' time. In 1971, the Miskolc Waterworks admitted that "*due to warm temperatures and increased demand (…) available water resources are becoming exhausted.*" To maintain uninterrupted water supply, "*in August (…) we will purchase water from the Sajó-bank waterworks (of the Northern-Hungarian Regional Waterworks).*"[59]

Pressure on the water supply system in Miskolc increased in 1972 due to dry weather conditions and the decreasing output of karst springs. The Miskolc Waterworks reported that they were unable to satisfy increasing demand from shrinking resources. Temporary solutions to mend this critical water situation included the use of Tapolca and August 20 thermal bath springs, which normally provided water for city baths. Such temporary measures had also been employed in the 1950s during periods of severe water supply crisis. Despite these efforts, the amount of produced water decreased from 22.3 million cubic meters to 20.8 million cubic meters per annum between 1971 and 1972. Simultaneously, the amount of water purchased from ÉRV Regional Waterworks increased from 0.9 million cubic meters to 1.84 million cubic meters per annum.[60]

Water scarcity continued in 1972. Water purchased from ÉRV continued to increase and posed an extra financial burden of over 4.3 million Ft on the Miskolc Waterworks in 1972. In the first three-quarters of 1971, 0.47 million cubic meters of water were purchased from ÉRV; this amount rose during the first three-quarters of 1972 to 1.26 million cubic meters. In 1972, Miskolc Waterworks carried out an investigation into industrial users to ease the city's water supply situation. As a result, industrial water use dropped somewhat from 6.84 million cubic meters down to 6.22 million cubic meters during the first three-quarters of 1972. Unfortunately, the company report does not indicate what exact measures were taken or how they contributed to the reduction of water use in 1972. The decreasing local industrial water use trend, however, correlated with a national trend of decreased industrial water use. Meanwhile, the residential water supply slightly grew from 5.33 million cubic meters to 5.59 million cubic meters between 1971 and 1972. As result, the overall consumption stagnated.[61] The slight decrease in water use did not mean a decreased amount of pollutants discharged in wastewaters in Miskolc in the early 1970s. The Miskolc Waterworks was the collector of most industrial and residential wastewaters in Miskolc and released approximately 15 million cubic meters of waste water in 1971 and 1972.[62]

The water supply issues received close public and media attention in Miskolc after 1956. The rise of public attention and discourse over water supply and wastewater treatment began decades earlier in Miskolc than it has been suggested for Hungary and the rest of East-Central Europe by a large amount of the scholarly accounts cited in the bibliographical chapter of this dissertation. Water supply projects were constructed and received public attention parallel with local water-related infrastructural investments, such as the rationalization of the Szinva Creek. The rationalization of the Szinva Creek included cementing long segments of this flow and covering stretches of the riverbed in central areas of Miskolc. The discussion over water supply projects also coexisted with the discourse over wastewater treatment projects. But during the FFYP, the acceleration of the wastewater networked lagged significantly behind the construction of the water supply network. After 1956, in regional scientific journals, planners warned about the health and environmental concerns over new housing blocs which were equipped with water supply but were not connected to waste water system of Miskolc. The gap between the water supply and wastewater network should have been closed, according to contemporary whistle blowers, but such a goal was never.

Notes

1. Robert W. Davies, *Soviet Economic Development from Lenin to Khruschev* (Cambridge-New York: Cambridge University Press, 1998), 69.
2. Davies, *Soviet Economic Development from Lenin to Khruschev*, 72.
3. A Nagy Imre vonal. Dokumentumválogatás. Válogatta és a bevezető tanulmányt írta Dér Ferenc. Reform, 1989. 248–267. l.
4. The crisis of the economic system was marked with "disruption of food supplies, the collapse of the energy system, frequent power cuts and widespread shortages" both in Hungary, and in East-Central Europe. Ivan T. Berend, *The Hungarian economic reforms, 1953–1988* (Cambridge-New York: Cambridge University Press, 1990), 17.
5. Preface: "Uralkodóvá vált a mennyiségi fejlődés hajszolása, közben a gazdaságosság, a minőségjavítás, a termelés költségeinek csökkentése és

a nemzetközi együttműködés követelményei háttérbe szorultak."1958. évi II. törvény az 1958–1960. évi hároméves népgazdaságfejlesztési terv irányelveiről (Act. II. in 1958 on on the guidelines of the 1958–1960 three year people's-economy development plan.) Enacted in Budapest, Hungary.

6. I. FEJEZET. "A hároméves terv fő feladatai." (Chap. I. "Main goals of the three year plan") 9. § Ibid.
7. The iron-, and steel works in Stalintown (Sztálinváros) were named as Stalin Ironworks (Sztálin Vasművek) and was renamed to Danube Ironworks (Dunai Vasmű) in 1956, and Stalintown was renamed to Dunaújváros in 1961.
8. László Szitkey, "Szennyízcsatornázásunk helyzete 1958. év végén (The Level of Waste Water Management at the end of 1958 in Hungary)," *Vízügyi Közlemények* 41, no. 3 (1959). 315.
9. Ibid., 330. Figure 6. Magyarország megyéinek csatornázottsága (Waste water coverage in the counties of Hungary).
10. Ibid., 328. Figure 5. Városi, falusi és az összlakosság szennyvízcsatorna ellátottsága (Waste water coverage in villages, towns and in general in Hungary).
11. "A szennyvízcsatornázás hiánya miatt keletkező közegészségügyi ártalmak mellett legalább ugyanolyan mértékű károkat okoznak a *tisztítás nélkül kibocsátott szennyvízek is.*" Ibid., 327.
12. Ibid., 327–328.
13. "Szennyvíztisztitó-telepek viszont csatornaműveink többségénél hiányoznak. A meglévő tisztítóberendezések részben nem biztosítják az előírt tisztítást, részben túlterheltség miatt alacsony hatásfokkal, vagy gyakorlatilag eredménytelenül működnek." Ibid., 328.
14. Ibid.
15. Ibid., 331.
16. Ádám Fázold, "Környezetvédelem alakulása Borsod megyében különös tekintettel a vízminőségvédelemre (The history of Environmental Protection in Borsod County with special notice on water quality control)," *Proceedings of the XXIXth Annual Conference of the Hungarian Hydrology Association, Eger 2011.* http://www.hidrologia.hu/vandorgyules/29/dolgozatok/fazold_adam.html (accessed on August 20, 2013).
17. „Szakvélemény. Északmagyarországi Vízügyi Igazgatóság Vízminőségvizsgáló Csoport. Ügyszám: 6087/1962, LKM szennyvízének hatása a Szinva patakra (Specialist's Report. Northern Hungarian Water Superintendence Water

Monitoring Group. Case 6087/1962, The impact of LKM waste waters to the Szinva Creek)," Környezetvédelmi és Vízügyi Levéltár (Environmental and Water Archives) VI. 9. Miskolci Kulturmérnöki Hivatal Vizikönyvek 1867–1971 (Miskolc „Culture" Engineering Office „Waterlogs"), 291 box. 4006 / I. dossier. Lenin Kohászati Művek 1962–1970. (Lenin Metallurgical Works 1962–1970).

18. In the Cold Rolling Plants of the LKM ("LKM Húzóműhelyek") steel was formed between rolls of low temperature. Cold Rolling strengthened steel and improved the surface in low temperature.
19. A similar type of acid bath treatment was used in the Smith Plant, where metal parts were cleaned in warm sulphuric acid, or occasionally in 10–15 per cent hydrochloric bath on 60–65 Â°C degrees. Occasionally acid was not rinsed off with water, but was neutralized in lime bath and was rinsed off only at the end of this process.
20. „Jegyzőkönyv. Északmagyarországi Vízügyi Igazgatóság Vízminőségvizsgáló Csoport. Az LKM szennyvízkezelésének vizsgálata Az 1/1961 Korm. rendelet végrehajtása során (Minutes. Northern Hungarian Water Superintendence Water Monitoring Group. The examination based on the 1/1961 Governmental Order)" 1 June 1962, Környezetvédelmi és Vízügyi Levéltár (Environmental and Water Archives) VI. 9. Miskolci Kulturmérnöki Hivatal Vizikönyvek 1867–1971 (Miskolc „Culture" Engineering Office „Waterlogs"), 291 box. 4006 / I. dossier. Lenin Kohászati Művek 1962–1970. (Lenin Metallurgical Works 1962–1970).
21. Documents of the LKM 1962—1968. Környezetvédelmi és Vízügyi Levéltár (Environmental and Water Archives) VI. 9. Miskolci Kulturmérnöki Hivatal Vizikönyvek 1867–1971 (Miskolc „Culture" Engineering Office „Waterlogs"), 291 box. 4006 / I. dossier. Lenin Kohászati Művek 1962–1970. (Lenin Metallurgical Works 1962–1970).
22. „Jegyzőkönyv. Északmagyarországi Vízügyi Igazgatóság Vízminőségvizsgáló Csoport. Az LKM szennyvízkezelésének vizsgálata Az 1/1961 Korm. rendelet végrehajtása során (Minutes. Northern Hungarian Water Superintendence Water Monitoring Group. The examination based on the 1/1961 Governmental Order)".
23. Ádám Fázold, *Proceedings of the XXIXth Annual Conference of the Hungarian Hydrology Association, Eger 2011*. http://www.hidrologia.hu/vandorgyules/29/dolgozatok/fazold_adam.html (accessed on August 20, 2013).

24. ÓKÜ had a joint sewer system that handled industrial waste waters and waste waters from bathrooms and showers jointly.
25. "Északmagyarországi Vízügyi Igazgatóság, Vízminőségvizsgáló Laboratórium, Hatósági és Felügyeleti Csoport. Ózdi Kohászati Üzemek szennyezésének vizsgálata az 1/1961-es. sz. korm. r. alapján (Northern Hungarian Water Superintendence, Water Quality Monitoring Laboratory, Authority and Supervisors Group. The Inspection of the Water Pollution of the Ózd Metallurgical Plants based on the 1/1961 Governmental Order)."
Környezetvédelmi és Vízügyi Levéltár (Environmental and Water Archives) VI. 9. Miskolci Kulturmérnöki Hivatal Vizikönyvek 1867–1971 (Miskolc „Culture" Engineering Office „Waterlogs"), 296 box. 4019 dossier, Ózdi Kohászati Üzemek szennyvízkezelése (Waste Water Treatment at the ÓKŰ.)
The Ózd Steel Mills purchased water from the Borsod County Waterworks. The Waterworks had built riverbank filtering wells along the Sajó River. The Ózd Steel Mills had a joint wastewater system for industrial and community waters. To separate these two types of waste waters a part of the community sewage was connected to the sewage network of the city of Ózd.
Sewage from ÓKŰ was discharged to the Hangony Creek at three points: 1. domestic canal 2. the discharge site at Lake Nagy 3. the discharge site at the Ózd Creek (that was the site where sewage was discharged from the Doór sedimentation plant as well.)
26. "Északmagyarországi Vízügyi Igazgatóság, Vízminőségvizsgáló Laboratórium, Hatósági és Felügyeleti Csoport. Ózdi Kohászati Üzemek szennyezésének vizsgálata az 1/1961-es. sz. korm. r. alapján (Northern Hungarian Water Superintendence, Water Quality Monitoring Laboratory, Authority and Supervisors Group. The inspection of the water pollution of the Ózd Metallurgical Plants based on the 1/1961 governmental order)" 1. In: Környezetvédelmi és Vízügyi Levéltár (Environmental and Water Archives, KVL) VI. 9. Miskolci Kulturmérnöki Hivatal Vizikönyvek 1867–1971. 296 box. 4019 dossier.
27. VIZITERV was established in 1954 and it was the largest water management planning company in Hungary under state socialism.

28. „Hozzászólás: Tervek Miskolc vízellátásának javítására (Comment: Plans to Improve Water supply in Miskolc)," *Észak-magyarország*, 30 December 30, 1966, 3.
29. Ibid.
30. "Részben ezt a célt szolgálta az OVH által (1968) augusztus 9-én Miskolcon kezdeményezett megbeszélés is, amelynek során a város vezetőivel a csúcsvízmű hitelforrásait is nagyrészben sikerült tisztázni. Elsősorban a tanácsnak kell határoznia, hogy a vízellátás kérdését miképpen rangsorolja a kétségtelenül szintén fontos más szükségletekkel szemben. Mindenesetre helyes volna, ha az ez évi aszály tanulságait kellőképpen megszívlelnék."Vincze Oszkár, "Miskolc Vízellátása," *Borsod Szemle* 12, No. 3. (1968): 98.
31. "Felsőzsolcáról is kapunk vizet, Intézkedések a vízellátást javítására (We Get Water from Felsőzsolca, Measures to Improve Water Supply)," *Déli Hírlap*, 12 January 1973. "Miskolcon megszűnik a vízhiány (Water Shortage is Ceasing in Miskolc)," *Déli Hírlap*, 6 November1969, nov 6, 5.
32. "Felsőzsolcáról is kapunk vizet, Intézkedések a vízellátást javítására (We Get Water from Felsőzsolca, Measures to Improve Water Supply)," "Miskolcon megszűnik a vízhiány (Water Shortage is Ceasing in Miskolc)."
33. „Tervek Miskolc vízellátásának javítására (Plans to Improve Water supply in Miskolc)". *Észak-magyarország*, 30 December 30, 1966, 3.
34. "Az ÉRV Zrt. Kialakulásának Története Korabeli Dokumentumok Alapján (The History of ÉRV Corp. Based on Contemporary Documents)," *Északmagyarországi Regionális Vízművek Rt. Company Website*, http://www.ervrt.hu/cgi-bin/index.php?hlid=10 (accessed on August 20, 2013).
35. "Százötven kilométerre bővítik a regionális vízmű fővezetékét. Törpe vízműveket létesítenek. Több gondot fordítanak a kutak közegészségügyi ellenőrzésére (Regional Water Supply Mains are Extended to be 150 km Long. Small Waterworks are Installed. More Attention is Being Paid to the Public Health Control of Wells)," *Észak-Magyarország*, 6 November 1958, 3.
36. "Az ÉRV Zrt. Kialakulásának Története Korabeli Dokumentumok Alapján (The History of ÉRV Corp. Based on Contemporary Documents)."

37. 4354/1955 (VII.18) Kormány Határozat (4354/1955 (VII.18) Order of the Council of Ministers), 18 July, 1955, Budapest, Hungary.
38. Construction works of the BRV I. lasted between 1956 and 1965 with the budget of 110.4 million Forints. BRV I consisted several units. The largest of these units, the Kazincbarcika II. waterworks was constructed with 3500 cubic meter per day capacity. Further construction sites included the pumping stations of Alacska I/1, Szuhakálló II/1, Ormosbánya II/2, and Herbolya II/3.
39. "Az ÉRV Zrt. kialakulásának története korabeli dokumentumok alapján (The history of ÉRV Corp. based on contemporary documents)," *ÉRV Zrt. Company Website,* http://www.ervrt.hu/cgi-bin/index.php?hlid=10 (accessed on August 20, 2013).
40. Ibid.
41. Ibid.
42. Ibid.
43. „Miskolc vízellátási gondjairól, Beszélgetés a Miskolci Vízművek főmérnökével (Water Supply Problems in Miskolc, Talk with the Chief Engineer of the Miskolc Waterworks) *Észak-Magyarország,* 1 October 1963, 2. Egy ankét margójára, Miskolc város vízellátásáról (On the Margin of a Conference, About Water Supply in Miskolc)," Észak-magyarország, 9, February 9, 1964. 5.
44. "Miskolci vízművek, Fürdők és Csatornázási Vállalat 1964. I. negyedéves Mérlegbeszámoló (Miskolc Waterworks, Baths and Drains Company 1964. I. quarterly Balance Report) 31 March 1964". No page numbers, Chap. V. 1. Borsod-Abaúj-Zemplén Megyei Levéltár, Mezőcsát Fióklevéltár (Borsod-Abaúj-Zemplén County Archives Mezőcsát Branch Archives) XXIX. 113. Miskolci Vízművek Iratai. 33 box.
45. *"Legnagyobb forrásunk a tapolcai oly kevés mennyiségben adott vizet, hogy az a megfigyelésünk szerint az 1913-as üzembehelyezéstől kezdődően még nem volt."* "Miskolci vízművek, Fürdők és Csatornázási Vállalat 1964. I. negyedéves Mérlegbeszámoló (Miskolc Waterworks, Baths and Drains Company 1964. I. quarterly Balance Report) March 31, 1964". 27. Borsod-Abaúj-Zemplén Megyei Levéltár, Mezőcsát Fióklevéltár (Borsod-Abaúj-Zemplén County Archives Mezőcsát Branch Archives) XXIX. 113. Miskolci Vízművek Iratai. 33 box.
46. A város lakói még emlékeznek az 1964-es vízhiányra. Egymást követték akoriban az ankétok, a megbeszélések. Szakemberek százainak

véleményét hallgatták meg, hogyan lehet és kell megoldani a város gondjait. Egyöntetű volt a megállapítás, hogy bármilyen nagy összegbe is kerül *sürgősen meg kell építeni a város úgynevezett keleti csúcsvízművét."* "Emlékezünk még 1964. nyarára, amikor gyönyörű, új házsorok lakóinak egy része az emeletről a földszintre járt vízért. Jónéhány utca lakóinak kimosott, fertőtlenített öntözőkocsikban szállították az ivóvizet. Akadt kerületi tisztiorvos, aki járványveszélytől rettegett, mert a lakosság végszükségből régi, fertőzött kutak vizét fogasztotta." Ismét hiánycikk lehet a leerősebb ital! Két miskolc újító aggodalma. Pozsonyi Sándor, Ápril 24, 1966 5. In: Észak-magyarország.

47. "Miskolci vízművek, Fürdők és Csatornázási Vállalat 1964. I. negyedéves Mérlegbeszámoló (Miskolc Waterworks, Baths and Drains Company 1964. I. quarterly Balance Report) 31 March 1964". 27. Borsod-Abaúj-Zemplén Megyei Levéltár, Mezőcsát Fióklevéltár (Borsod-Abaúj-Zemplén County Archives Mezőcsát Branch Archives) XXIX. 113. Miskolci Vízművek Iratai. 33 box.
48. "Miskolci vízművek, Fürdők és Csatornázási Vállalat 1965. éves Mérlegbeszámoló (Miskolc Waterworks, Baths and Drains Company 1965 Annual Balance Report)". 5. Borsod-Abaúj-Zemplén Megyei Levéltár, Mezőcsát Fióklevéltár (Borsod-Abaúj-Zemplén County Archives Mezőcsát Branch Archives) XXIX. 113. Miskolci Vízművek Iratai. 34 box.
49. "Miskolci vízművek, Fürdők és Csatornázási Vállalat 1965. éves Mérlegbeszámoló (Miskolc Waterworks, Baths and Drains Company 1965 Annual Balance Report)". 3. Borsod-Abaúj-Zemplén Megyei Levéltár, Mezőcsát Fióklevéltár (Borsod-Abaúj-Zemplén County Archives Mezőcsát Branch Archives) XXIX. 113. Miskolci Vízművek Iratai. 34 box.
50. "Miskolci vízművek, Fürdők és Csatornázási Vállalat 1965. éves Mérlegbeszámoló (Miskolc Waterworks, Baths and Drains Company 1965 Annual Balance Report)". 3–5. Borsod-Abaúj-Zemplén Megyei Levéltár, Mezőcsát Fióklevéltár (Borsod-Abaúj-Zemplén County Archives Mezőcsát Branch Archives) XXIX. 113. Miskolci Vízművek Iratai. 34 box.
51. "Miskolci vízművek, Fürdők és Csatornázási Vállalat 1966. éves Mérlegbeszámoló (Miskolc Waterworks, Baths and Drains Company 1966 Annual Balance Report)". 8. Borsod-Abaúj-Zemplén Megyei Levéltár, Mezőcsát Fióklevéltár (Borsod-Abaúj-Zemplén County

Archives Mezőcsát Branch Archives) XXIX. 113. Miskolci Vízművek Iratai. 34 box. "Miskolci vízművek, Fürdők és Csatornázási Vállalat 1967. éves Mérlegbeszámoló (Miskolc Waterworks, Baths and Drains Company 1967 Annual Balance Report)". 3. Borsod-Abaúj-Zemplén Megyei Levéltár, Mezőcsát Fióklevéltár (Borsod-Abaúj-Zemplén County Archives Mezőcsát Branch Archives) XXIX. 113. Miskolci Vízművek Iratai. 35 box.

52. "Miskolci vízművek, Fürdők és Csatornázási Vállalat 1967. éves Mérlegbeszámoló (Miskolc Waterworks, Baths and Drains Company 1967 Annual Balance Report)". 4. Borsod-Abaúj-Zemplén Megyei Levéltár, Mezőcsát Fióklevéltár (Borsod-Abaúj-Zemplén County Archives Mezőcsát Branch Archives) XXIX. 113. Miskolci Vízművek Iratai. 35 box.
53. "Általánosságban megállapítható, hogy a vállalatunknál képződő saját beruházási alap, valamint a felettes szervünk hozzájárulása és az egyéb hozzájárulások éves viszonylatban 22-25 mFt-ot tesznek ki. Ez az összeg elegendő a kisebb volumenű fejlesztések megvalósítására, de alkalmatlan arra, hogy ebből víztermelés, szennyvíz elvezetés és tisztítás, valamint fürdő rekonstrukciós nagy beruházások megvalósítást nyerjenek." Miskolci vízművek, Fürdők és Csatornázási Vállalat 1967. éves Mérlegbeszámoló (Miskolc Waterworks, Baths and Drains Company 1967 Annual Balance Report) 8–9. Borsod-Abaúj-Zemplén Megyei Levéltár, Mezőcsát Fióklevéltár (Borsod-Abaúj-Zemplén County Archives Mezőcsát Branch Archives) XXIX. 113. Miskolci Vízművek Iratai. 35 box.
54. "Miskolci vízművek, Fürdők és Csatornázási Vállalat IV. 5. Éves Terv Szöveges Indoklása (Miskolc Waterworks, Baths and Drains Company 4th Five Year Plan Textual Reasoning) June 21, 1971". 1. Borsod-Abaúj-Zemplén Megyei Levéltár, Mezőcsát Fióklevéltár (Borsod-Abaúj-Zemplén County Archives Mezőcsát Branch Archives) XXIX. 113. Miskolci Vízművek Iratai. 36 box.
55. „A termelékenységet jobb és több géppel, folyamatos műszaki fejlesztéssel kívánjuk növelni, már eddigis, a jövőben pedig fokozottabban kívánjuk gépesíteni a fizikai munkát a szolgáltatásban, az építőipari tevékenységgel és karbantartásoknál." "Miskolci vízművek, Fürdők és Csatornázási Vállalat 1971. I. féléves Mérlegbeszámoló (Miskolc Waterworks, Baths and Drains Company 1971. I. Half Year Balance Report)". 3. Borsod-Abaúj-Zemplén Megyei Levéltár, Mezőcsát

Fióklevéltár (Borsod-Abaúj-Zemplén County Archives Mezőcsát Branch Archives) XXIX. 113. Miskolci Vízművek Iratai. 36 box.

56. "Miskolci vízművek, Fürdők és Csatornázási Vállalat 1971. I. féléves Mérlegbeszámoló (Miskolc Waterworks, Baths and Drains Company 1971. I. Half Year Balance Report)". Without page number. Borsod-Abaúj-Zemplén Megyei Levéltár, Mezőcsát Fióklevéltár (Borsod-Abaúj-Zemplén County Archives Mezőcsát Branch Archives) XXIX. 113. Miskolci Vízművek Iratai. 36 box.
57. "Szöveges értékelés az MSZMP-MVB 257.1972. Számú Tájékoztató Adatszolgáltatásához (Textual Report on Hungarian Workers' Socialist Party's Miskolc City Committee 257. 1972 Information Service)". 1. Borsod-Abaúj-Zemplén Megyei Levéltár, Mezőcsát Fióklevéltár (Borsod-Abaúj-Zemplén County Archives Mezőcsát Branch Archives) XXIX. 113. Miskolci Vízművek Iratai. 36 box.
58. "Miskolci vízművek, Fürdők és Csatornázási Vállalat 1971. I. féléves Mérlegbeszámoló (Miskolc Waterworks, Baths and Drains Company 1971. I. Half Year Balance Report)". 8. Borsod-Abaúj-Zemplén Megyei Levéltár, Mezőcsát Fióklevéltár (Borsod-Abaúj-Zemplén County Archives Mezőcsát Branch Archives) XXIX. 113. Miskolci Vízművek Iratai. 36 box.
59. "A nagy meleg és a fokozódó igények miatt a növekvő termelés mellett a város rendelkezésére álló vízforrások kimerülőben vannak, augusztus hóban a zavartalan vízellátás érdekében a Sajó-menti vízműtől fogunk ivóvizet átvenni." "Miskolci vízművek, Fürdők és Csatornázási Vállalat 1971. I. féléves Mérlegbeszámoló (Miskolc Waterworks, Baths and Drains Company 1971. I. Half Year Balance Report)". Without page number. Borsod-Abaúj-Zemplén Megyei Levéltár, Mezőcsát Fióklevéltár (Borsod-Abaúj-Zemplén County Archives Mezőcsát Branch Archives) XXIX. 113. Miskolci Vízművek Iratai. 36 box.
60. "Miskolci vízművek, Fürdők és Csatornázási Vállalat 1972. évi Gazdálkodás Adatai (Miskolc Waterworks, Baths and Drains Company Economic Report 1972)". 1–2. Borsod-Abaúj-Zemplén Megyei Levéltár, Mezőcsát Fióklevéltár (Borsod-Abaúj-Zemplén County Archives Mezőcsát Branch Archives) XXIX. 113. Miskolci Vízművek Iratai. 37 box.
61. "Miskolci vízművek, Fürdők és Csatornázási Vállalat 1972. I–III. Negyed Évi Teljesítések (Miskolc Waterworks, Baths and Drains Company 1972. I–III. Quarterly Reports)". 1. Borsod-Abaúj-Zemplén

Megyei Levéltár, Mezőcsát Fióklevéltár (Borsod-Abaúj-Zemplén County Archives Mezőcsát Branch Archives) XXIX. 113. Miskolci Vízművek Iratai. 37 box.

62. "Miskolci vízművek, Fürdők és Csatornázási Vállalat 1972. I. Félévi Gazdálkodás Adatai (Miskolc Waterworks, Baths and Drains Company 1972. I. Half Year Economic Report)". Without page numbers. Borsod-Abaúj-Zemplén Megyei Levéltár, Mezőcsát Fióklevéltár (Borsod-Abaúj-Zemplén County Archives Mezőcsát Branch Archives) XXIX. 113. Miskolci Vízművek Iratai. 37 box.

6

Technological Reform and Environmental Performance in Hungary in the 1960s

6.1 The Rise of Environmentalism in West Germany in the 1960s–1970s

In West Germany, environmental concerns were subdued by economic and social concerns in the postwar reconstruction era. Following economic development, urbanization, and industrialization, environmental concerns rose again after World War II. Mass membership rise in four conservation groups mirrored the rise in social interest for environmental problems. Membership in the League for Bird Protection, League for Conservation in Bavaria, Isar Valley Society, and the Society for Nature Parks drastically declined from around 90,000 in 1940 to around 40,000 in 1945. The most popular of these four was the League for Bird Protection, a recipient of government subsidies in the 1950s. The group also contributed to the promotion of the German translation of Rachel Carson's *Silent Spring*, which heightened public environmental awareness, especially matters related to bird protection. As a result, the organization's membership was up to 57,000 in 1965. Such growth could not be sustained, and membership again dropped in the late 1960s to below 70,000. During the 1970s, the trend reversed, and

V. Pál, *Technology and the Environment in State-Socialist Hungary*,
DOI 10.1007/978-3-319-63832-4_6

by 1975 the league's membership reached 1940 levels, but by 1980, membership surpassed 120,000. It is important to note, however, that membership only reached 1940 levels again in the second half of the 1970s. Membership in the other three conservation groups researched by Dominick followed similar patterns.[1]

Soon after the beginning of postwar economic growth, the conditions of certain West German water resources were horrific. Newspapers and magazines often reported on water pollution scandals and their bitter aftermath. On June 3, 1954, the *Hamburger Abendblatt* warned its readers that the "Water Cycle is in the Greatest Danger!" Another journal preferred by industrialists headlined: "Water: A Commodity in Short Supply." One and a half decades later, *Die Welt* reported on the Rhine with the headline, "20 Million Drink from Germany's Largest Sewer."[2] Media attention to environmental issues between 1950 and 1970 rose continuously. One of the country's most prominent papers, *Frankfurter Allgemeine Zeitung (FAZ)* reported on environmental issues with growing frequency, especially between 1950 and 1960 when, according to Dominick, environmental coverage exploded from around 60 column inches annually to nearly 450 column inches per year within a decade. Such dedication to environmental issues, however, was not sustained and began to slowly decline by 1970. Between 1957 and 1961, environmental coverage reached its height and compared closely to coverage of educational issues in *FAZ*. After 1961, the prominence of environmental issues began to drop slightly in the newspaper. Meanwhile, the length educational articles climbed from 500 column inches per annum to nearly 2000 column inches per year. Dominick carried out similar research on reporting by *Die Zeit*. His four two-year periods of investigation of articles in *Die Zeit*; 1954–1955, 1959–1960, 1964–1965 and 1969–1970 showed similar curves. Apart from similarities, the peak in *Die Zeit* appeared at the end of 1969–1970. Compared to *FAZ*, column length devoted to ecology at *Die Zeit* was significantly lower throughout 1969–1970. Dominick found similar differences in the case of the Hofolding forest and the controversy over a proposed airport in Munich. *Münchener Merkur* reported vehemently on the subject, while Munich's other prominent daily, *Süddeutsche Zeitung* gave significantly less attention to this environmental debate.[3] Dominick found that environmental controversies in West Germany were often discussed only in the local press until the 1960s. He did not find another newspaper other than *Münchener Merkur* concerned about the Hofolding affair.

Local environmental problems added together and developed nationally horrifying environmental conditions in West Germany. According to *Der Spiegel's* massive 11-page coverage of water pollution on November 18, 1959, German industry's wastewater caused more devastation to water resources than residential water use and discharges. Residential wastewater discharge increased and caused problems because of the introduction of bathrooms and increased per capita consumption, but according to *Der Spiegel*, this was dwarfed by problems associated with industrial growth. Between 1951 and 1959, German residential water usage grew from 3.4 to 3.9 billion m^3. Concurrently, industrial water needs grew from 4.4 to 6.5 billion m^3. This exposé especially blamed Germany's chemical industry both for disproportionate water use and water pollution. Similar trends unfolded in Hungary ten years later. Increased residential water use in Hungary after 1958 unfolded especially because of changing standards and practices of personal hygiene. Massive discharge of industrial effluent by the chemical industry happened after the buildup of Hungary's major chemical production capacity in the second half of the 1960s and in the 1970s. In 1959 in Germany, only 17% of municipal industrial wastewater, and 43% of industrial wastewater was treated. Such a statistic was similar in Hungary, where more industrial establishments operated wastewater treatment plants than municipalities.[4] *Der Spiegel* mentioned positive instances as well. During the 1950s, the German metallurgy industry introduced water recycling; a method which was employed by Hungarian metallurgical plants in the 1960s. As a result, the Germans reduced water need/production ton from 20 to 5 tons.[5]

Dominick also investigated whether journalistic accounts were in favor of environmental protection or were only presenting the facts of environmental destruction. He found that approximately 30% environmentally concerned articles in *FAZ* and *Die Zeit* between 1957 and 1964 displayed environmental attitudes beyond just highlighting episodes of destruction.[6] Accounts in the media were not far from reality. Dr. Thienemann, a hydrologist, reported that in the half century since the beginning of WWI, the Rhine salmon harvest dropped from 160,000 to 3000 fish annually. In addition, according to Dr. Thienemann, that meager catch was useless because of the high chemical contamination.[7]

One of the most important German conservation groups at the time was the Alliance for the Protection of Germany's Waters (Vereinigung deutscher Gewässerschutz) founded in Frankfurt am Main in 1951. The impetus to establish such an association came from fishermen because their entire industry or recreational activity was endangered by water pollution from West Germany's booming industry and urban centers. The aims of the organization included cleaning up surface and groundwater resources, getting a national Water Law passed which would provide adequate management of water resources, and harmonize the interests of various pressure groups engaged in the water quality dialog. The alliance was able to communicate with players in both industry and government circles. In fact, the Alliance for the Protection of Germany's Waters worked very closely with government officials. The President of the Republic and federal ministers contributed to the alliance's conferences, educational programs, and exhibits. For example, at the 1959 Annual Alliance Conference, Professor Siegfried Balke, Federal Minister for Atomic Energy and Water Supply, who at the same time was also the head of the Alliance, gave the keynote speech in which he declared that water conditions in West Germany were life-threatening. Such close collaboration between the Alliance and the government partly resembled the situation in ECE. Here government organizations managed environmental "grassroots" activities exclusively until the late 1970s. The effectiveness of the Alliance also resembled the situation in ECE in the 1950s, because even though the organization had very close ties to the highest strata of the Federal German Government, very little happened to reverse the depletion of water resources until the late 1960s.[8]

Environmental concerns reentered mainstream discourse after World War II only in the 1960s, with the second wave of environmental awakening unfolded in the 1970s–1980s. During the first environmental upheaval, the state of the economy was less of a concern for German society because *Wirtschaftswunder* was producing an unprecedented level of economic prosperity. During the 1970s, when the economy slowed down and the Oil Crisis hit the global economy in 1973–1974, the economic situation changed. In 1965, only 30% of Germans viewed the economy as one of the most pressing problems of German society, rising to 40% in 1970, and shooting up to 85% in 1975 two years after the Oil Crisis.[9] Ecological problems rose to main federal level political topics in West Germany when Willy Brandt included environmental issues in his unsuccessful campaign for the chancellorship in 1961. When Brandt and the Social Democrat Party finally won the election in 1969, the earlier pro-industry policies of the Christian Democrats were contested, and a comprehensive governmental program was put in place to begin to curtail pollution nationwide. Environmental issues emerged as a top priority for a wide array of politicians, and the establishment of the Green Party in 1981 also signified the growing importance of the environment shared by a large segment of society. As a result, environmental conditions improved in many respects. The share of completely untreated household sewage decreased from 40% in 1957 to 12% in 1978. After over a century, water quality in the Rhine began to improve permanently by the early 1980s. On the other hand, some environmental problems worsened. Car traffic and air pollution caused damage to forests, a phenomenon called *Waldsterben*; and nitrates continued to accumulate in ground water. According to Dominick's assessment, however, the overall environmental quality in West Germany was better in 1989 than twenty years earlier.[10] Unfortunately, the opposite situation held true in East Germany. Results of East Germany's worsening environmental record were clearly visible in 1989–1990 when lurid accounts became more frequent in western scientific and popular journals.

Environmental matters in West Germany did not gain much support from the federal government until Willy Brandt was elected chancellor in 1969. Despite Germany's worsening environmental record, federal politics had been, until then, dominated by the pro-industry, pro-growth Christian Democratic Party (CDU).[11]

In September 1970, in order to gain some control over environmental issues, Brandt introduced an Immediate Program (*Sofortprogramm*); including the reduction of lead in gasoline, trash removal reform, as well as tackling water and air pollution issues. This program was the first step eventually leading to comprehensive environmental reform. Between 1971 and 1974, 1399 laws, ordinances and administrative regulations were enforced or prepared by the government. According to Dominick, media coverage, public opinion, and governmental activity interacted with each other and thus helped environmental issues to gain more prominence. Environmental activists had a major role in shaping German public opinion. Their role should not be underestimated when one takes into account the influx of environmental education on various levels of society.

At the same time, because of the plurality of the political system in West Germany, positive environmental changes on the federal level were in fact more difficult to implement and were delayed until the pro-environment Brandt Administration took office. Even so, the pro-environmental *thinking* was not shared by all West German deputies in 1979. Dominick researched delegates from various major political parties in Germany and examined who voted in favor of stronger environmental legislation at the annual major party congresses. According to Dominick, only 25% of Christian Social Union (CSU) and 31% of CDU delegates voted in favor of tightening environmental protection. Meanwhile, 72% of the Social Democratic Party (SPD) delegates favored pro-environmental pieces of legislation. Dominick further emphasizes that this voting "meter" could be an indicator of the overall environmental attitudes of German political parties and their representatives.[12] Since the CDU backed pro-industry policies, it was not until Willy Brandt, the leader of the SPD was elected chancellor in 1969, that environmental issues were effectively raised in postwar West Germany. The SPD claimed that the Adenauer Administration was not able to establish effective environmental protection standards since it was rooted in the traditional pro-industry policies of the CDU. According to SPD politicians, when the Adenauer Administration finally appointed a committee to draft an air pollution ordinance, approximately 75% of the committee members represented industrial interests.[13]

Outside of the political arena, traditional forms of environmental protection and conservation efforts included the *Natur- und Landschaft* magazine which often attacked materialism and the consumer lifestyle brought about by economic development. Traditional conservation groups such as the Swabian Alps Society enticed conservationists and provided opportunities to express their environmental views during various gatherings. In the 1950s–1960s, members of the Germany clergy also supported conservationists' efforts. In 1955, Dr. Kunst, a Lutheran minister prayed during his Bonn-based radio show for better air quality in the Ruhr. In 1957, the West German Evangelical Church sponsored a conference on air pollution in Westphalia. Christian debate over environmental matters was quite concerned over the Christian interpretation of the human–nature relationship. Gardeners and garden clubs were also anxious about conservation issues. West German gardening and landscape magazines such as *Garden and Landscape* (*Garten und Landschaft*) often published environmental commentaries. Scientific and technological associations concerned with production and industrial issues, such as the Society of German Engineers (*Verein Deutscher Ingenieure*), also became concerned about environmental matters. The tourist industry held a joint conference with traditional conservationists in 1959 with a focus on hiking and walking in nature. The rise of new environmental movements in West Germany was a result of multiple factors. Structural change, the rise of the service sector, and the change in attitudes concerning material possessions contributed to the appearance of a new environmental movement. Average West German working hours declined from 48 to 42 hours a week between 1950 and 1967, providing more leisure time. The share of the population that was able to take longer than 6-day holidays rose from 21% in 1949 to 36% in 1957, and 50% in 1964. Attitudes towards material possessions and work, versus enjoyment of life and leisure began to change in West Germany during the 1960s. A poll question asked West Germans about their life goals, whether they (A) "considered life as an assignment" which they had to "carry out" even if it proved "to be difficult," or they wanted to (B) "enjoy life," "avoid unnecessary exertion" and "make the most of it." In 1960, at the height of the economic miracle, 60% answered (A), compared to 29% for (B). By 1973, the gap between (A) and (B) narrowed, and 48% responded (A) while 35% responded (B).[14]

Although fields of environmental discussion were present in state socialism as early as the beginning of the 1960s, media coverage and the expression of public opinion were state-controlled, and therefore, more restricted than in West Germany. Regarding the political system, the plurality and the relatively easy access to the political arena in West Germany provided more room for democratic dialog; especially after the end of the 1960s when the federal government began to actively support environmental clean-up.[15]

6.2 The *Economical Shift* in Hungary in the 1960s–1970s

The most progressive elements of the planned reforms remained in theory. Cutting back on the most advanced elements of reform ideas and taking a more moderate path direct impact on Hungary's economic, technological and environmental future. As a result of accelerated development in the 1950s, which moderated somewhat, but were not completely abandoned in the 1960s, the water supply and waste water situation became critical nationally. Improvements, however weighted out the negative factors. Economic reforms and technological improvements of the 1960s intertwined with new economic philosophy and management practices. These sprang up from the reforms of the 1950s and were extended in the 1960s. These factors combinedly led to an *economical shift,* that both mean the prevalence of new, economical management philosophy and practices and the launch of new economical and profitable industries.

In the 1960s and 1970s, the Kádár regime prioritized investment in new technologies, especially in the chemical industry. This changed the composition of industry in Hungary, enhanced its export compatibility and profitability. State-socialism also had a competitive advantage over capitalism on certain fields. The pivotal economic role of the state was an advantage in the 1950s–1960s, when large steel and chemical production capacities were created in Hungary. Massive investment was needed for the establishment of these industries, which at the time, could only reasonably come from state funds. With limited discourse and democratic practices, economic decisions were made quicker and investments were carried out easier and more effectively. Simultaneously, environmental efforts were experiencing the same dynamic to industrialization. The pivotal role of the state enabled state agencies to rapidly and effectively implement measures when the central decision was made. For example, the implementation of the Hungarian natural gas grid and the rapid connection of heavy industrial plants to that grid enabled the heavy industry to reduce the discharge of phenols more quickly than in Western Europe. Also, other economic measures such as the recycling of industrial water discharges, and some degree of industrial symbiosis could be implemented within a short period of time by governmental orders and decisions.

After the mid-1960s the Kádár Regime worked to make the economy and industries more economical and competitive in the international market. According to Pál Germuska, the leadership acknowledged that cooperation solely within the Comecon system could not secure the successful development of Hungary. An economic turn to the West was based on the recognition that "Eastern integration" failed in economic terms and for economic survival, the country needed closer ties with the West.[16] According to Germuska, the second half of the 1970s was a turning point in Hungarian foreign policy as the country's economy turned more and more to the West. During the 1970s, economic contacts were fortified with Western European states. Hungary became a member of GATT (General Agreement on Tariffs and Trade) in 1973, and the IMF (International Monetary Fund) and World Bank in 1982.[17] In economic terms, this western orientation became inevitable and dominant after 1977.

The reorientation of Hungarian economic ties towards the West affected how economical production methods and environmental protection investments were planned. These methods and investments ultimately determined the environmental impact of Hungarian industry. For example, the Ministry of Metallurgy and Machine-Building began negotiations between 1968 and 1970 with the Nissan Company over a possible car factory. This project eventually failed. However, if it had succeeded, modern Japanese technology would have probably reduced the amount of discharged pollutants per unit. In 1967, the Hungarian Wagon and Machine Factory (*Magyar Vagon- és Gépgyár*,

MVG) purchased a diesel engine manufacturing license from the MAN Company (West Germany) and built several products based on MAN technology. From 1967, Rába-MAN engines were incorporated into the new Ikarus 200 bus series and were also placed in the legendary Rába-Steiger 250 tractor.[18]

In 1973, Rába began manufacturing the Rába-Steiger 250 tractor under license from the Steiger Company (USA). A year later, Rába USA was established and Rába exported 700 million USD worth of products to the US between 1974 and 1992.[19] The 250 series was a product that withstood competition in Western markets. It was powered by a 6-cylinder, 250 horsepower diesel engine and had four-wheel drive. Inside the 250, various components were Western-made. Pumps and governors were produced by the Bosch Company (West Germany), and fine filters were made by one of the largest filter manufacturers in the world, the Donaldson Company (US). It is difficult to estimate the positive environmental impact of the influx of Western technology in the 1970s, but it can be assumed that purchased Western patents were in most cases superior to domestically developed products and technology imported from Eastern Europe. Therefore, it is presumed that their environmental impact was less than those of Comecon origin.[20]

Despite the turn to the West, Hungary was not ultimately able to export highly finished products and technology. In most cases, manufacturers assembled Western technology or contributed to foreign assembly processes. For example, Ikarus, Hungary's bus production company and one of the big Comecon bus manufacturers, teamed up with the American Crown Coach in 1976.[21] The production of the Crown-Ikarus 286 lasted from 1980 to 1986, and the company delivered 243 buses to the US. Only body shells were built in Hungary, which were then shipped to the USA and assembled in Crown Coach's California plant. The largest orders for Crown-Ikarus 286s came from Tri-Met, Portland, Oregon (87 buses), Houston (50 buses), and Milwaukee (40 buses) (Fig. 6.1).

Within a short time, the Crown-Ikarus 286 manifested various technical problems in Portland. These technical faults were most probably the result of incompetent assembly in the USA. Breakdowns were frequent, and maintenance costs of these buses were high. Tri-Met

Fig. 6.1 Ikarus 280 bus in Budapest, 1975. *Photo* FORTEPAN / NAGY GYULA

eventually filed a lawsuit against the manufacturers and as a result, the introduction of Ikarus to the American market failed.[22] Between 1986 and 1989, Ontario Bus Industries produced similar buses for the Canadian market under the brand name of Orion-Ikarus 286. Bodies and chassis were again made in Hungary and then shipped to Canada to be fully assembled. Unlike its engineering products, Hungarian agriculture targeted Western markets with better success. Exports of cash crops, food products, and domestically developed agrarian technologies found more welcoming markets.

Ivan T. Berend suggested that Hungary operated in a continuously opening global market from the 1960s. This claim is supported by Germuska's analysis, based on HSWP party documentation of the redirection of the national trade and export policy in the 1970s. According to Germuska, the shift from Comecon partnerships to Western partnerships was facilitated by the reforms of 1968 and the Oil Crisis of 1973. The reforms of 1968 had a direct positive impact on economic planning and the rising importance of profitability. Moreover, they had an indirect impact on environmental quality, including the discharge of wastewaters.

The Oil Crisis of 1973 and the drastic price rise that followed had a gradual impact on energy and production costs in the Comecon area. In Hungary, there was a direct relation between the rise of raw material and energy costs and the mounting importance of environmental matters. Where production costs rose, economic and environmental protection efforts by industrial actors strengthened.

Hungarian economic reforms were launched on January 1, 1968, providing more freedom to individual production plants and industrial ministries. Allowing more independence to the Hungarian Socialist Workers' Party (HSWP) from the central bodies aimed to strengthen productivity. The reforms triggered growth in Hungary that topped 7–11% in 1968–1969 and was planned to level out between 5 and 6% during the coming years. For example, in May 1970 the Political Committee of the HSWP added an extra 30% investment for the coming five-year plan period compared to the previous one. The HSWP's investment aimed to curtail externalities and to enhance the productivity and profitability of the national economy.[23]

A more flexible economy led to more foreign contacts and a growing influx of Western machinery and know-how. Imports already drastically grew between 1969 and 1972. According to Germuska, more imports were probably the result of very high demand for investment and up-to-date machinery, know-how and technologies. During the years that followed, hard currency-poor Hungary suffered from an unfavorable foreign trade balance. The rapid rise of imports was a further threat to the state budget deficit. Due to its unfavorable foreign trade balance, Hungary was particularly vulnerable during the Oil Crisis of 1973 when the prices of imported commodities briskly increased. Immediately after the Oil Crisis, import prices increased by 8–10%. Export prices also increased, but only by 6–8%. These combined factors increased the negative impacts of the unfavorable trade balance on the Hungarian market that operated with semi-fixed prices. As a result, the Hungarian Government extended the already existing system of state subsidies on both exported and imported goods. However, the extension of subsidies was not financially sustainable.[24]

When Hungary turned increasingly toward Western trade after 1968, it became increasingly vulnerable to changes in the volatile world market. Price increases in the world market during the 1970s inevitably affected domestic prices. Eventually, the Kádár Regime had to introduce a radical price rise on "energy sources, fuels, metallurgical, chemical and clothing products" on January 1, 1975. This price increase did not include foodstuffs or most consumable goods because the Government did not want to disturb the living standard of the population. In any case, energy and raw materials prices indirectly led to the increase in the production costs of consumer goods.[25]

Prices for consumer goods were normally fixed by the National Office of Prices and Materials and should have been increased. However, the State Planning Committee and the Party leadership of the HSWP were not in favor of burdening consumers. On the other hand, the main branches of Hungarian industry, for example, the iron, steel, and the chemical industries were not able to cover the financial gap between high import and low export prices. On the contrary, according to a Price Office report produced in March 1976 the iron, steel, and chemical industries were in need of high state subsidies. After 1973, it became inevitable that Hungary's price system was unsustainable in the rapidly changing economic environment. Hungary's state socialist regime should have introduced hasty changes to adapt to the new economic order. Change in the economic system would have had a direct impact on more cost-effective production and should have resulted in the gradual abandonment of industrial processes with the highest energy and raw material demand. Ultimately, that shift should have eventually reduced the amount of discharged pollutants. In January 1977, the Ministry of Finance together with the National Office of Materials and Prices investigated some of the most severe economic issues of the Hungarian state socialist economy. This report concluded that in the case of most products, producer costs were higher than the sales prices.

In other words, even though an extremely wide spectrum of industrial products received direct state subsidies, and even so, and were not profitable. It was clear that in a fierce economic climate with escalating energy, transport, and raw material costs, this economic structure was untenable and had to be reformed. Such reforms should have contained considerable price increases and the drastic reduction of state subsidies. Rising prices would be painful for the population and could contribute to the erosion of public support for the Kádár Regime. Unsurprisingly, this made state socialist leaders worry.[26]

After 1973, scientific and political debates erupted with the aim to analyze issues of the economic crisis. In many senses, these debates resembled the reform discussions of the mid-1950s. Reformers in 1954–1955, and especially after 1957 concentrated on the successful modernization, increased competitiveness, cost-effective production, and energy use in Hungarian industry. During the 1960s, the achievement of such goals was beyond reach. Hungarian economic experts and ministry officials were anxious to find a remedy for Hungary's painful economic issues, especially when the European and world economy showed signs of economic slowdown and even exhaustion in 1973. After 1975, the Central Committee of the HSWP commissioned hundreds of experts and organized these specialists into six sub-committees focused on finding the answers to Hungary's escalating economic woes. Working groups of the post-1975 era delivered very similar answers to those of the mid-1950s. Most experts agreed that the expansion of exports to Comecon countries, and especially to Western capitalist states was vital. This was because similarly to the ambitious goals of the Second Three-Year Plan (1958–1961), experts of the 1975 subcommittees hoped to satisfy Hungary's need for hard currency through the export of highly finished and sophisticated products which would sell for a relatively high price on the world market. Reformers in 1975 assumed that pharmaceuticals, petrochemicals, herbicides, pesticides, and electronics would produce enough convertible currency to revive Hungary's suffering economy.[27]

6.3 The *Economical Shift* and the *Energy Shift* in the Borsod Basin in the 1960s–1970s

The 1962–1968 wastewater discharge fine system was partly effective with factories which discharged their pollution into smaller waterways. ÉVÍZIG's measures were especially effective with LKM, where pollution was discharged into the tiny Szinva Creek causing an eyesore for the residents of the large industrial town of Miskolc. However, the 1962–1968 fine system was ineffective with factories which discharged their wastewaters into larger water bodies. In general, the relatively mild wastewater pollution fine rates between 1962 and 1968 were not strict enough for many industrial plants. After the introduction of economic reform policies in 1968, the methodology and pollution fine rates changed. The new system led to higher fines for numerous industrial plants. Simultaneously, the Hungarian Government invested a growing share of the total industrial investment budget into environmental protection measures.

During the course of the Fourth Five-Year Plan (1971–1975), Hungarian heavy industry spent about 1.7 billion Ft for environmental protection investments. Water quality protection investment gained precedence, absorbing 60.4% of the total environmental budget. Air pollution came second with 33%, and the remainder of the environmental budget was spent on other types of pollution abatement. For example, 2% targeted hazardous waste and 0.6% addressed noise pollution. The chemical industry received 932.7 million Ft (54.8%) out of the total national 1.7 billion Ft environmental budget from 1971 to 1975. The sector's environmental spending pattern closely mirrored the national budget. Out of its environmental budget, the chemical industry invested 68.9% on water protection, 27.7% on air emissions, 2.3% on hazardous waste treatment, and 0.58% on noise pollution. Between 1971 and 1975, environmentally-related investment in Hungary totaled around 2–2.3% of all industrial investments and 0.8–0.9% of the country's GDP. However, environmental funding was not coming from central sources alone. About 50% of environmental funding came from the companies' own resources, further complemented by 34.7% matching funds from the central authorities, and 14.1% in bank loans. Despite the growing importance and the rising effectiveness of environmental investments, not nearly enough was done to rectify the grim situation. According to a 1978 report by the Hungarian Chemical Industry Union (*Magyar Vegyipari Egyesülés*, MVE), the 2–2.3% of all industrial outlays spent on wastewater management was not enough to stop or even significantly reduce industrial water pollution. The MVE estimated that about 6.7–7.5% of the industrial investment budget would need to be devoted to environmental investments in order to actually improve the state of the environment.[28]

The MVE pointed out that 2–2.3% was not even enough to stabilize the present level of environmental quality. In fact, it estimated that about 4.3–5% of the industrial investment budget should have been devoted to environmental investments to peg environmental quality at the 1975 level. The chemical industry's environmental claims were listened to by decision-makers, and its environmental budget was doubled from 933 million during the Fourth Five-Year Plan (1971–1975) to 1.992 billion Ft during the Fifth Five-Year Plan period (1976–1980). The MVE knew that Hungarian chemical plants were under intense pressure because of their discharges and emissions. The environmental impact of the chemical industry, especially on water resources was significantly more severe than from the other branches of the economy. By the early 1970s, Hungarian chemical plants such as BVK grew into major polluters and became more prominent targets for tightening environmental measures and fines. The MVE was aware of the change, but it was uncomfortable to accept the reality of this new unfavorable situation. The MVE criticized the post-1968 environmental fine and environmental funding system, because: "*When plants install wastewater treatment equipment, the service and operation costs might scale up to several million forints annually. In the case of the Nitrochemical Industrial Plants (Nitrokémiai Vegyipari Művek), these (environmental) costs were 8.2 million Ft in 1977. Simultaneously, many of these (chemical) plants were due to pay pollution fines besides their treatment facility operation costs.*" The MVE regarded the post-1968 system as contradictory because while finance for wastewater protection works was still as difficult to obtain as pre-1968, wastewater discharge fines had escalated significantly from bee stings to painful bites.[29]

Simultaneously, with the rise of more environmentally friendly attitudes in Western, and East-Central Europe, newly born chemical industries across the continent radically transformed the composition of industrial pollutants released into surface waters. While the iron and steel industry jeopardized water resources with phenols, oils and ore sludge, continental Europe's emerging chemical industry polluted rivers such as the Rhine with a wide array of organic pollutants and toxic substances. Postwar Europe's newborn chemical industry and its massive load of new pollutants dwarfed previous discharges by the iron and steel industry. Yet, again, what unfolded in Western Europe also consequently occurred on a smaller scale in East-Central Europe. Soon after the introduction of Hungary's chemical program, new chemical conglomerates began discharging toxic pollutants. Rapidly mounting toxic emissions triggered environmentally-conscious economic measures, state-funded end-of-pipe technologies, and a heightened social awareness (Fig. 6.2).

The Khrushchev Administration supported the development of large-scale chemical and petrochemical projects in the Soviet Union and in other Comecon countries. The abundant fossil fuel resources of the USSR would provide a solid base for the massive development of the chemical industries in state socialist countries. In 1958, Comecon member countries decided to place an emphasis on the development of their chemical industries. Chemical production developments would emerge and dominate industrial investment programs in many Comecon member states between 1958 and 1975.[30]

In Hungary, where the iron and steel industry did not fulfill the promise to bridge the economic gap between the East and West, petrochemical products and thermoplastics provided a new hope for overtaking the West in an important production area. Since Hungary was poor in raw materials compared to other ECE states, the Kádár Regime was especially keen to develop new chemical production capacities. Chemical production could be based on cheap imported raw materials. In order to implement large-scale PVC manufacturing, access to the Soviet Union's cheap, abundant oil and natural gas supplies was vital.

Fig. 6.2 Dunamenti Petrochemical Company, Oil Refinery Unit, Százhalombatta 1971. *Photo* FORTEPAN / URBÁN TAMÁS

Eventually, prodigious funds were directed to establish large chemical combines such as BVK, the Tisza Chemical Combine (*Tiszai Vegyi Kombinát*, TVK) in Leninváros, and an oil refinery and industrial symbiosis system in Százhalombatta.

In the 1960s, it was cheaper, easier, more flexible, and more competitive to use crude oil and natural gas supplied by the USSR than to continue the use of domestic and imported coal. This did not mean that Hungary shifted from a coal regime to an oil and natural gas regime instantly. Much of the *energy shift* unfolded between 1958 and 1973 as part of the *economical shift*. The Hungarian economy slowly shifted from a coal economy towards oil and natural gas-based economy. In the 1960s, the domestic coal industry slightly increased its production volume. Meanwhile, to decrease production costs, coal mining underwent intensive mechanization. When we compare the use of coal with the use of crude oil and natural gas during this period, coal was rapidly losing importance to new fossil fuels. By the late 1970s, Hungarian coal mining had changed significantly. A series of highly mechanized open-pit lignite mines opened. In addition, operations at several uneconomical mines were shut down, forcing thousands of miners to change their professions. After the 1950s, social changes soon made it difficult to find workers for the dangerous and grueling work in mines. Even though the coal industry retained its annual volume of production throughout the researched period, coal slowly lost significance to other fossil fuels. Hungarian energy use, despite reforms and efficiency campaigns, was steadily rising in the 1960s–1970s. Mining received renewed impetus in the mid-1980s when investment in mining reached new heights.[31]

The slow decline of the coal mining industry in Hungary in the 1960s–1970s ran parallel with a soaring use of oil and natural gas. A production boom of oil and gas-based products followed. After modest beginnings in the early 1960s, national PVC production grew rapidly during the second half of the 1960s and the 1970s.[32]

By the late 1970s, BVK emerged as the primary PVC producer and one of the flagship heavy chemical plants in the country. The BVK's PVC I production unit initially produced 6000 tons annually, less than a third of the national PVC production capacity between 1961 and 1965. PVC I began operation in 1962, and BVK grew during the following decade from a single product, provincial nitrogen fertilizer factory into a large multi-product chemical combine.

During the 1960s, PVC production at BVK went through three large expansion phases. As a result, BVK wastewater discharges increased approximately tenfold in the decade following 1962. Water protection measures which produced some successes in the cases of Diósgyőr and Ózd during the 1960s rapidly lost relevance against the massive amount of oils, acids, and ammonia being released from BVK.[33]

Fig. 6.3 Borsodi Power Plant, Kazincbarcika 1965. *Photo* FORTEPAN / MORVAY KINGA / PHOTO BY MORVAY LAJOS

BVK's nitrogen fertilizer production line was also broadened. In 1958, production at Plant I was consolidated; improving its annual production capacity to 132,000 tons/year. In 1960, it was decided that the plant's production capacity was to be doubled.[34] Two years later, an additional fertilizer production unit and caprolactam[35] production lines were added, triggering the decision to build Plant II (Fig. 6.3).[36]

Simultaneously, BVK's energy system was modernized and the factory shifted from the use of coal to natural gas. Imported coke was also replaced by natural gas for ammonia production in 1962–1963. In the late 1950s, coke was expensive in Hungary because it was mostly imported from Czechoslovakia. Moreover, coke used over 2.5 times more energy per production ton than pressurized natural gas-based methods.[37] Upon the introduction of natural gas-based ammonium production, energy need per ton dropped sharply. At the same time, phenols disappeared from BVK's wastewater.[38]

Coke-based	26 x 106 kcal
Natural gas-based	17 x 106 kcal
Pressurized natural gas-based	10 x 106 kcal

Fig. 6.4 BVK energy consumption for a ton of ammonium. *Source* Frisnyák, *Kazincbarcika földrajza*, 217

These modernization projects were part of the partial economic reform processes in Hungary that aimed to boost Hungarian industry into a more economical and energy-efficient pattern (Fig. 6.4).

Tendencies with both positive and negative environmental impacts were present at BVK in the 1960s. For example, the shift from coal to natural gas eliminated phenols in the wastewater, but the extension of the fertilizer production line produced more wastewater then was previously discharged. Also between 1962 and 1978, three stages of the PVC unit came on line, causing the scale and composition of wastewaters to change dramatically. Western technology and know-how dominated, especially during the construction of PVC II and PVC III. However, the use of high-tech Western technology did not coincide with the construction of adequate wastewater cleaning facilities until 1975.[39]

Imported western technology included everything from single machines to complete production units. At PVC I, the Hoechst-Hde's (West Germany) carbide-acetylene patent was employed.[40] The chloride-alkali plant at PVC I used patents of the French Krebs Company. Here, transformers and rectifiers were delivered by Siemens. The use of Western technology prevailed, but cheap raw materials were supplied from Comecon sources. Carbide and industrial salts were imported from Czechoslovakia, East Germany, and China. Natural gas came from domestic fields around Hajdúszoboszló and from the USSR via the Brotherhood (*Testvériség*) Pipeline (Fig. 6.5).[41]

Initially, BVK's PVC I unit was an independent factory constructed approximately 1 km from the nitrogen fertilizer plants in the village of Berente. In 1963, the fertilizer plants and the PVC unit merged, and the multi-product BVK began manufacturing. PVC I began regular operation in June 1963 and reached full capacity a year later in May 1964.[42]

Year	Electricity (MWh)	Water (1000 m^3)
1958	55,988	1,992.1
1963	246,689	5,605.2
1967	281,406	7,785
1971	483,728	14,343.4
1975	623,621	12,635.7
1977	645,094	13,086.6

Fig. 6.5 Borsod Chemical Combine energy and water consumption, 1958–1977. *Source* Frisnyák, *Kazincbarcika földrajza*, 228

BVK's PVC I produced Ongrovil, a semi-finished PVC product in dust form, and a granulate brand called Ongrolit.[43] BVK aimed to maximize profits through the marketing of finished products. Therefore, the production of plastic doors, windows and insulation walls began as early as 1967. The finished PVC production line was based on a patent and machinery of the Covema Company (Italy).[44] Sources suggest that the finished Covema product line could be seen as the manifestation of entrepreneur-like behavior by BVK. Producing a finished product to make a higher profit may symbolize the profit-oriented attitude of several Hungarian factories in the partially-reformed Hungarian economic system in the 1960s. Expansion of PVC output capacity continued during the Second Five-Year Plan. An additional 10,000 ton/year unit was added to the initial 6000 ton/year capacity of PVC I.

Between 1964 and 1967, the nitrogen fertilizer factory was also enlarged and modernized for the third time.[45] Eastern European machinery from the 1950s was replaced by a new production line from the American-Belgian Coppée-Rust Company.[46] Rust-Coppée was an odd business choice in Cold War politics because its mother company in the US was also an important contractor of the US Army Corps of Engineers.[47] During the third extension of the nitrogen fertilizer unit, coke-based fertilizer production was abandoned and pressurized natural gas and vacuum technology were introduced. Modern machinery and production methods significantly decreased the per ton energy needs. Western technological orientation became inevitable. During the design and construction phase of the new nitrogen fertilizer unit, Belgian,

West German, and Dutch experts traveled to Kazincbarcika to supervise construction.[48]

PVC I was soon followed by additional facilities. The 25,000 ton/year capacity PVC II plant and the Caprolactam Unit were built by 1969.[49]

The Caprolactam Unit was initially planned as a component of the North Hungarian Chemical Plants (*Észak-Magyarországi Vegyiművek*, ÉVM) a little over 10 km south-southeast from BVK. However, the decision was changed and the investment went to BVK where hydrogen, ammonium and ammonium-nitrate production was already happening. These products were all essential raw materials for caprolactam production.[50]

The new Caprolactam Unit was erected in 1966 beside the old nitrogen fertilizer plant. Equipment for the factory was supplied by domestic producers. Popular products included polyamide fibers and artificial silk, which was delivered mostly to the Hungarian Viscose Fabric Factory (*Magyar Viscosia Gyár*). The unit also produced specialized plastics such as "Bonamid," a sturdy substitute for imported and expensive non-ferrous metals in heavy machinery—especially in the mining industry.[51]

By-products of the Caprolactam Unit were also reutilized. Ammonium-sulfate was recycled into nitrogen fertilizer production.[52] Markets for by-products such as sodium-hydroxide (NaOH), sodium hypochlorite (NaOCl), hydrochloric acid, ammonia water, chloride, ammonia, nitrous oxide (Dinox) or "laughing gas," and cyclohexanol were also searched or they were recycled.[53]

PVC I was followed by PVC II, doubling production capacity by an additional 24,000 tons/year. Machinery at PVC II was mostly supplied by Italian and West German companies. Some instruments were imported from Czechoslovakia. During the 1960s, various subdivisions at PVC I were modernized. For example, a new acetylene production plant was built in 1965 using a patent and equipment imported from the Montecatini Company (Italy).[54]

As a result of large-scale investments at BVK and TVK, domestic PVC production reached 100,000 tons per year by the early 1970s. This was approximately ten times higher than the national PVC output a decade earlier. Despite the sharp rise, the Union of the Hungarian Chemical Industry (*Magyar Vegyipari Egyesülés*, MVE) estimated that domestic and foreign demand for PVC was 40–50% higher than current production.[55]

During the Third and Fourth Five-Year Plans (1966–1970 and 1971–1975), the importance of foreign markets to BVK increased, and exports rose sharply to 238 million Ft by 1972.[56]

PVC II was completed in 1971, soon followed by PVC III in 1977. PVC III added another 150,000 ton annual capacity to BVK's production system that alone now represented more than the entire national PVC output in 1970. PVC III was a very expensive 11.3 billion Ft investment that represented about 80% of BVK's total investment budget between 1971 and 1977.[57]

PVC III included a vinyl chloride plant that produced 60,000 tons per year. Vinyl chloride production in Kazincbarcika was based on the 80,000 tons of ethylene produced annually in Leninváros supplied to BVK via a pipeline.[58] An Electrolysis Unit was also part of PVC III. With an annual capacity of 120,000 tons, it was the largest concern of its kind in Hungary.[59] According to the MVE, BVK's polymer unit had the fourth largest production capacity in the world by the mid-1970s. It was preceded only by Japanese and two American production plants.[60]

High-technology was employed within the PVC production unit. Chloride production was based on the De Nora Company's (Italy) patent.[61] Equipment at the monomer unit was based on a Goudricke patent and was supplied by the Badger Company (US). Machinery at the polymer unit was automated, computerized and delivered by the Shin Etsu Company of Japan.[62]

Production technology at PVC III was substantially more efficient than earlier polyvinyl chloride plants in Hungary. For example, PVC II devoured 500 grams of mercury for each ton of chloride produced, while PVC III used only 50 grams of mercury per ton of chloride.[63] In addition, PVC III was one of the first heavy industrial investments in Hungary that included substantial funds for comprehensive wastewater cleaning technologies.[64] Trial runs at PVC III began on April 4, 1978. Simultaneously, a three-phase wastewater treatment plant was installed in the vicinity of the factory.[65]

6.4 The Environmental Impact of the *Economical Shift* and the *Energy Shift* in Hungary in the 1960s–1970s

Shortly after the Barcika nitrogen fertilizer plant began production in 1958, large amounts of ammonia were detected in the Sajó River. Ammonia was the first large-scale pollutant emanating from BVK. According to contemporary factory documentation, company management was surprised by the ammonia discharges.[66] Normally, BVK's fertilizer production technology would not allow ammonia to leak. Despite the theoretically safe technology, ammonia discharges remained significant during the following years.

The fertilizer plant discharged a large *amount* of grease as well. However, when wastewater discharge fines were introduced in Hungary in 1962, BVK was fined only for its ammonia pollution. According to the then current law, when a factory discharged several pollutants and did not have the means to clean its wastewater, fines for only the most severe type of pollution should be imposed.[67]

During the early 1960s, the accumulated wastewater fines for BVK dwarfed its contemporaries, such as fines given to the steel giants of the Borsod Basin. For example, fines just for BVK's waterborne ammonia discharges (115 mg/l) came to 330,000 Ft. in 1962.[68] This amount was only about 10–15% of the fines set for LKM and ÓKÜ in the first half of the 1960s. One of the major factors that led to low wastewater discharge fines at BVK was that ÉVÍZIG superintendents claimed that the ammonia discharge was not primarily the fault of the plant. According to ÉVIZIG staff, the ammonia leak was the result of a defect in the plant design. Consequently, the annual discharge fine for BVK was significantly lower than the fine it would normally earn for such a leak.[69]

BVK was only paying 20 filler per liter instead of the maximum of 40 forints per liter.[70] Moreover, a low 0.5 multiplier was set instead of 1 or 2. Superintendents "did not yet want to punish BVK for environmental harm," because the most severe water pollution was not initially the result of misdeeds by the plant. Superintendents obliged BVK to apply an ammonia extraction technology by August 1964 (within

14 months). If that condition could not be met by the deadline, superintendents from 1964 onwards would sanction BVK and calculate penalties with a higher per liter rate and greater than 1.0 multiplier.[71]

ÉVÍZIG attempted first to draw the plant's attention to a prevailing problem and facilitate BVK's cooperation within an action framework designed by the regulators. If such an approach did not work, then ÉVÍZIG would shift to the use of financial penalties aimed to maximize fines until the desired goals were achieved.[72]

The second factor that led to relatively low wastewater discharge fines at BVK was that the 1962–1968 wastewater fines system monitored the impact of polluters on water flows. If for example, a polluter discharged its wastewater into a relatively large water flow such the Sajó River, the initial concentration of pollution would be greatly diluted and lead to a reduced fine (Fig. 6.6).

It is not known exactly how much water was discharged from BVK on a daily and annual basis between 1962 and 1968 because BVK remained reluctant to cooperate with ÉVÍZIG. What is known is that production greatly intensified in Kazincbarcika in the 1960s, but such growth and the proliferating amount of discharged pollutants was not entirely reflected in the scale of fines. BVK paid 330,000 Ft in 1962, escalating only to 1.2–1.4 million Ft by 1965–1968. Meanwhile, the factory grew to be one of the rising heavy chemical plants in the country.[73]

BVK's wastewater was somewhat diluted in the already polluted Sajó River; meaning that monitoring was limited to determining its negative impact in the already contaminated river water. BVK also successfully avoided attempts by ÉVÍZIG to determine the exact amount of wastewater discharged from the factory. As a result, BVK emerged as a negative example of the inefficiency and ambiguity of the 1962–1968 wastewater fine system. ÉVÍZIG reports were full of bitter comments concerning the unlawful actions of BVK which often remained non- or partly sanctioned (Fig. 6.7).[74]

In the mid-1960s, BVK defended itself by claiming that pollution discharges were not the result of the plant's unlawful conduct but in fact the unavoidable side-effect of the technology used in the factory. BVK further argued that construction and operation of this equipment had

Fig. 6.6 Borsodi Chemical Combine, Kazincbarcika 1967. *Photo* FORTEPAN / LECHNER NONPROFIT KFT. DOKUMENTÁCIÓS KÖZPONT / PHOTO BY VÁTI

been approved by the OT and ÉVIZIG, and it was the responsibility of the central planners and regional superintendents that provided licenses to the BVK.[75]

In 1966, Gyula Harencsár, a representative of BVK defended his company at the OVF, the court of the second instance in water pollution issues. Mr. Harencsár stated that BVK had already applied for and had been promised sufficient credit by central authorities to invest in wastewater treatment technologies. According to Harencsár, it was not BVK's fault that at the time of its appeal to the OVF such environmental protection funds from the government had not yet been received. He argued that due to its high costs, the construction of an effective wastewater treatment facility at BVK could only be financed by the

Year	Fine (in Ft)
1962	330.000
1963	N/A
1964	1,252,000
1965	1,242,000
1966	1,379,000
1967	N/A
1968	N/A

Fig. 6.7 Initial discharge fines levied against Borsod Chemical Combine, 1962–1968. *Source* Decree Series on the waste water discharge fee based on the waste water treatment monitoring of he BVK between 1962 and 1968. évre.' In: Környezetvédelmi és Vízügyi Levéltár (Environmental and Water Archives, KVL) VI. 9. Miskolci Kulturmérnöki Hivatal Vizikönyvek 1867–1971. 304 box. 4034 / II. dossier

central authorities. BVK alone was powerless to prevent its own industrial water pollution to be discharged into the Sajó River. Harencsár also pointed out that even though BVK was unable to install a full wastewater treatment facility on its own, the company had already purchased several wastewater cleaning machines. Some of this equipment, for example, an ammonium-sulfate extracting machine, had not yet been installed due to technical problems but would begin operation in the near future. Harencsár added that some pollutants, e.g. carbide sludge should not have been taken into account when calculating BVK's annual water pollution fine because they were discharged into the Sajó River with a ÉVÍZIG permit. Harencsár concluded that given these circumstances, BVK denied any responsibility for environmental harm caused to water quality in 1966.[76]

OVF dismissed many of Harencsár's claims but found some of his arguments justified.[77] Miklós Breinrich, the vice-director of OVF based the final decision on 25.§ of Governmental Order 32/1964. He acknowledged that the technology in BVK's fertilizer plant should not have discharged ammonium into the Sajó River. The judge also found the company's argument justified that the installed technology was responsible for the ammonium discharges. Breinich accepted that the plant did not have the necessary financial resources to access effective wastewater technologies.[78]

The OVF dismissed BVK's argument concerning the discharge of carbide sludge, lime, and other pollutants. The OVF noted that even though a discharge permit for carbide sludge was given to BVK in 1962, it limited discharges to 200 m^3/day. Monitoring in 1966 proved that the 200 m^3 daily limit had been far exceeded. In fact, BVK discharged 3000 m^3/day of carbide sludge into the Sajó River.[79]

BVK notoriously misinterpreted environmental bylaws between 1962 and 1968. In several cases, BVK constructed wastewater treatment facilities without the ÉVÍZIG's permission. In other cases, the factory did gain permission from the superintendents but did not follow the guidelines set by ÉVÍZIG. In 1968, Dr. Gusztáv Wolf explained such cases to Sándor Vezse, ÉVIZIG director in a report: "*When planning the installation of new equipment for the plant, BVK asked a permission from ÉVÍZIG. But after permission was granted, construction blueprints were changed regularly. These changes were initiated by BVK, and negative environmental impacts were not taken into account. For example, the carbonite production unit released wastewater without a permission into the municipal waste water treatment plant of Kazincbarcika, which could not treat such wastewaters properly.*"[80]

BVK's wastewater discharges grew more dangerous when PVC I began operation. The PVC unit discharged more environmentally harmful wastewater than the fertilizer plant. In 1966, pollution fines remained roughly on a similar scale as in 1962, with the PVC plant fined nearly 1.4 million Ft., while the fertilizer plant was fined only a little over 300,000 Ft.[81]

The relatively large diluting capacity of the Sajó River absorbed wastewater from the PVC unit. Theoretically speaking, if the PVC unit had discharged its wastewater into the Szinva Creek instead, it would have been severely fined and environmental criticism would have risen immediately because of the acute pollution.

However, the wastewater fine system was dilution-based between 1962 and 1968 and could not put enough financial pressure on plants which discharged their wastewaters into larger water flows. Weak financial pressure translated into minimal motivation at BVK to speed up the installation of end-of-pipe wastewater treatment technologies.

Although there were plans to build a central wastewater treatment plant at BVK between 1968 and 1972, the 1962–1968 wastewater fine system was too feeble to pressure BVK effectively. As a result, the central wastewater treatment plant remained as just blueprints until the reform of the wastewater fine system in 1968.[82]

Notes

1. Dominick, *The Environmental Movement in Germany*, 121–124.
2. Ibid., 139–140.
3. Ibid., 184–187.
4. Ibid., 188.
5. Ibid., 189.
6. Ibid.
7. Ibid., 140.
8. Ibid., 140–141.
9. Ibid., 210.
10. Dominick, Raymond, "Capitalism, Communism and Environmental protection, Lessons from the Germany experience", 320–321.
11. Dominick, *The Environmental Movement in Germany*, 194.
12. Ibid., 198–203.
13. Ibid., 202.
14. Ibid., 206–209.
15. Ibid., 194–196.
16. Pál Germuska, "Failed Eastern integration and a partly successful opening up to the West: the economic re-orientation of Hungary during the 1970s" *European Review of History* 21, No. 2 (2014): 273–275.
17. Ibid., 274.
18. Ibid.
19. *Cégtörténet (Company History). Rába Company Website*, http://www.raba.hu/cegtortenet.html, (accessed on September 18, 2013).
20. *Rába-Steiger 250*, http://trakesz.gportal.hu/gindex.php?pg=11460994&PHPSESSID=41daa3408ba705c71ff1bdea625fd98d, (accessed on September 18, 2013).

21. Anders, George, "Soviet Bloc Bus Builder Hits Bumpy Road in U.S.," *The Wall Street Journal*, March 28, 1984, Eastern Edition, 1.
22. Stan Federman, "Tri-Met readies bendable buses," *The Oregonian*, 30 November 1981, B1. Stan Federman, "Tri-Met sues over articulated bus defects," *The Oregonian*, 5 November 1981, B5. Stan Federman, "Settlement due on bus defects," *The Oregonian*, 13 February 1986, A17.
23. Germuska, "Failed Eastern integration and a partly successful opening up to the West: the economic re-orientation of Hungary during the 1970s", 274–277.
24. Ibid., 275.
25. Ibid., 276.
26. Ibid., 277.
27. Ibid., 277–278.
28. *Tájékoztatás az iparág és a tagvállalatok környezetvédelméről (Information about the Environmental Protection of the [Chemical] Industry and its Member Companies)* (Magyar Vegyipari Egyesülés: Budapest, 1978), 2–3.
29. Ibid.
30. Eli Rubin, *Synthetic Socialism: Plastics and Dictatorship in the German Democratic Republic* (Chapel Hill: University of North Carolina Press, 2008), 27–31.
31. Germuska, "Failed Eastern integration and a partly successful opening up to the West: the economic re-orientation of Hungary during the 1970s", 284.
32. "Jelentős előrehaladást kell elérni a műanyagok hazai előállítása terén; a termelést az 1960. évi 11 400 tonnáról 1965-ben mintegy 33 000 tonnára kell növelni. (...) Elsősorban a hőre lágyuló műanyagok termelését kell fokozni. Üzembe kell helyezni a második ötéves terv folyamán a Berentei Vegyiművek PVC üzemét. Hozzá kell kezdeni egy további nagykapacitású PVC üzem és egy polietilén üzem létesítéséhez. (...) Korszerűsíteni kell a műanyag-feldolgozást. A Berentei Vegyiműveknél új PVC feldolgozó üzemet kell létesíteni. ('We need to achieve considerable development in the production of domestic plastics. Production needs to be enchanced from 11.400 tons to 33.000 tons between 1961–5. (...) Primarily thermoplastic production needs to be raised. During the Second Five Year Plan at the Berente Chemical Plants a PVC unit needs to be installed. Construction of a large scale

PVC and polyethylene plant should began. (...) Plastic processing should be modernized. A new PVC processing plant needs to be built at the Berente Chemical Plants)" 1961. évi II. törvény a Magyar Népköztársaság második ötéves népgazdaság-fejlesztési tervéről az 1961. január 1-jétől 1965. december 31-ig terjedő időszakra (Act. II in 1961 on the Second Five Year Plan of the People's Republic (effective) for the period from January 1, 1961 to December 31, 1965) Enacted in Budapest, Hungary. II. Fejezet. Az ipar, az építőipar, és a közlekedés fejlesztése. C, Vegyipar. 16. §Chapter II. Development of industry, construction and transportation. C, Chemical Industry. 16. §

33. Documents of the BVK. In: Környezetvédelmi és Vízügyi Levéltár (Environmental and Water Archives, KVL) VI. 9. Miskolci Kulturmérnöki Hivatal Vizikönyvek 1867–1971. 303 box, 4034/I. dossier and 304 box. 4034 / II.
34. "Document 89.324/III/59" 1–2. In: Környezetvédelmi és Vízügyi Levéltár (Environmental and Water Archives, KVL) VI. 9. Miskolci Kulturmérnöki Hivatal Vizikönyvek 1867–1971. 304 box. 4034 / II. dossier.
35. Caprolactam (CPL) is an organic compound with the formula (CH2)5C(O)NH. This colourless solid is a lactam or a cyclic amide of caproic acid. Approximately 4.5 billion kilograms are produced annually. Caprolactam is the precursor to Nylon 6, a widely used synthetic polymer.
36. "II. Sz. Üzem építéséről GB.10.1084/1962 határozat (10.1084/1962 Economic Committee Decree about the Construction of the II. Plant)" and "Kaprolaktám üzem: OT elnök "M" 1811/62 határozat (Caprolactam Factory: OT President "M" 1811/62 Decree" In: Környezetvédelmi és Vízügyi Levéltár (Environmental and Water Archives, KVL) VI. 9. Miskolci Kulturmérnöki Hivatal Vizikönyvek 1867–1971. 304 box. 4034 / II. dossier.
37. Hungary possessed some modest natural gas fields already deployed around Hajdúszoboszló. The Hajdószoboszló field was in the relative proximity of the BVK, therefore the supply of natural gas was possible before the construction of the natural gas pipeline from the U.S.S.R.. A shift from coke to natural gas seemed to be a straightforward choice for that plant. "Gazdasági Bizottság.10.203./1959 határozat (Economic Committee Decree 10.203./1959)" June 13, 1963. In: Környezetvédelmi és Vízügyi Levéltár (Environmental and Water

Archives, KVL) VI. 9. Miskolci Kulturmérnöki Hivatal Vizikönyvek 1867–1971. 304 box. 4034 / II. dossier.

38. Documents of the BVK. In: Környezetvédelmi és Vízügyi Levéltár (Environmental and Water Archives, KVL) VI. 9. Miskolci Kulturmérnöki Hivatal Vizikönyvek 1867–1971. 303 box, 4034/I. dossier and 304 box. 4034 / II.
39. Documents of the BVK. In: Környezetvédelmi és Vízügyi Levéltár (Environmental and Water Archives, KVL) VI. 9. Miskolci Kulturmérnöki Hivatal Vizikönyvek 1867–1971. 303 box, 4034/I. dossier and 304 box. 4034 / II.
40. This production method has been abandoned by producers in recent decades, because it isn't not cost effective.
41. Documents of the BVK. In: Környezetvédelmi és Vízügyi Levéltár (Environmental and Water Archives, KVL) VI. 9. Miskolci Kulturmérnöki Hivatal Vizikönyvek 1867–1971. 303 box, 4034/I. dossier and 304 box. 4034 / II.
42. Peak capacity was 6000 t/y pvc-dust and 10,000 t/y chloride, The main production profile of the plant was carbide based acetylene, polyvinyl-chloride dust, and natrium-chloride based 97,5% clear caustic soda and chloride gas. Documents of the BVK. In: Környezetvédelmi és Vízügyi Levéltár (Environmental and Water Archives, KVL) VI. 9. Miskolci Kulturmérnöki Hivatal Vizikönyvek 1867–1971. 303 box, 4034/I. dossier and 304 box. 4034 / II.
43. Attila Papp, *Ismerkedjünk Kazincbarcikával (Introduction to Kazincbarcika)* (Kazincbarcika: Kazincbarcikai Városi Könyvtár, 1974), 48.
44. Frisnyák, *Kazincbarcika földrajza*, 218.
45. Caprolactam was used as a raw material for polyamide artificial fibers.
46. Documents of the BVK. In: Környezetvédelmi és Vízügyi Levéltár (Environmental and Water Archives, KVL) VI. 9. Miskolci Kulturmérnöki Hivatal Vizikönyvek 1867–1971. 303 box, 4034/I. dossier and 304 box. 4034 / II.
47. Rust was a Birmingham, AL. based company established in 1905, that created its international affiliate: Coppée-Rust in 1962 in Brussels. Rust and Coppée-Rust were internationally renowned companies with large corporal projects between 1958 and 1969. Rust project in the USA included the Granite City Steel mill expansion in Granite City, IL., American Viscose Co. rayon plant edition in Front Royal, VA., design of the mobile service structure for NASA's Launch Complex 39

at Merrit Island, FL. Rust also participated in a joint venture in the Air Force Titan facilities program. Rust provided architectural and engineering services until 1963.

48. Documents of the BVK. In: Környezetvédelmi és Vízügyi Levéltár (Environmental and Water Archives, KVL) VI. 9. Miskolci Kulturmérnöki Hivatal Vizikönyvek 1867–1971. 303 box, 4034/I. dossier and 304 box. 4034 / II.
49. Ibid.
50. Ibid.
51. Ibid.
52. Nitrogen fertilizer produced here was 21% clean.
53. Frisnyák, *Kazincbarcika földrajza*, 216.
54. The Montecatini method was based on hydrocarbons, an acetylene production method developed by BASF in the 1920s. The new acetylene plant supplied the PVC I. and II. with Vinil-chloride, one of the most important ingredients of PVC production. Vinil-chloride was produced with reaction of acetylene and hydrochloric acid. Montecatini Company was established in 1888, and merged with Edison in 1966. The merged consern was operational between1966 and 2002 under the name of Montedison. The company merged into the Edison S.p.A. in 2002.
55. *Tájékoztatás az iparág és a tagvállalatok környezetvédelméről (Information about the Environmental Protection of the [Chemical] Industry and its Member Companies)* (Magyar Vegyipari Egyesülés: Budapest, 1978), 1–6.
56. More PVC and hence more PVC factories were needed. Central planners were aware of this problem and in addition to the BVK another PVC production plant was constructed in Leninváros (Lenintown). The Tiszai Vegyi Kombinát (Tisza Chemical Combine, TVK) was established near the confluence of the Sajó and Tisza Rivers.*Tájékoztatás az iparág és a tagvállalatok környezetvédelméről (Information about the Environmental Protection of the [Chemical] Industry and its Member Companies)* (Magyar Vegyipari Egyesülés: Budapest, 1978), 1–6
57. Documents of the BVK. In: Környezetvédelmi és Vízügyi Levéltár (Environmental and Water Archives, KVL) VI. 9. Miskolci Kulturmérnöki Hivatal Vizikönyvek 1867–1971. 303 box, 4034/I. dossier and 304 box. 4034 / II.
58. Papp, *Ismerkedjünk Kazincbarcikával*, 42–54.

59. *Tájékoztatás az iparág és a tagvállalatok környezetvédelméről (Information about the Environmental Protection of the [Chemical] Industry and its Member Companies)* (Magyar Vegyipari Egyesülés: Budapest, 1978), 1–6.
60. Ibid.
61. It is unclear whether the machinery was produced and shipped from Italy, or it was patented from Italy and produced in Romania, or just a number of part of the equipment were purchased from Romania.
62. Documents of the BVK. In: Környezetvédelmi és Vízügyi Levéltár (Environmental and Water Archives, KVL) VI. 9. Miskolci Kulturmérnöki Hivatal Vizikönyvek 1867–1971. 303 box, 4034/I. dossier and 304 box. 4034 / II.
63. Ibid.
64. *Tájékoztatás az iparág és a tagvállalatok környezetvédelméről (Information about the Environmental Protection of the [Chemical] Industry and its Member Companies)* (Magyar Vegyipari Egyesülés: Budapest, 1978), 1–6.
65. Papp, *Ismerkedjünk Kazincbarcikával*, 42–54.
66. Interview with János Latorczai, Veszprém, Hungary, July 20, 2007.
67. Documents of the BVK. In: Környezetvédelmi és Vízügyi Levéltár (Environmental and Water Archives, KVL) VI. 9. Miskolci Kulturmérnöki Hivatal Vizikönyvek 1867–1971. 303 box, 4034/I. dossier and 304 box. 4034 / II.
68. "ÉVÍZIG Határozat Borsod Vegyi Kombinát szennyvízkezelésének vizsgálata alapján megállapított szennyvíz-bevezetési díj kiszabása 1962. évre. (ÉVÍZIG Decree on the waste water discharge fee based on the waste water treatment monitoring of the BVK for 1962)" 1–2 June 13, 1963. In: Környezetvédelmi és Vízügyi Levéltár (Environmental and Water Archives, KVL) VI. 9. Miskolci Kulturmérnöki Hivatal Vizikönyvek 1867–1971. 304 box. 4034 / II. dossier.
69. Ibid.
70. 100 Fillér equals to 1 Forint.
71. "ÉVÍZIG Határozat Borsod Vegyi Kombinát szennyvízkezelésének vizsgálata alapján megállapított szennyvíz-bevezetési díj kiszabása 1964. évre." (ÉVÍZIG Decree on the waste water discharge fee based on the waste water treatment monitoring of the BVK for 1964) 1–2. In: Környezetvédelmi és Vízügyi Levéltár (Environmental and Water

Archives, KVL) VI. 9. Miskolci Kulturmérnöki Hivatal Vizikönyvek 1867–1971. 304 box. 4034 / II. dossier.

72. Ibid.
73. Decree Series on the waste water discharge fee based on the waste water treatment monitoring of he BVK between 1962 and 1968. évre.' In: Környezetvédelmi és Vízügyi Levéltár (Environmental and Water Archives, KVL) VI. 9. Miskolci Kulturmérnöki Hivatal Vizikönyvek 1867–1971. 304 box. 4034 / II. dossier.
74. "ÉVÍZIG Határozat Borsod Vegyi Kombinát szennyvízkezelésének vizsgálata alapján megállapított szennyvíz-bevezetési díj kiszabása 1962. évre." (ÉVÍZIG Decree on the waste water discharge fee based on the waste water treatment monitoring of the BVK for 1962) 1–2. Vizügyi Levéltár. 13.06.1963. In: Környezetvédelmi és Vízügyi Levéltár (Environmental and Water Archives, KVL) VI. 9. Miskolci Kulturmérnöki Hivatal Vizikönyvek 1867–1971. 304 box. 4034 / II. dossier.
75. Decree Series on the waste water discharge fee based on the waste water treatment monitoring of he BVK between 1962 and 1968. évre.' In: Környezetvédelmi és Vízügyi Levéltár (Environmental and Water Archives, KVL) VI. 9. Miskolci Kulturmérnöki Hivatal Vizikönyvek 1867–1971. 304 box. 4034 / II. dossier.
76. Ibid.
77. "ÉVÍZIG Határozat Borsod Vegyi Kombinát szennyvízkezelésének vizsgálata alapján megállapított szennyvíz-bevezetési díj kiszabása 1966. évre. (ÉVÍZIG Decree on the waste water discharge fee based on the waste water treatment monitoring of the BVK for 1966)" In: Környezetvédelmi és Vízügyi Levéltár (Environmental and Water Archives, KVL) VI. 9. Miskolci Kulturmérnöki Hivatal Vizikönyvek 1867–1971. 303 box, 4034/I. dossier and 304 box. 4034 / II. dossier.
78. Ibid.
79. "Borsod Vegyi Kombinát szennyvízkezelésének vizsgálata alapján megállapított szennyvíz-bevezetési díj kiszabása 1966. évre. (ÉVÍZIG Decree on the Waste Water Discharge Fee Based on the Waste Water Treatment Monitoring of the BVK in 1966)" 1–2. In: Környezetvédelmi és Vízügyi Levéltár (Environmental and Water Archives, KVL) VI. 9. Miskolci Kulturmérnöki Hivatal Vizikönyvek 1867–1971. 304 box. 4034 / II. dossier.

80. "Tájékoztató jelentés a BVK-ról Dr Wolf Gusztáv HÉF alosztály vezetőtől. (Report on BVK from Dr Gusztáv Wolf head of HÉF sub-department)" August 26, 1968. In: Környezetvédelmi és Vízügyi Levéltár (Environmental and Water Archives, KVL) VI. 9. Miskolci Kulturmérnöki Hivatal Vizikönyvek 1867–1971. 304 box. 4034 / II. dossier.
81. The final payable fine set by the OVF was 1,379,400 HUF. BVK I., the fertilizer plant was fined 351,385 Ft, and the BVK II., the PVC plant, was fined 1,028,016 Ft. "Országos Vízügyi Főigazgatóság, Határozat. Tárgy: Borsod Vegyi Kombinát 1966. évi szennyvízbirsága elleni felebezés. (National Water Directorate, Decree. Subject: Appeal to the 1966 waste water discharge fine of the BVK) October 24, 1967" In: Környezetvédelmi és Vízügyi Levéltár (Environmental and Water Archives, KVL) VI. 9. Miskolci Kulturmérnöki Hivatal Vizikönyvek 1867–1971. 304 box. 4034 / II. dossier.
82. Decree Series: "ÉVÍZIG Határozat Borsod Vegyi Kombinát szennyvízkezelésének vizsgálata alapján megállapított szennyvíz-bevezetési díj kiszabása 1962–68. évre. (ÉVÍZIG Decree on the waste water discharge fee based on the waste water treatment monitoring of the BVK for 1962)" 1–2. In: Környezetvédelmi és Vízügyi Levéltár (Environmental and Water Archives, KVL) VI. 9. Miskolci Kulturmérnöki Hivatal Vizikönyvek 1867–1971. 304 box. 4034 / II. dossier.

7

Capacity Building in Environmental Services and the *Environmental Shift* in Hungary in the 1960s and 1970s

7.1 Reform of the Pollution Tax System in Hungary After 1969

Individual plants immediately felt the bite when Governmental Order 40/1969 completely reformed the wastewater discharge calculation system. For example, fines at BVK grew tenfold within a couple of years.[1] In the mid-1960s, BVK paid 1.2–1.4 million Ft in wastewater discharge fines. Five years later, following the introduction of the new wastewater discharge calculation system, its fines jumped to 22–25 million Ft per annum (Fig. 7.1).[2]

Although monitoring methods remained fundamentally similar during that five-year period, what changed was the calculation system. After 1968, polluters paid according to their raw pollution, not based on diluted pollutants in rivers and streams. This was a dramatic change for polluters who regularly discharged their wastewaters into relatively large rivers such as the Sajó. At the same time, pollution limits also gradually grew stricter during the 1970s.[3]

Large industrial plants were forced to react to pressing wastewater fines and tightening regulations. According to a complex environmental

V. Pál, *Technology and the Environment in State-Socialist Hungary*,
DOI 10.1007/978-3-319-63832-4_7

Year	Discharge Fine on First degree / Second degree in Ft
1962	330,000 / N/A
1963	N/A / N/A
1964	1,252,000 / 999,400
1965	1,242,000 / 1,242,000
1966	N/A / 1,379,000
1967	2,922,513 / N/A
1968	3,782,000 / N/A
1969	23,595,000 / 22,287,000
1970	25,672,000 / 22,017,000 Ft
1971	12,284,000 / N/A

Fig. 7.1 Discharge Fines Levied Against Borsod Chemical Combine, 1962–1970. *Source* "ÉVÍZIG Határozat Borsod Vegyi Kombinát szennyvízkezelésének vizsgálata alapján megállapított szennyvíz-bevezetési díj kiszabása 1962–71. évre. (ÉVÍZIG Decrees on the waste water discharge fee based on the waste water treatment monitoring of the BVK between 1962 an 1971)" 1–2. In: Környezetvédelmi és Vízügyi Levéltár (Environmental and Water Archives, KVL) VI. 9. Miskolci Kulturmérnöki Hivatal Vizikönyvek 1867–1971. 303 box, 4034/I. dossier and 304 box. 4034/II. dossier

report commissioned by BVK in 1972, the volume of discharged pollution in wastewaters already decreased by 25% between 1968 and 1972. The authors of this report predicted that the decreasing trend would continue for the coming three-year period. Despite the environmentally positive direction foreseen by the authors, they also predicted that given the financial means available to the company in 1972–1973, wastewater discharge fine limits would tighten at a quicker pace than BVK was capable of decreasing the amount of pollutants in its waste water. For example, some of the discharged pollutants fined in 1971 using a 3.0 multiplier would now be calculated using a 5.0 multiplier by 1973. The BVK report concluded that positive environmental changes paradoxically would not be reflected in the company's wastewater discharge fines unless significant improvement was carried out in the wastewater fine system itself (Fig. 7.2).[4]

	1975 (V. FYP)	1980 (VI. FYP)	1985 (VII. FYP)	1990
Total discharge water used by industry (million m3/yr)	2,640	4,250	8,200	13,500
Industrial waste water (million m3/yr)	640	1,380	1,900	2,500
Properly treated	30%	45%	65%	90%
Partially treated	37%	35%	25%	10%
Untreated	33%	20%	10%	0%
Total investment cost (billion Ft)	7 (V. FYP)	13.5 (VI. FYP)	20 (VII. FYP)	

Fig. 7.2 Projected Development of Discharge and Treatment of Industrial Wastewater in Hungary 1975–1990. *Source Tájékoztatás az iparág és a tagvállalatok környezetvédelméről (Information about the Environmental Protection of the [Chemical] Industry and its Member Companies)* (Magyar Vegyipari Egyesülés: Budapest, 1978), Table 4

Despite BVK's chorus of complaints, the conclusions of the 1972 environmental report and rapidly accumulating fines swiftly mobilized the company into action. Between 1971 and 1975, BVK invested 68.3 million Ft on wastewater treatment methods from its own financial resources. Nearly 70 million Ft was still not enough for a complex wastewater treatment plant, but the sum could fund some effective environmental investments.[5]

The construction of two 100,000 m^3 oil and grease settling ponds were commissioned. These were BVK's largest wastewater treatment projects between 1971 and 1975. The settling ponds were complemented by five air blowers in 1975. Air blowers increased oxygen content in the settling ponds and hence sped up the cleaning process.[6]

In addition to the settling pond project, a handful of smaller wastewater cleaning investments were completed independently from one another. These isolated cleaning units eliminated certain pollutants in individual production facilities between 1971 and 1975.

- An arsenic remover was installed in the fertilizer factory;

- A pollution filter was installed in the cooling system of the fertilizer factory to prevent pollutants from entering the cooling water;
- Small settling ponds were installed at Polymer I;
- A post-production sedimentation unit was constructed at Polymer II;
- Ammonia and ammonium (NH_3, NH_4^+) extractors and chemical neutralizers were built at the Caprolactam Factory; and
- Additional investments included organic waste stripping, hydrogen-chloride and carbide sludge extraction at the vinyl chloride plant.[7]

The above-mentioned set of environmental investments combined, considerably improved the quality of discharged wastewater. A breakthrough when BVK would substantially eliminate pollutants from its wastewaters, however, was not achieved until the end of the 1970s. Between 1971 and 1975, preparation works began for BVK's three-phase complex wastewater unit and adjacent sludge lagoon.

Wastewater treatment technologies installed at BVK between 1971 and 1975 increased operational costs. This was because wastewater treatment systems grew more complex and their operation required more manpower, energy, and maintenance than previous systems. In 1972, water treatment cost BVK 19,683,500 Ft per annum, equivalent to the company's wastewater discharge fines during the same year. By 1979, and after the installation of the three-phase wastewater treatment unit, operation costs rose dramatically. BVK spent 26.1 million Ft of its own resources and received 80.2 million Ft in government funding to operate existing units and install smaller environmental protection technologies.[8]

Notwithstanding the investments and the rising operational costs of environmental systems, BVK accrued 22 million Ft in discharge fines in 1972.[9] Much of this sum (17,751,747 Ft) was due to the floating material discharged from PVC II. This type of discharge, however, was a temporary nuisance. When eliminated in 1975, BVK's fines decreased to 3.6 million Ft.[10]

During the 1960s, BVK was the black sheep among heavy industrial plants in the Borsod Region. It was reluctant to cooperate with ÉVIZIG, did not provide data, and aimed to obstruct the work of environmental authorities whenever it was possible. Within a decade, BVK management was changed and new leaders brought environmental attitudes which radically differed from those in the 1960s.

The first signs that environmental protection and the demands of regional superintendents would not be neglected occurred after BVK received approximately 60 million Ft in annual fines within three consecutive years between 1969 and 1971. BVK finally realized that in the future, cooperation with the environmental authorities may be their best strategy.

7.2 The *Environmental Shift* in Hungary in the 1970s

In 1970, István Körtvélyes was named the BVK's new general director. During the Körtvélyes years, environmental protection emerged as an important management concern. By the end of the 1970s, BVK stood out regionally as an environmentally-conscious, positive example of state socialist industry.[11]

István Körtvélyes was born in 1931 and worked at the Péti Nitrogen Works during the late—1950s and early—1960s. He was then offered the position of director of technology at BVK in 1963. In 1970, Körtvélyes was promoted to general director.[12]

Within ten years, Körtvélyes dramatically transformed BVK's environmental performance. First, a Department of Environment was established in 1973. This small but independent unit marked the beginning of a new era when environmental concerns gained in importance. Körtvélyes recruited János Latorczai, a fresh graduate from the Budapest University of Technology (*Budapesti Műszaki Egyetem*, BME) to lead the new environmental department. Latorczai was given funds and equipment to mend the situation.

János Latorczai was born in Szuhakálló, a village neighboring BVK on the opposite bank of the Sajó River. Because of his local upbringing, he fundamentally understood the environmental impact and the water pollution situation of BVK. Latorczai remembered that as a child: "*I was regularly playing with my mates on the banks of the Sajó. We knew it was polluted. I believe the local people knew about the pollution and most people just accepted that it (the Sajó River) was polluted.*"[13] Latorczai gained insight into heavy industry at a very early age through his father, who was a production engineer at the Borsod Coal Company. He followed his father's footsteps into the industry and studied chemical engineering. During an interview in 2008, Latorczai claimed that he had only scarce and elementary knowledge of environmental protection when recruited by BVK. An environmental curriculum was not yet a central piece in the chemical engineering university's education in the late 1960s and early 1970s. However, Latorczai recalled that textbooks and seminars by Professor Somlói, an expert on chemical engineering processes and CEO of Chemical Planning Company (*Vegyterv*) included information on complex wastewater treatment systems and dust pollution reduction. Latorczai summed up his university training as such: "*Even though environmental protection was represented in the curriculum, it was rather a side issue.*" (Fig. 7.3)[14]

Nevertheless, environmental themes were beginning to emerge into the mainstream at the engineering university during the late 1960s. As part of this process, Latorczai wrote his master's thesis on the solid waste disposal strategies of BVK and how they could be improved. His core idea was that solid waste should be recycled back into the production process. For example, the oily waste from the Caprolactam Plant should not be disposed in landfills, but could instead be an additional energy source for production. Latorczai worked at BVK until the end of the 1970s. He was promoted to a state socialist elite business school in Esztergom for two semesters in 1978. Upon the completion of his supplementary training, Latorczai was promoted to Chief Engineer at the PVC Profile Factory (*PVC Profil Üzem*) in Szekszárd. Körtvélyesi and Latorczai built a small team of young engineers who brought new, environmentally-conscious perspectives to BVK. At the beginning, Department of Environment associates included István Nagy, József Bezovics, Ágoston Vízi, and Ferenc Stefán.[15] The new BVK environmental department was equipped with a laboratory where experiments and monitoring tests were carried out. Up-to-date, professional information

Fig. 7.3 Borsodi Chemical Combine in the background, Kazincbarcika in the foreground, 1967. *Photo* FORTEPAN/LECHNER NONPROFIT KFT. DOKUMENTÁCIÓS KÖZPONT/PHOTO BY VÁTI

on industrial environmental protection efforts and technologies was provided via BVK's Technological Library (*Műszaki Könyvtár*).[16]

At the Technological Library, a team of translators reviewed international professional and general press published in France, Germany, Switzerland and the UK. Information related to chemical engineering was translated from Comecon countries, especially from Poland, the USSR, and Czechoslovakia. Articles translated for the staff of the Department of Environment included methodological findings and applied environmental protection measures. Since most engineers in the Department of Environment did not speak a foreign language, translations were vital in acquiring current professional information.[17] For example, the 1974 press review of international press for the Department of Environment included articles on wastewater discharge regulation methods in Poland, the Chisso Company mercury scandal in Japan, and the establishment of the French Ecopol environmental association. New end-of-pipe technologies had an important place in the press review. In 1974, wastewater cleaning methods by British Aluminum, new oil and chemical pollution removal technologies in Belarus, a new biological treatment method at Bayer AG in Germany, acid and toxic steam pollution neutralization technology and "the'*Filtration totale de L'Air*' method" in Paris were introduced as part of the press reviews. The publication was based on original articles from peer-reviewed journals such as: *Anti-Corrosion Methods and Materials*, *Chemical Age International*, *European Chemical News*, *VWD Chemie*, *Process Technology* and the *International Journal of Environmental Pollution Control*. General Soviet dailies such as *Izvestija* and *Pravda* were also included in the press review.[18]

Department of Environment engineers also gained experience about wastewater treatment technologies via foreign on-site visits. Before and during the construction process of BVK's central wastewater treatment plant, specialists visited a number of sewage treatment plants in both Comecon countries and Western states. Field trips also included visits to domestic factories such as the Nitrokémia Company in Fűzfő and the Komárom Petrochemical Company (*Komáromi Kőolajipari Vállalat*) in Szőny. The experts also visited the Buna Works (*Buna Werke*) in Schkopau in the GDR, the Blachownia Petrochemical Plant in Poland, and the Devnya Chemical Plant in Bulgaria. While it was important to learn about domestic and Comecon experiences, BVK still planned to install Western technology in its central wastewater treatment plant. Since Japan had some of the most sophisticated wastewater treatment technologies for the chemical industry in the 1970s, it was crucial to access Japanese technology via site visits. West German experiences were also very important because located along the Rhine River, the country had one of Europe's largest and most advanced chemical capacities. In May 1972, representatives of Farbwerke Hoechst AG were invited to a workshop in Budapest where they outlined their wastewater treatment practices to BVK's environmental engineers.

Latorczai remembered this meeting as "deeply formative and impressive."[19] Hoechst engineers stressed that their environmental efforts had been effective because in 1971 about 10% of every industrial investment was spent directly on environmental protection projects. Latorczai recalled that BVK engineers were shocked by the high German figure when they compared it to the 2–2.3% Hungarian standard of the early 1970s. This meeting with Hoechst was a milestone for BVK engineers, who from that point on became obsessed with also achieving the 10% figure.

BVK aimed to earmark about 10% of the total PVC III investment budget directly for environmental protection.[20] During the planning phase, probably the most formative site visit to complex wastewater treatment plants was paid by Elemér Teleki, a member of BVK's environmental staff, to the Fukashiba United Wastewater Treatment Plant in the Ibarak Prefecture of Japan during the summer of 1976. In Teleki's detailed report, he described the technological methods and efficiency of the plant. He concluded his report by recommending the Fukushiba plant as a prime example for BVK. Fukushiba had a 330,000 m^3/day capacity and cleaned the industrial waters of the Kashima Crude Oil and Petrochemical Plants. Teleki was particularly interested in the successful collaboration between the factory and the wastewater plant because occasional discharges containing higher concentrations of heavy metals and other toxic substances would have endangered the effectiveness of the active sludge process. Communication and cooperation between the chemical plants and the wastewater treatment plant were essential to achieving success. Teleki was amazed by the efficiency of the active sludge treatment process at Fukushiba. He was convinced that if good collaboration could be achieved between the production plant and the planned wastewater treatment plant at BVK, environmental impacts could be minimized.[21]

It is important to note that the staff of the Department of Environment not only paid site visits and read scientific literature; they also published scientific articles based on their environmental and engineering experiences in peer-reviewed journals such as the *Journal of Hungarian Chemists* (*Magyar Kémikusok Lapja*).[22]

7.3 The Technological Impact of the *Environmental Shift*

When BVK's new Department of Environment was established in 1973, it was incorporated into the Service Factory Unit (*Szolgáltató Gyáregység*) and was supervised by the then Director of Energy

Supply (*Energiaellátási Igazgató*) Ottó Tóth. The establishment of the Department of Environment and its staff's subsequent site visits were preliminary to the construction of the central wastewater treatment plant. Similarly to Director Körtvélyesi, Ottó Tóth also considered environmental issues and environmental investments one of the priorities of the company. In an interview, Latorczai asserted that Tóth and Körtvélyesi both lobbied heavily and that their activity was key to BVK's success in grabbing the highest possible chunk of funding for environmental investments at PVC III. Their goal was to equal the 10% claimed as the environmental budget for Hoechst in West Germany in 1971. As a result of this effective lobbying, the central authorities designated 1.1 billion Ft to BVK out of the total 11.3 billion Ft investment budget for wastewater treatment and air filtering technologies.[23]

In 1980, Tóth summed up the changing role of environmental protection at BVK throughout the 1960s and 1970s: "In the first two phases (PVC I & II), environmental protection was in a subordinated position, and the focus (of BVK) was on production. In the last ten years (during the 1970s) environmental protection emerged to be equally as important as production."[24] Tóth's statement may have been an exaggeration of the constantly improving environmental conditions at BVK. Nevertheless, Tóth's assertion is a powerful symbol of a psychological adjustment I call the *environmental shift*. Environmental protection had been neglected at BVK, and could be considered a foster child of industrial production until the introduction of the PVC III project. During the construction of PVC III, environmental protection efforts emerged as one of BVK's main concerns and responsibilities. Central wastewater treatment was constructed between 1975 and 1978. Trial runs of ended on December 31, 1979. In 1980, BVK's complex wastewater treatment unit treated all BVK wastewaters. The central wastewater treatment plant incorporated three treatment phases: mechanical, chemical, and biological. The mechanical phase removed large parts of solid waste from the wastewater. Then, wastewaters passed through chemical and biological treatment. Chemical treatment aimed to stabilize the activity of the hydrogen content in the water at around 7 ph. During the chemical treatment, alkaline and liquid acid were treated to match the requirements of the biological treatment phase. After the chemical treatment process, inorganic water was pumped into capacious settling ponds and organic wastewater was pumped into the biological treatment process where aerobic bacteria digested organic pollution.[25]

A Tabata Aerator was installed at BVK to increase the efficiency of the active sludge process. The aerator was patented by the Nishihara Environmental Sanitation Research Corporation Ltd. (Japan) and was designed to increase oxygen flow into the biological treatment process.[26] The final output produced fresh water and carbon-dioxide in addition to the large volume of treated sludge awaiting disposal. The budget for the three-phase wastewater treatment plant included the replacement of the discharge pipes. Originally, BVK discharged wastewater via ceramic pipes. These proved to be vulnerable to toxic substances and cracked regularly. Therefore, the Chemical Company Planning Company (*Vegyiműveket Tervező Vállalat*) designed a new above-ground polypropylene pipe system for BVK which was installed in 1978.[27]

The installation of the new wastewater treatment plant was essential. During the 1970s, wastewater discharges from BVK grew at a staggering rate and pressure from pollution sources jeopardized environmental resources in multiple ways. When the wastewater discharge fine system resulted in higher penalties and BVK's emission limits grew stricter, the company aimed to reduce the volume of pollutants discharged directly to the Sajó River where its pollution was being monitored. The growing volume of pollution led to the company's sludge lagoons where some of the most notorious components of waste sludge were stored. If these toxic materials had been dumped into the Sajó, extremely high fines would have been incurred.[28]

By the summer of 1976, BVK's sludge lagoons were close to full capacity. The lagoons stored the polluted wastewater, allowing the water content to evaporate while leaving behind the hazardous solids and reducing its volume to make way for more sludge. Sludge lagoon cells (*zagykazetták*) covered a 100 × 200 meter area. Dikes formed a physical barrier around the lagoon and between individual cells. It is unknown whether earth dikes were covered or not. Dikes were 3–4 meters wide on the top. Sludge from BVK, and later from the wastewater treatment plant was transported here via a flexible pipeline system that could be altered and directed to fill up individual cells. In June 1976, a team from BVK's Department of Environment visited this site and reported their findings. The experts warned decision-makers that if sludge was not quickly removed from these cells to decrease pressure on the levees these earthwork barriers would breach, and thousands of cubic meters of toxic sludge would enter the Sajó and cause an environmental disaster.[29]

However, the relocation of sludge seemed an impossible hurdle. BVK received 1 billion Ft to have its own wastewater treatment plant constructed. The construction of the wastewater treatment plant was the top environmental priority at BVK between 1975 and 1980 and it seemed out of the question to squeeze more money from the central authorities to manage the sludge issue effectively. János Latorczai remembered the sludge lagoon issue: "Legally, we could not solve the problem of the sludge lagoons. Financial resources did not enable relocation and safe storage elsewhere. On the other hand, if the levees failed, carbide, electrolysis and salt sludge,[30] soot,[31] surplus bleach, and chloride whitewash from the chloride annihilation unit would have entered the Sajó River and caused unprecedented environmental destruction to the Sajó, and downstream in the Tisza River."[32]

Latorczai and his team understood that when burned, sludge would shrink in size, and an "accidental" fire would also prevent a disastrous spill. Hence, BVK Department of Environment employees set fire to the sludge lagoon. When the sludge was burning properly in the lagoon, BVK employees notified fire departments in Kazincbarcika and Miskolc. Upon arrival, firefighters were unable to douse the fire in a timely manner and much of the stored hazardous chemicals burned. The fire produced thick, black smoke visible even from the city of Miskolc, but the Sajó River was saved and the pressure on levees was eased. BVK also got rid of its unwanted by-products. The local media did not report this event, neither much is known about the air pollution and health effects of this event. From 1978, the BVK wastewater treatment plant gradually entered operation. The plant was a major step towards reducing the factory's environmental impact on water resources. As a result, wastewater discharges dramatically declined. Paradoxically, upon the installation of the wastewater treatment unit the significance of sludge disposal issues emerged.[33]

Notes

1. 40/1969 (XI.25) korm.sz.rendelet (Governmental Order). Enacted on November 25, 1969 in Budapest, Hungary.
2. Decree Series on the waste water discharge fee based on the waste water treatment monitoring of he BVK between 1962 and 1968. évre.' In: Környezetvédelmi és Vízügyi Levéltár (Environmental and Water Archives, KVL) VI. 9. Miskolci Kulturmérnöki Hivatal Vizikönyvek 1867–1971. 304 box. 4034/ II. dossier.
3. Decree Series on the waste water discharge fee based on the waste water treatment monitoring of he BVK between 1962 and 1968. évre.' In: Környezetvédelmi és Vízügyi Levéltár (Environmental and Water Archives, KVL) VI. 9. Miskolci Kulturmérnöki Hivatal Vizikönyvek 1867–1971. 304 box. 4034/ II. dossier.
4. Multipliers were raised from 3.0 to 5.0 in the cases of certain components discharged.
   "A Borsod Vegyi Kombinát szennyvízhelyzete a IV. Ötéves tervben. (Waste water treatment in the Borsod Chemical Combine in the Fourth Five Year Plan)" 2. In: Private Archives.
5. "A Borsod Vegyi Kombinát szennyvízhelyzete a IV. Ötéves tervben. (Waste water treatment in the Borsod Chemical Combine in the Fourth Five Year Plan)" 2. In: Private Archives.
6. Ibid.
7. Ibid.
8. "Jegyzőkönyv. 1980.03.20. BVK 1979. évi szennyvízbírságának hatósági tárgyalása (Minutes. 20 March, 1980. The court hearing of the 1979. Waste Water Discharge Fine of the BVK)" In: Private Archives.
9. Ibid.
10. "A Borsod Vegyi Kombinát szennyvízhelyzete a IV. Ötéves tervben. (Waste water treatment in the Borsod Chemical Combine in the Fourth Five Year Plan)" 2. In: Private Archives.
11. Decree series between 1962 and 1975. In: Környezetvédelmi és Vízügyi Levéltár (Environmental and Water Archives, KVL) VI. 9. Miskolci Kulturmérnöki Hivatal Vizikönyvek 1867–1971. 304 box. 4034/ II. dossier and Private Archives.
12. Interview with János Latorczai, Veszprém, Hungary, July 20, 2007
13. Ibid.
14. Ibid.

15. Ibid.
16. "BVK Műszaki Propaganda osztály. Vegyipari Gazdasági Hírek. Környezetvédelem. 1974. Ápr. 2. Nr.34. (BVK Tecnological Propaganda Department. Economic News of the Chemical Industry. Environmental Portection. April 2, 1974)" In: Private Archives.
17. Ibid.
18. Ibid.
19. Ibid.
20. "Környezetvédelemmel kapcsolatos hazai és külföldi tapasztalatcserék (Environmental protection related domestic- and international exchanges)" In: Private Archives.
21. "78/1968, Energiaellátási Főosztály, Tóth Ottó Főov. Et. Részére. Tárgy: Szennyvízkezelő üzemben tett látogatás. Kazincbarcika 1976. aug. 2. Készítette Teleki elemér és Iszsó Gábor (Power Supply General Department File No. 78/1968, Report by Elemér Teleki Elemér and Gábor Izsó to Ottó Tóth General Director of Department, Object: Visit at the Waste Water Treatment plant. August 2, 1976)" In: Private Archives.
22. Interview with János Latorczai, Veszprém, Hungary, July 20, 2007.
23. Ibid.
24. "196/80/Körny. Környezetvédelem a Borsod Vegyi Kombinátban 1980 Jan. 11 (Environmental Protection at the Borsod Chemical Combine. Document 196/80/Körny. January 11, 1980)" 2. In: Private Archives.
25. Ibid.
26. Ádám Fázold, *Proceedings of the XXIXth Annual Conference of the Hungarian Hydrology Association, Eger 2011*. http://www.hidrologia.hu/vandorgyules/29/dolgozatok/fazold_adam.html (accessed on August 20, 2013).
27. "196/80/Körny. Környezetvédelem a Borsod Vegyi Kombinátban 1980 Jan. 11 (Environmental Protection at the Borsod Chemical Combine. Document 196/80/Körny. January 11, 1980)" 2. In: Private Archives.
28. Interview with János Latorczai, Veszprém, Hungary, July 20, 2007.
29. Sludge lagoon cassettes covered an approximately 100 × 200 meter area. Dykes formed physical barrier around the area and between individual cassettes. Earth dykes were 3–4 meters wide on the top. Sludge from the factory and later from the waste water treatment plant was transported here by a flexible pipe line system, which could be directed into individual cassettes, when one became full.Ibid.

30. Salt sludge was released into casettes until the installation of salt drying lagoons in 1975.
    Ibid.
31. Soot was produced in the natural gas based Montecatini plant during cleaning executed by fuel oil.
    Ibid.
32. Ibid.
33. Ibid.

8

Economic Stagnation and Failed Environmental Reform in the 1970s

8.1 Limits of the *Environmental Shift* During the Economic Stagnation of the 1970s

BVK was an exception to the rule, and a lucky one in terms of received environmental protection funding. Most industrial plants in Hungary did not receive cutting-edge wastewater technology, or if they did, they had to wait many years before actually acquiring it. For example, the Miskolc Waterworks discharged municipal wastewater as well as the liquid waste from several local industrial plants into the Sajó throughout the 1970s. This is why the Miskolc Waterworks Company's wastewater fines included sums to be paid for both municipal and industrial pollution. These penalties were higher than the fines set for several industrial plants in the Borsod Basin. The Miskolc Waterworks received an 8 million forint annual wastewater discharge fine in 1971. According to the monitoring calculations of ÉVÍZIG, Attila József Str. wastewater main discharged 10,000 m^3/day directly into the Sajó without any form of treatment. In addition, 16,000 m^3/day was "treated" in the dilapidated settling ponds of the Miskolc Waterworks. These pools worked with minimal cleaning efficiency, if any, and the wastewater that was

V. Pál, *Technology and the Environment in State-Socialist Hungary*,
DOI 10.1007/978-3-319-63832-4_8

discharged from here could be realistically perceived as untreated or hardly treated.[1]

ÉVÍZIG was especially critical towards the Miskolc Waterworks. Environmental inspectors tackled this company's wastewater situation in an uncompromising manner. A decision handed down by ÉVIZIG in 1972 contained powerful arguments wrapped in administrative and legislative language. ÉVÍZIG stated in this document that they had already warned Miskolci Waterworks in 1970, and once again in 1971, about the poor condition of its settling ponds and the high degree of sediment accumulated at the municipal "waste water plant." ÉVÍZIG added that they monitored Miskolc Waterworks' wastewater discharges on May 7, 1971 and sent the results of the chemical and biological analysis to the company prior to the initial fine. Agents noted in a frustrated manner that according to the 1/1969 (XI.25) bylaw of the Secretary of State (*Államtitkár*), Miskolc Waterworks had the right to respond and disagree with the document. However, Miskolc Waterworks did not respond to the criticism. ÉVIZIG attempted to force Miskolc Waterworks to respond by claiming that a decade had passed since Governmental Order 1/1961 sanctioned water polluters for the first time. Between 1961 and 1971, the annual wastewater discharge in Miskolc rose from 6.74 to 15.33 million m^3. Having this rapid growth in mind, ÉVÍZIG assumed that Miskolc Waterworks would have invested considerably into the rundown state of its wastewater cleaning facility and prevent pollution from entering the Sajó. ÉVÍZIG challenged the company about why even rudimentary maintenance works on the "sediment pools" had not been carried out.[2]

ÉVÍZIG further assumed that the ruinous state of the wastewater treatment plant could have been at least cleaned and repaired by Miskolc Waterworks to provide some degree of mechanical treatment. ÉVÍZIG also complained that notices from the regional superintendent in 1970 and 1971 were left unanswered. Personal tensions and sentiments that filtrated into business correspondence also appeared in printed monitoring reports. ÉVÍZIG monitoring reports in 1970 and 1971 emphasized the depressing conditions at the wastewater discharge locations of the Miskolci Waterworks (Fig. 8.1).[3]

Fig. 8.1 Szinva creek in central Miskolc, 1957. *Photo* FORTEPAN/UVATERV

Municipal wastewater dominated Miskolc Waterworks discharges, which is why chemical oxygen demand (*dikromátos oxigén fogyasztás*, COD) levels were closely monitored by ÉVIZIG. The first monitoring in 1971 was carried out at the Attila József Str. sewer pipe. The results showed approximately 3.65 million m^3 of wastewater were discharged here, with a correspondingly dramatic high 715 mg/l oxygen demand. The second monitoring session measured a 560 mg/l oxygen demand at the same location by using identical monitoring methods.[4] Both of these results were well above the 75 mg/l legal threshold. A second wastewater main, dubbed "the Substitute" (*Mentesítő*), carried 5.84 million m^3 of wastewater into the Sajó River annually. Water discharged via this sewer main was somewhat cleaner than the one at Attila József Str. The first monitoring session in the first half of 1971 measured 405 mg/l oxygen demand, and a second monitoring session during the latter part of that year measured 280 mg/l of COD. Besides the two sewer mains which discharged wastewater directly into the Sajó, approximately third of the wastewater was discharged into the Sajó via the Miskolc's old wastewater treatment facility. According to monitoring data from 1971, the settling ponds at the old wastewater treatment plant hardly provided any cleaning, even though they "handled" 5.8 million m^3 of water. During that year, ÉVÍZIG monitored 415 mg/l oxygen demand at the first monitoring session. This figure dropped to 320 mg/l by the time the second monitoring was conducted. Miskolc Waterworks appealed to the court of second degree because it believed that ÉVÍZIG "*did not consider the facts with necessary accuracy.*" Most industrial plants questioned the validity of monitoring results in their appeals. The difference in Miskolc Waterworks' appeal was that it did not question the validity of ÉVÍZIG's monitoring; instead, it doubted the facilitative attitude of ÉVIZIG towards Miskolc Waterworks. From the company's point of view, ÉVIZIG should have placed the situation at the Miskolc Waterworks into a larger context: "*(ÉVIZIG) did not investigate why the (wastewater treatment) plant is too outdated to function and operate properly. (…) During the course of a deeper investigation, it (ÉVIZIG agents) should have realized that the current settling ponds cannot be regarded as a treatment plant.*" [5]

Miskolc Waterworks' appeal raised a very important point:

> According to our assessment, our company is not responsible for the fact that Governmental Order 1/1961 was not executed in coordination with the National Housing Plan - significantly higher authorities than us. (…) Our company claimed at every meeting that preceded the construction of the new housing estates (in Miskolc), that water supply and wastewater treatment for a new housing estate could only be secured via the construction of the new Eastern Peak Waterworks and a new central wastewater treatment plant. (…) The heavy penalty (that our company has just received) will not achieve its goal because it does not encourage our company (to collaborate with ÉVIZIG). It is beyond our company's

technological and economic competence to solve such (large) problems which have been remained (unsolved) for decades [6]

This quote shines a light on the way environmental protection was intertwined with Hungary's economic performance. A better performing economy would have been a prerequisite to a more efficient environmental protection system. This was one of the major reasons why it was so difficult to obtain adequate funding for up-to-date end-of-pipe technologies under state socialism. For example, Miskolc was first promised funds for a new, large-scale mechanical wastewater treatment plant in 1955. At the time, construction costs were estimated to be around 35 million forints. Funds were eventually allocated but then withdrawn by the OT, and Hungary's second largest city was effectively left without wastewater treatment.[7]

The construction of a new wastewater treatment plant for Miskolc was taken up again between 1963 and 1965. On November 25, 1963 Miskolc Waterworks commissioned the MÉLYÉPTERV Company to plan a complex wastewater treatment plant for the city. Mélyévterv presented blueprints to the OVF during the course of 1964 and 1965, and two variants (II/a and II/a-1) were selected for further consideration. Yet again, construction funds for the project were withdrawn and the project was removed from the Third Five-Year Plan. Finally, after two unsuccessful attempts, the permitting process for the new wastewater treatment plant began on May 26, 1972. By that time, the estimated construction costs for the project grew to 400 million forints. This sum equaled the total budget of the Miskolc Waterworks for the next five years.[8]

Any new wastewater treatment unit had to take into account an accelerated amount of water because Miskolc went underwent rapid growth between 1955 and 1972. That growth was accompanied by a rising level of water consumed and discharged. Water use continued to increase after the Oil Crisis of 1973, and Miskolc discharged 19.3 million m^3 of water in 1972, rising to 20.6 million m^3 in 1976 and 24.6 million m^3 in 1977.[9]

The mechanical phase of Miskolc's wastewater treatment plant began test operations in December 1976. This phase entered operation after a nearly twenty-year delay if we consider the duration between drawing up the first blueprints and going online. The facility was installed, as planned, in two major phases. The first 70,000 m^3/day unit was operational as of the beginning of 1977. A second 70,000 m^3/day unit was fully functional only by 1984.[10]

Due to the long delay between the planning and construction process, as well as the accelerated discharge of water during the intervening years, water discharge fines correspondingly increased. Given this increasingly negative situation, Miskolc Waterworks lobbied heavily for funds to build a wastewater treatment plant. It was not the Miskolc Waterworks, but rather the central authorities that halted this project for over two decades. That is why I would expect large reductions of wastewater fines on second degree. Such decisions would have underlined stereotypical presumptions about state socialist wastewater fine systems. In fact, the court of second court of instance halved the 8 million forint fine of the first court to 4 million Forints. However, following the court decision György Illés, the vice-director of OVH interfered with the case and personally reevaluated it. In his decision of November 20, 1972 Illés assumed that the first court of instance correctly interpreted the empirical data and that the subsequent 50% reduction was not supported by the evidence. Illés withdrew the milder OVH decision and required Miskolc Waterworks to pay the full original 8 million forint fine.[11]

The relatively high fine could not be realistically collected without a government subsidy. The 8 million forint fine represented 10% of the company's 80 million forint annual budget during the first half of the 1970s. The budget of the Miskolc Waterworks was significantly lower than the budget of the industrial giants' in the Borsod Basin. The Miskolc Waterworks had difficulties to pay the 8 million forint fine. Moreover, it was out of the question for the company to mobilize its own resources to develop a wastewater treatment plant with an estimated budget of 200 million forints that would be able to treat wastewater discharged by 200,000 residents as well as several dozen small and medium-sized industrial plants in the city. ÉVIZIG applied Hungarian environmental law especially effectively in the case of the Miskolc Waterworks. ÉVIZIG neither took into account the ineffective state of the old wastewater treatment plant, nor did it soften its position after the typical "victimization" argument made by the company. In 1971, both ÉVIZIG and the OVH took for granted that the Miskolc Waterworks had a "central wastewater treatment plant." They both referred to the old city wastewater plant in ruins.[12]

This facility was constructed in 1913 to serve only the central areas of Miskolc, then a provincial town of merely 40,000 inhabitants. Assuming that ÉVIZIG and OVH must have understood that the old wastewater plant was in a half-demolished state and lacking regular maintenance, it could not possibly serve a bustling and rapidly growing city of 200,000 residents and its rapidly increasing water use per capita. Furthermore, the environmental authorities must have also understood that the Miskolc Waterworks was not primarily at fault for the highly polluted wastewater discharges from the city. Despite this knowledge, ÉVIZIG set a large fine to pressure the Miskolc Waterworks into compliance, a fine eventually enforced by OVH. Therefore, evidence may support that the environmental authorities were fully aware of their roles and aimed to pressure polluters to acquire central funds for effective end-of-pipe technologies.[13]

Miskolc Waterworks was on the opposite side of this game and it aimed to protect its own interests and pay less in fines. In 1971, Miskolc Waterworks sent an inquiry to the Szeged Waterworks about their first- and second-degree fines. In this document, chief bookkeeper József Vinárcsik aimed to acquire precise data regarding wastewater fines in Szeged. Vinárcsik was particularly interested in the content of fines; the counter-arguments employed by Szeged; and how effectively those arguments had decreased the fines. Vinárcsik also requested copies of appeal documents.[14] At the end of his inquiry into such a delicate matter, Vinárcsik wanted to ensure his peers at the Szeged Waterworks that any data provided would be treated confidentiality, which they did upon the receipt of required documents. Vinárcsik stressed that documents "will be reviewed only by leaders of the (Miskolc Waterworks) company, and will not be released to a third party."[15]

It must be stated that even though the wastewater situation was a very important concern for the Miskolc Waterworks, problems related to water supply remained the top priority. Construction of the Eastern

Peak Waterworks water supply line was experiencing delays, but in 1972 the Alsózsolca Waterworks launched operation.[16]

From Alsózsolca it was possible to supply 8000 m^3/day to Miskolc, easing the scarcity of drinking and industrial water in the city. Initially, the Alsózsolca waterworks were not planned to supply water to Miskolc because they were originally meant to be the industrial waterworks for the Alsózsolca Prefabricated Housing Plant. Alsózsolca's wells were well filtrated and provided a reliable quality of water that could have been used for both industrial and residential purposes. The Alsozsolca Waterworks were connected to Miskolc's water grid as soon as the advantages were realized. The 16 million forint construction costs for Alsózsolca were dwarfed next to the several tens of millions invested in the Eastern Peak Waterworks. In other words, Alsózsolca provided water of better quality at a lower price than the Eastern Peak Waterworks, one of the largest water supply-related investments in Borsod in the 1970s. Alsózsolca gained importance in 1971–1972 when construction works on the Eastern Peak Waterworks began to lag significantly behind schedule. Simultaneously, water requirements in Miskolc were escalating. Given these critical circumstances, the supply capacity of Alsozsolca could have provided an instant remedy for Miskolc's pressing water shortage.[17] Water from Alsózsolca was also cheaper than water purchased from the ÉRV (Észak-Magyarországi Regionális Vízművek, Northern Hungarian Regional Waterworks). However, since Alsózsolca's water was pumped by electric pumps, this added 0.45 kWh/m^3 to Miskolc Waterworks' electricity bill.[18]

In conclusion, the Alsózsolca project proved to be successful. Whereas the construction schedule for the anticipated Eastern Peak Waterworks was postponed several times, Phases I and II at Alsózsolca provided relatively cheap, clean water. Alsózsolca's Phase III supplied an additional 4000 m^3/day to thirsty Miskolc from September 27, 1974.[19] Simultaneously, with the development of Alsózsolca facilities, the amount purchased from ÉRV escalated to 2.74 million m^3/yr in 1974. The more water Miskolc purchased from ÉRV, the larger financial burden imposed on Miskolc. ÉRV sold a cubic meter of water for 5.6 forints, which was then resold by the Miskolc Waterworks on a much lower price level at 2.1 Ft/m^3. For Miskolc Waterworks this was an expensive trade. Water from ÉRV represented only 10% of the total water supplied to Miskolc, but it produced 9.6 million forints in extra costs. This amount nearly equaled the total 11.5 million forint construction and development funds for the period between 1971 and 1973. Miskolc Waterworks could not have maintained this inefficient system without assistance from the OVH, which reimbursed the company 6.15 million forints (around two-thirds of the extra costs incurred). In Miskolc, and generally in state socialist Hungary, water supply lagged behind the water needs brought on by extensive growth. In addition, the maintenance costs of the existing infrastructure put further financial and organizational stress on the already overloaded and underfunded water supply and wastewater management system. In 1974, Miskolc Waterworks had less than 10 million forints budgeted for maintenance work and reconstruction projects. This sum was especially low compared to the total value of the water infrastructure in Miskolc with a probable value of 1 billion (estimated by OVH) to 2 billion forints (estimated by Miskolc Waterworks). Generally speaking, it would have taken between 100 and 200 years for the Miskolc Waterworks to fully reconstruct its old pipelines and replace its old generators with funding available in 1974.[20]

Extensive infrastructure growth should have been accompanied by economic growth on a comparable scale to run the new and extensive infrastructure successfully and efficiently. Instead, from the beginning of the 1970s, and especially after the Oil Crisis of 1973, ECE economies slowed down and state socialist economic systems were soon unable to run their infrastructure successfully. Between 1971 and 1975, water production at the Miskolc Waterworks increased by 27% overall. Output of the Tapolca and Tavi Springs decreased slightly due to prolonged dry periods. The Szinva Spring increased production after an enlargement project in 1973. Alsózsolca Phases I, II and III supplied as much 3.6 million m^3 of water in 1975, enough to meet a third of the city's water needs.[21]

Moreover, the long awaited Eastern Peak Waterworks was put into test operation in 1975. During testing, and not full operation, it only produced 455 m^3. The Eastern Peak Waterworks first phase was finally put into operation on April 10, 1977, providing a 15,000 m^3/day water intake capacity. In 1977, pumps at the Alsózsolca Waterworks were upgraded, increasing the facility's capacity from 12,000 m^3 to 15,000 m^3/day.[22]

Between 1976 and 1977, the total annual water intake increased from 31 million m^3 to 33.4 million m^3 in Miskolc. Water supply disruptions disappeared by 1977, and both industrial and residential consumers were satisfactorily supplied with water. In 1976 and 1977, industry was supplied with between 10.6 and 11.6 million m^3 of water by the Miskolc Waterworks. Residential users were consuming 11.3 million m^3 of water in 1976 and 12.7 million m^3 water in 1977. In conclusion, the introduction of new water resources to the water supply system of Miskolc were important in providing a safe and reliable water supply for the capital of the Borsod industrial area. Immediate water supply was essential because, unlike the Ruhr area in Germany where gigantic reservoir capacities had been built from the nineteenth century, Miskolc had a meager 17,450 m^3 water storage capacity in the mid-1970s. That capacity was increased to 21,200 m^3 in 1977 when the Vadgalamb Str. Reservoir was built. It is important to note however, that separate water storage facilities were created for industrial water use. The Alsózsolca versus Eastern Peak Waterworks case represented essential problems with Hungarian environmental planning. The Alsózsolca site was initially planned to be a temporary supply plant and its construction was significantly cheaper than the Eastern Peak Waterworks. Alsózsolca eventually helped the Miskolc Waterworks through the hardest years of the water shortage in the mid-1970s when the construction of the Eastern Peak Waterworks fell behind. Interestingly, as of 1977 the Alsózsolca wells still produced more water (4.8 million m^3/yr) than wells at the Eastern Peak Waterworks (4.3 million m^3/yr).[23]

In 1977, future water supply prospects for the City of Miskolc were brighter than any time since World War II. Between 1976 and 1980, the Miskolc Waterworks expected to produce an extra 27,000 m^3/day; a 25% rise from the new and extended water intake plants.[24] Extra water capacity was expected to be delivered through the completion of Phase II of the Eastern Peak Waterworks (15,000 m^3/day) and from the Garadna Springs (5000 m^3/day) in 1978. In 1980, the first phase of the Sajólád Waterworks was planned to be installed, adding a further 10,000 m^3/day in capacity.[25]

New water intake plants came with rising electricity costs because with few exceptions they used electric water pumps. During the first half of 1976, daily electricity consumption surpassed levels during the first half of 1975 by 1320 kWh (34% growth). This figure increased during the second part of 1976 and into 1977. Over 80% of that growth came from the increased energy drawn to power water pumps. The rest (210 kWh/day) was produced by gravitation pumps (*átemelő gépházak*) within the city.[26]

Water pumps at the Eastern Peak Waterworks accounted for 68% (756,000 kWh/yr) of the extra demand. An additional 30% (332,000 kWh/yr) was consumed by an increased production capacity at existing water pumping stations at other locations.[27]

Soaring energy bills curtailed Miskolc Waterworks' annual budget. In dire need for funding, the company aimed to reduce its costs. For example, management in 1975 aimed to reduce annual fuel consumption by 3%, save over 100,000 forints on material use, and save 3000 forints by a more economical use of stationery supplies. System loss was also to be reduced, potentially saving 150,000 m^3 of water already within the system.[28]

Extensive developments in production resulted in the growth of the Miskolc Waterworks. New positions were created, for example, an energeticist (*energetikus*) was hired on January 1, 1972. The energeticists' responsibility included the supervision of energy production and analysis of energy consumption and energy efficiency at the company.[29] At first, wastewater and wastewater fine issues were also assigned to the energeticist, but from 1976 the position of a wastewater fine-specialist (*szennyvízbírságolási előadó*) was introduced. The wastewater fine-specialist's responsibility included all matters related to wastewater and wastewater pollution issues. [30]

According to the mid-year report of the Miskolc Waterworks in 1978, water shortages and severe water supply problems seemed to be memories of the past. The report begins with an optimistic and self-confident statement that had been atypical for much of the 1960s and 1970s: "We have not had such a balanced water supply for many years (...) our capacity surpassed needs. In certain cases we needed to decrease production (...)."[31]

By the end of 1977, Miskolc Waterworks was able to supply approximately 125,000 m^3/day at maximum capacity. This amount was nearly nine times greater than the system's capacity in 1945.[32] But water demand was once again catching up with supply capacity, and prospects for water supply in Miskolc were not entirely bright in the 1980s. Water needs stagnated briefly at around 100,000 m^3/day between 1977 and 1979, but were expected to rise to 110,000 m^3/day by the end of 1979 and 120,000 m^3/day by the end of 1980. The company expected daily water demand to reach 145,000 m^3 by 1985.[33]

In reality, the decades of rapid growth were over. The Hungarian economy was struggling by the end of the 1970s, and much of the extra water demand came from new housing estates and not from thriving industrial plants. For example, industrial water demand in Miskolc dropped from 15.79 million m^3 in 1977 to 14.74 million m^3 in 1979.[34] Water demand continued to slow down after the end of the 1970s. Although water supply capacity surpassed 34.1 million m^3 in 1980, slightly less than 29 million m^3 of water was actually supplied during the same year. Industrial water demand decreased to 10.12 million m^3 in 1980. During the same year, residents consumed 14.24 million m^3 (Fig. 8.2).[35]

Water and wastewater prices were also indicators that the Hungarian economy was struggling. Water and wastewater prices were subsidized by the government but stagnated after the mid-1960s. However, rising energy costs and the Oil Crisis of 1973 began to have its impact on

	1975	1976-77	1978-79	1980
Water price	2.1	2.3	2.6	3.4
Wastewater price	1.4	1.6	1.9	2.2

Fig. 8.2 Water Supply, and Wastewater Pricing in Miskolc, 1975–1980. (Ft/m^3). *Source* "Tájékoztató jelentés Miskolc város vízellátási helyzetéről és a fejlesztés feladatairól. 1979 április 17 (Report on the Situation of Water Supply and Duties of Development in the City of Miskolc. April 17, 1979.) 8. Borsod-Abaúj-Zemplén Megyei Levéltár, Mezőcsát Fióklevéltár (Borsod-Abaúj-Zemplén County Archives Mezőcsát Branch Archives) XXIX. 113. Miskolci Vízművek Iratai. 40 box

Hungarian price levels. Water distributed by the Miskolc Waterworks increased by over 60% between 1975 and 1980. Prior to 1975, price increases were significantly slower. Water prices in Miskolc rose by 50% between 1958 and 1975.[36]

8.2 Limits of the *Environmental Shift* During the Economic Stagnation of the Early 1980s

As a result of the *environmental shift* in economic and industrial planning, several environmental protection investments were installed in Hungary. This investment were especially beneficiary in the chemical industry, where the variety and volume of pollutants represented significant environmental threat especially to water bodies. One of the most successful examples of such environmental protection investments was the wastewater treatment plant at the Borsod Chemical Combine (BVK). Although, it was energy-intensive, and therefore costly to run the new treatment unit, it significantly reduced the annual wastewater discharge fines for the company. In 1978, for example, wastewater pollution fines for BVK were only 2.4 million Ft compared to the massive water pollution fines of the early 1970s.[37]

In 1978, BVK requested special limits for its ammonium discharges until its wastewater treatment plant came fully online. The Ammonium Sulfate Factory released an average of 600 mg/l ammonium, well above the 350 mg/l pollution limit.[38] Nitrogen discharges were also problematic. BVK's designated discharge limit was reduced to 6 tons of nitrogen annually in 1976–1977. However, BVK's Nitrogen Fertilizer Plant discharged between 1400 and 2100 tons of fertilizer a year. Other sources of wastewater were the Carbide (karbamid) and Caprolactam Plants.[39]

In 1978, national environmental regulations on emissions were tightened once more. Ammonium discharge fines per pollution unit increased by 50 times between 1977 and 1979. This restriction was part of a long-term process. For example, between 1969 and 1977 mercury fines grew by 200 times.[40]

Technological investment could hardly keep pace with tightening environmental limits. Governmental Order 40/1969 limited mercury discharges to 2 mg/l. A few years later, BVK ordered the construction of a wastewater treatment plant. The specifications for the plant were eventually designed to allow a maximum mercury discharge of 0.5 mg/l.[41] In the meantime, a new and stricter governmental order in 1977 lowered the mercury discharge limit to 0.02 mg/l and simultaneously raised the annual fine for mercury discharges from 5000 to 10,000 Ft/kg.[42] Even though BVK was carrying out a large-scale wastewater investment program that included the strict control of mercury discharges, during the course of eight years mercury limits became ten times stricter and fines for the same amount of mercury discharge were raised by 20 times between 1969 and 1977. Given this situation, BVK turned to the regional superintendents in 1977 in an attempt to gain exception for its mercury releases.[43]

Despite certain environmental issues, the installment of the new wastewater treatment plant reduced liquid waste discharges to such a degree that contemporaries no longer perceived them to be dangerous. After 1978, BVK was able to keep the waste content of its discharged wastewaters well below limits. Nevertheless, when one major wastewater treatment problem was solved, several others emerged.

Since BVK was able to manage its wastewater discharges fairly well after 1978, its posttreatment sludge and solid hazardous waste disposal issues became more and more visible. Postbiological treatment sludge, alkaline waters, and heavy metals such as mercury were extracted during the cleaning process. The question remained, what should be done with these solid pollutants?

Since the 1 billion Ft three-phase wastewater treatment plant solved only the majority of the BVK's environmental problems, the issue was very complicated. Keeping in mind that many other factories did not have any access to effective wastewater cleaning technology at all, a little extra funding could have solved the sludge issue as well. In addition, it was expensive and energy demanding to run the new wastewater treatment plant. Whenever it was possible, by-products were recycled back into the production process rather than treated as waste.[44]

For example, BVK planned to rid itself of up to 80–90% of its nitrogen rich wastewaters as fertilizer for nearby farmlands via an irrigation system. Several Western European countries had already experimented with similar projects, producing controversial results with devastating environmental and health effects. BVK planned to use an automated irrigation system including gravity flow plastic pipes to direct nitrogen-rich wastewater to agricultural land during harvest and tilling times. A "Rain-roll"-type mobile irrigation system was purchased to disperse the waste. This automated equipment turned out to be very costly to run and was abandoned shortly.[45]

After the failure of the automatic irrigation system, the BVK Department of Environment planned to transport nitrogen fertilizer waste in large containers to the fields two–three times annually. This plan was abandoned for unknown reasons.

Finally, the fertilizer project planning team and its project leader Dr Márton Stéfán decided to collect nitrogen fertilizer waste at three permanent storage sites in proximity to designated farmlands where fertilizer waste would be used. The team assumed that via these permanent storage facilities, liquid fertilizer would be made ready to use. Cseres Valley, close to the village of Ziliz and 11 km east of BVK was designated as a storage facility. A second container station was placed at the Batta (Bartha) farm close to the village of Boldva, 13 km southeast of BVK. The third location was built at the *Kép-szer oldal* area in the village of Sajóvámos, 16 km southeast of BVK. The joint capacity of the three temporary dumping stations was between 30,000 and 60,000 cubic meters. Stefán and his team did not foresee that the containers would eventually leak. The BVK planning team assumed that fertilizer wastewaters would be isolated from the environment and sealed safely until further use in the fields. Unfortunately, Stefán and his project team misjudged the situation.[46]

By the mid-1980s leakage from the containers was visible and activists from civil organizations such as the Borsod County Environmental Protection Association (*Borsod Megyei Természetvédelmi Egyesület*, BMTE) began to visit and report on several BVK dumping sites, including the fertilizer waste containers. The BMTE was established in Miskolc in 1981 by Iván Gyulai and his circle of environmentally conscious friends. It was the first independent environmental association in Hungary. A BMTE monitoring team led by biologist Dezső Nagy carried out a staggering amount of work documenting legal and illegal dumping chemical industry sites throughout the Borsod Basin between 1985 and 1995. State socialist local media also followed the fertilizer dumping drama. The first attempts to use fertilizer waste in agriculture had seemed promising, but they eventually led to a small-scale disaster. At the beginning of the nitrogen fertilizer project, the agricultural use of industrial wastewaters provided an opportunity to claim that chemical industrial activities could coexist with agriculture and the environment. In 1972, *Észak-Magyarország* praised the possibilities of high ammonium content wastewaters for use in agriculture. *Észak-Magyarország* reported on the joint experiment of BVK and the New Life Cooperative (*Új élet Teremlő Szövetkezet*) in Múcsony. The article mentioned that experts considered the use of ammonium-rich wastewaters for the irrigation of pea and corn fields, as well as use in industrial pig production. Required scientific know-how for this project was provided by the Agrarian Science University (*Agrártudományi Egyetem*) in Keszthely. What *Észak-Magyarország* did not later report was that this project, among others, was a complete failure.[47]

Similarly to the nitrogen wastewaters, the treatment of sludge from the biological treatment unit emerged as a major concern. To deal with this new form of pollution, BVK considered the purchase of industrial combustion equipment to dry and reduce the amount of postsediment sludge. In the end, this machinery was not purchased and sludge was not dried effectively until the economic changes of the early 1990s. As a result, postsediment sludge emerged as the main environmental threat at BVK after 1978. [48]

Some sludge was stored in old BVK gasometers converted in 1980 into storage facilities capable of holding 20,000 cubic meters of toxic waste. According to BVK Department of Environment experts, this storage option was a satisfactory mid-range solution but could only store a limited amount of waste. The sludge lagoon that was ignited in 1976 was still in operation in the early 1980s. After the installation of the wastewater treatment plant, a significantly smaller volume of sludge was deposited there.[49] Here too, BVK environmental management was satisfied with the situation and considered it to be a "mid-range" solution. Deposited sludge in lagoon cells remained out of the public eye. In addition, BVK was not fined because wastewater fines did not consider discharges into settling ponds. The author is convinced that this was one of the reasons why BVK began to practice illegal and legal dumping on an increased scale in the 1980s, and to abuse loopholes in the environmental protection system. [50]

By the early 1980s, BVK and the Borsod Power Plant agreed to construct a new joint sludge and scale disposal site on the left bank of the Sajó River. This site was only a few kilometers from both BVK and the power plant, but it was also in the vicinity of the villages of Mucsony and Dusnokpuszta.[51] Storage cells were dug 15 m deep and 10 m wide and were protectively lined on the sides, but not at the bottom or on the top. This type of isolation prevented direct leakage to the Sajó, but did not prevent the filtration of pollutants into groundwater. Cells were basically unlined holes in the ground, enabling easy filtration of heavy metals and other dangerous materials into groundwater. Therefore, when pollutants leaked there was a high probability that they would eventually end up in the Sajó River only few hundred meters away. Additional risk was posed in dry seasons when dust was blown from the cells by the wind and covering local houses with a layer of toxic dust.[52]

During the 1980s, dumping became even more problematic than before. After its environmental risks were revealed by whistle-blowers, local media and residents, growing pressure was applied to encourage BVK to find new ways of reselling, relabeling, and recycling by-products to reduce the amount of sludge deposited in settling ponds. New ways were sought to sell BVK's waste. Possibilities in marketing and selling the waste seemed promising to Ottó Tóth, the second head of the Department of Environment: "*Market research work shall be continued to find new markets for our waste.*"[53]

Tóth's efforts were eventually fruitful. From 1979, sulfuric acid, a by-product of the Electrolysis Plant that had until then been discharged into the Sajó, was instead marketed. In 1979, 5100 tons of sulfuric acid was sold, generating 3.4 million Ft revenue for BVK. A year later, domestic demand for sulfuric acid increased and BVK doubled its sales. In 1980, water softener sludge was also marketed successfully. This material was reused during the neutralization process of wastewaters in certain industrial plants. For example, the Northern Hungarian Chemical Plants (*Észak-Magyarországi Vegyiművek*, ÉMV) purchased 1100 m^3 of water softener sludge in 1980. Smaller quantities were sold to the Gyöngyösoroszi Ore-Dressing Plant (*Gyöngyösoroszi Ércelőkészítőmű*) and the Spišská Nová Ves Ore Mining Company in Czechoslovakia. Spišská Nová Ve also purchased mercury catalyst sludge from BVK. The new BVK wastewater treatment plant was well suited for the neutralization of chloride and caustic soda. However, treatment of these substances was an energy- and money-intensive process. Therefore, BVK aimed to market these by-products as well. Chloride was mixed with milk of lime and iron chloride to produce sodium hypochlorite.[54]

At first, iron chloride was imported from Sweden, but this was an expensive raw material and raised production costs. Therefore, the Department of Environment researched how to replace iron chloride in the production process. Experiments on domestically available and cheap iron sulfate and chloride were carried out. Stand-alone iron sulfate produced inadequate results, but when it was combined with iron chloride the cleaning effectiveness of this compound was comparable to imported pure iron chloride.[55]

BVK PVC's Hydrochloric Acid Plant produced large quantities of saline wastewater. If all saline wastewater would be treated in the wastewater treatment plant, operation costs would have been raised considerably. Technologies to effectively recycle saline wastewater were unavailable and dumping was out of question due to the large quantities involved. BVK had to come up with a solution that would eliminate saline waters effectively, in an environmentally friendly way that would also secure a high degree of recycling for that by-product. The company cooperated with Chemiplan (*Vegyterv*) on this project, and jointly designed a vaporizing mechanism to speed up the evaporation of water and hence effectively reduce the humidity content in this by-product. The dried alkaline material could then be packaged and sold. The vaporizing system included massive Soviet-made titanium water cannons which shot water out over large, shallow cement vaporization ponds (*Sóstavak*). Water would have evaporated in the air and the remaining water in the compound would have evaporated from the shallow ponds. Titanium cannons were necessary because they had to cope with aggressive salinity. In the late 1970s, full titanium cannons in Western Europe were extremely expensive, and according to János Latorczai they would have cost 3–3.5 million Ft, as opposed to the 90,000–100,000 Ft price tag from the USSR.[56]

Vegyterv and BVK patented their new vaporizing system because it seemed to work. Experiments estimated the cost of vaporization to decrease to 2.4 Ft/m^3 as opposed to the current 300–400 Ft/m^3 utilizing already established vaporizing methods. However, the system was used only for a short time period. One of its inventors, János Latorczai, assumed that vaporization investment was a failure of planning: "*It had never really been in operation, because those production plants gradually stopped producing saline wastewater. The little saline wastewater that was discharged to the pools evaporated naturally, and did not need to be vaporized (by cannons).*"[57] The total cost of the saline vaporization system was about 105 million Ft. Since the production of saline wastewater gradually decreased, this system eventually stopped operation in 1980.[58]

The three-phase wastewater treatment plant effectively cleaned wastewater after 1978. Water pollution discharged per production ton continuously diminished. In 1974, BVK released 50 kg of waste per production ton. By the end of the decade, water pollution per production ton decreased to 27 kg. Subsequently, BVK's pollution fines also decreased significantly. In 1969, the company's wastewater pollution fines were 24 million Ft and the company produced 2 billion tons of products annually. By 1978, wastewater fines decreased to 2.4 million Ft, even though production tripled to 6 billion tons per year.[59]

BVK was one of the worst polluters of water resources in the Borsod Region in the early 1970s. By the end of that decade, BVK transformed itself into a positive example. During the 1970s, the company's management incorporated environmental planning into its production development agenda and aimed to "widen the environmental mindset throughout the factory," "include the environmental aspect in the planning process," and elevate environmental concerns to a level where "*technological departments of the factory would treat environmental issues as seriously as their production goals.*"[60] In 1980, Ottó Tóth, Head of the

Department of Environment, envisioned environmental protection: "*{during the} Sixth Five-Year Plan period, (...) BVK will be able to minimize the release of environmentally-harmful materials, and will possess a world class environmental protection system.*"[61]

The *environmental shift*, however, had tight limits in the Hungarian industry. It depended on technological solutions which depended on invested funds and the overall economic performance of the country. With a stagnating economy, the industrial environmental shift lost its cutting edge, modern flavor by 1980. As the state lost the grip to control environmental discourse and ride the waves of the environmental shift, grassroots projects took over and grabbed the control in environmental discourses. The mass mobilization force of the BMTE, a remote and powerless, rural environmental association signified the turn that was about to come in the following decades.

Notes

1. "Miskolci Vízművek, Fürdők és Csatornázási Váll. Miskolc központi szennyvíztisztító telep után fizetendő 1971. évi szennyvízbírság (Miskolc Waterworks, Baths and Drains Co. Waste Water Discharge Fine of the Central Waste Water Treatment Plant in 1971)". Without page numbers. Borsod-Abaúj-Zemplén Megyei Levéltár, Mezőcsát Fióklevéltár (Borsod-Abaúj-Zemplén County Archives Mezőcsát Branch Archives) XXIX. 113. Miskolci Vízművek Iratai. 36 box.
2. Ibid.
3. Waterworks, Baths and Drains Company documents in 1970 and 1971. In: Borsod-Abaúj-Zemplén Megyei Levéltár, Mezőcsát Fióklevéltár (Borsod-Abaúj-Zemplén County Archives Mezőcsát Branch Archives) XXIX. 113. Miskolci Vízművek Iratai. 36 box.
4. Ibid.
5. "(...) mélyebben nem vizsgálta hogy mi az oka, mely szerint a meglévő telep működése és állapota teljesen elavult (...). Ilyen mélyreható vizsgálat során ugyanis azt kell megállapítani, hogy a jelenlegi ülepítő medencék tisztítótelepnek nem nevezhetők (...)." June 1, 1972. "Miskolci Vízművek, Fürdők és Csatornázási Váll. Miskolc központi szennyvíztisztító telep után fizetendő 1971. évi szennyvízbírság

(Miskolc Waterworks, Baths and Drains Co. Waste Water Discharge Fine of the Central Waste Water Treatment Plant in 1971)". Without page numbers. In: Borsod-Abaúj-Zemplén Megyei Levéltár, Mezőcsát Fióklevéltár (Borsod-Abaúj-Zemplén County Archives Mezőcsát Branch Archives) XXIX. 113. Miskolci Vízművek Iratai. 36 box.

6. "Megítélésünk szerint vállalatunk nem lehet felelős azért, hogy az 1/1961. sz. Korm. Határozatot Miskolc vonatkozásában -nálunk jóval magasabb szinten—nem koordinálták az országos lakásfejlesztési programmal. (…) Vállaltunk minden új lakótelep építésén az azt megelőző tárgyalásokon kinyilatkoztatja, hogy az új lakótelep vízellátása és csatornázása csak a csúcsvízmű megépítésével, illetve az új központi szennyvíztisztító telep megépítésével biztosítható. Ennél többet tenni nem tudunk (…) A súlyos bírság kiszabása nem éri el célját, mert nincs vállalatunkra nézve ösztönző hatása, ugyanis vállalatunk műszaki és anyagi erejét meghaladja olyan intézkedések megtétele, amelyek az évtizedek óta fennálló súlyos problémánt egyik véről a másikra meg tudnánk oldani."
   Ibid.
7. Ibid.
8. Ibid.
9. "1976 évi terv I. féléves teljesítményének értékelése, III. fejezet, Szennyvízágazat költségelemzése (Evaluation of Performance in the 1st Half of 1976, Chap. III. Cost Analysis of the Waste Water Cleaning Sector)". 1. In: Borsod-Abaúj-Zemplén Megyei Levéltár, Mezőcsát Fióklevéltár (Borsod-Abaúj-Zemplén County Archives Mezőcsát Branch Archives) XXIX. 113. Miskolci Vízművek Iratai. 38 box.
10. "1977 évi gazdálkodás értékelés. Szöveges beszámoló (The Evaluation of Management in 1977. Textual Report)". In: Borsod-Abaúj-Zemplén Megyei Levéltár, Mezőcsát Fióklevéltár (Borsod-Abaúj-Zemplén County Archives Mezőcsát Branch Archives) XXIX. 113. Miskolci Vízművek Iratai. 38 box.
11. Ibid.
12. "Országos Vízügyi Hivatal. Miskolci Vízművek, Fürdők és Csatornázási Váll. Miskolc központi szennyvíztisztító telep után fizetendő 1971. évi szennyvízbírság (National Water Directorate. Miskolc Waterworks, Baths and Drains Co. Waste Water Discharge Fine of the Central Waste Water Treatment Plant in 1971)". 2. In: Borsod-Abaúj-Zemplén Megyei Levéltár, Mezőcsát Fióklevéltár (Borsod-Abaúj-Zemplén

County Archives Mezőcsát Branch Archives) XXIX. 113. Miskolci Vízművek Iratai. 36 box.

13. Ibid., 1.
14. "Szennyvízbírság. Szegedi Vízmű és Csatorna Vállalat Főkönyvelő kartás!. May 13, 1971 (Waste Water Discharge Fine. Szeged Waterworks and Drains Company)". 1. In: Borsod-Abaúj-Zemplén Megyei Levéltár, Mezőcsát Fióklevéltár (Borsod-Abaúj-Zemplén County Archives Mezőcsát Branch Archives) XXIX. 113. Miskolci Vízművek Iratai. 36 box.
15. "(...) csak vállalatunk vezetői fogják tanulmányozni, azokat nem adjuk ki (...)."
Ibid.
16. Waterworks, Baths and Drains Company documents between 1970 and 1972. In: Borsod-Abaúj-Zemplén Megyei Levéltár, Mezőcsát Fióklevéltár (Borsod-Abaúj-Zemplén County Archives Mezőcsát Branch Archives) XXIX. 113. Miskolci Vízművek Iratai. 36 box and 37 box.
17. Ibid.
18. "Miskolci Vízművek, Fürdők és Csatornázási Vállalat, 1973. évi gazdálkodás értékelése (Miskolc Waterworks, Baths and Drains Company, Evaluation of Management in 1973)". 9. Borsod-Abaúj-Zemplén Megyei Levéltár, Mezőcsát Fióklevéltár (Borsod-Abaúj-Zemplén County Archives Mezőcsát Branch Archives) XXIX. 113. Miskolci Vízművek Iratai. 37 box.
19. "Melléklet a Pü. 187/1975. Számú—Tanácsi vállalatok 1974 évi gazdálkodásának értékeléséhez (Attachment to the Pü. No. 187/1975.—Evaluation of the Management of Council Companies in 1974" 2. Borsod-Abaúj-Zemplén Megyei Levéltár, Mezőcsát Fióklevéltár (Borsod-Abaúj-Zemplén County Archives Mezőcsát Branch Archives) XXIX. 113. Miskolci Vízművek Iratai. 38 box.
20. Ibid.
21. "Víztermelés. Beszámoló jelentés a Miskolci Vízmű Vállalat tevékenységéről. 1976 január 20. (Water production. Report on the Activities of the Miskolc Waterworks Company. January 20, 1976)". Borsod-Abaúj-Zemplén Megyei Levéltár, Mezőcsát Fióklevéltár (Borsod-Abaúj-Zemplén County Archives Mezőcsát Branch Archives) XXIX. 113. Miskolci Vízművek Iratai. 38 box.
22. Ibid.

23. "1. számú melléklet. Víztermelés. Címzett: "Tisztelt Végrehajtó Bizottság" (Attachment No. 1. Water Production. Addressee: "Dear Execution Committee")". 3. Borsod-Abaúj-Zemplén Megyei Levéltár, Mezőcsát Fióklevéltár (Borsod-Abaúj-Zemplén County Archives Mezőcsát Branch Archives) XXIX. 113. Miskolci Vízművek Iratai. 38 box.
24. "1976–1980 középtávú tervek. Szöveges indoklása (Mid-range Plans 1976–1980. Textual Reasoning)". 1. In: Borsod-Abaúj-Zemplén Megyei Levéltár, Mezőcsát Fióklevéltár (Borsod-Abaúj-Zemplén County Archives Mezőcsát Branch Archives) XXIX. 113. Miskolci Vízművek Iratai. 39 box.
25. Ibid.
26. "1976 évi terv I. féléves teljesítményének értékelése. II. Fejezet—Ivóvíztermelés, szolgáltatási ágazat költségelemzése (The Evaluation of the I. Half-year Performance of the Plans of 1976. Chap. II.—Water Production, Cost Analysis of the the Service Branch)". 2. In: Borsod-Abaúj-Zemplén Megyei Levéltár, Mezőcsát Fióklevéltár (Borsod-Abaúj-Zemplén County Archives Mezőcsát Branch Archives) XXIX. 113. Miskolci Vízművek Iratai. 38 box.
27. Ibid.
28. "Vállalatunk 1974. évi gazdálkodásának értékelése (The Evaluation of Our Company's Management in 1974)". 4. In: Borsod-Abaúj-Zemplén Megyei Levéltár, Mezőcsát Fióklevéltár (Borsod Abaúj-Zemplén County Archives Mezőcsát Branch Archives) XXIX. 113. Miskolci Vízművek Iratai. 37 box.
29. "Miskolci Vízművek, Fürdők és Csatornázási Vállalat. Beszámoló a vállalat tevékenységéről. 1913–77. (Miskolc Waterworks, Baths and Drains Company. Report on the Activities of the Company between 1913 and 1977)". 13. In: Borsod-Abaúj-Zemplén Megyei Levéltár, Mezőcsát Fióklevéltár (Borsod-Abaúj-Zemplén County Archives Mezőcsát Branch Archives) XXIX. 113. Miskolci Vízművek Iratai. 39 box.
30. Ibid.
31. "Több éve ilyen kiegyensúlyozott, zavarmentes ellátás nem volt (...) kapacitásunk felülmúlta az igényeket. Egyes esetekben csökkenteni kellett a termelést (...)."

"Miskolci Vízművek, Fürdők és Csatornázási Vállalat. 1978 I. félévi tevékenység értékelése (Miskolc Waterworks, Baths and Drains Company. Assessment of the Activities in the First Half-year of 1978.)". 1. In: Borsod-Abaúj-Zemplén Megyei Levéltár, Mezőcsát Fióklevéltár

(Borsod-Abaúj-Zemplén County Archives Mezőcsát Branch Archives) XXIX. 113. Miskolci Vízművek Iratai. 39 box.

32. "Tájékoztató jelentés Miskolc város vízellátási helyzetéről és a fejlesztés feladatairól. 1979 április 17 (Report on the Situation of Water Supply and Duties of Development in the City of Miskolc. April 17, 1979.) 4. In: Borsod-Abaúj-Zemplén Megyei Levéltár, Mezőcsát Fióklevéltár (Borsod-Abaúj-Zemplén County Archives Mezőcsát Branch Archives) XXIX. 113. Miskolci Vízművek Iratai. 40 box.
33. Ibid.
34. Ibid., 8.
35. "Miskolci Vízművek, Fürdők és Csatornázási Vállalat. Beszámoló vállalatunk 1980. évi gazdálkodásának értékeléséről (Miskolc Waterworks, Baths and Drains Company. Evaluation Report on the Management of Our Company in 1980. Borsod-Abaúj-Zemplén Megyei Levéltár, Mezőcsát Fióklevéltár (Borsod-Abaúj-Zemplén County Archives Mezőcsát Branch Archives) XXIX. 113. Miskolci Vízművek Iratai. 40 box.
36. Ibid.
37. "196/80/Körny. Környezetvédelem a Borsod Vegyi Kombinátban 1980 Jan. 11 (Environmental Protection at the Borsod Chemical Combine. Document 196/80/Körny. January 11, 1980)" 6. In: Private Archives.
38. "A létesítmény technológiai, műszaki színvonalban egyenrangú a nemzetközi szakirodalomból eddig ismert víztisztító egységekkel." Ibid.
39. Ibid.
40. Ibid.
41. 40/1969 (XI.25) korm.sz.rendelet (Governmental Order). Enacted on November 25, 1969 in Budapest, Hungary.
42. *Tájékoztatás az iparág és a tagvállalatok környezetvédelméről (Information about the Environmental Protection of the [Chemical] Industry and its Member Companies)* (Magyar Vegyipari Egyesülés: Budapest, 1978), 2–3.
43. Ibid.
44. Interview with Ádám Fázold, Miskolc, Hungary, June 11, 2012.
45. "Dr. Stefán Márton, Javaslat a BVK-ban keletkező hulladék műtrágyák hasznosítására (Proposal to utilize produced fertilizer waste)" In: Private Archives.
46. Ibid.

47. Interview with Dezső Nagy, Miskolc, Hungary, September 7, 2007.
48. Interview with János Latorczai, Veszprém, Hungary, July 20, 2007. Interview with Dezső Nagy, Miskolc, Hungary, September 7, 2007.
49. Ibid.
50. Ibid.
51. Exact location is: http://maps.google.com/maps?ie=UTF8&ll=48.24594,20.685196&spn=0.107685,0.233459&z=12&om=1.
52. Interview with János Latorczai, Veszprém, Hungary, July 20, 2007. Interview with Dezső Nagy, Miskolc, Hungary, September 7, 2007.
53. "196/80/Körny. Környezetvédelem a Borsod Vegyi Kombinátban 1980 Jan. 11 (Environmental Protection at the Borsod Chemical Combine. Document 196/80/Körny. January 11, 1980)" 6. In: Private Archives.
54. Ibid.
55. Interview with János Latorczai, Veszprém, Hungary, July 20, 2007.
56. Ibid.
57. "De igazán soha nem üzemelt, mert lassan leálltak azok az üzemegységek amelyek sós vizet termeltek. Gyakorlatilag nem kellett forgatni a sós vizet mert bepárolta magát."
Ibid.
58. Ibid.
59. In 1975: 40 kg/t, 1976: 37 kg/t, 1977: 32 kg/t, 1978: 30 kg/t, 1979: 27 kg/t, Decreased almost by 50% in 5 years. "196/80/Körny. Környezetvédelem a Borsod Vegyi Kombinátban 1980 Jan. 11 (Environmental Protection at the Borsod Chemical Combine. Document 196/80/Körny. January 11, 1980)" 6. In: Private Archives.
60. "A gyáraknál lévő technológiai osztályoknak feladatává kell tenni, hogy környezetvédelmi kérdésekkel (...) ugyanúgy foglakozzanak mint az üzemek termelő tevékenységével."
Ibid.
61. "Fenti feladatok VI. Ötéves tervidőszakban való megvalósítása esetén biztosítható, hogy a BVK minimálisra csökkentse környezetszennyező anyagainak kibocsátását és világszínvonalú környezetvédelemmel rendelkezzen."
Ibid.

9

The Environmental Movement and Political Opposition in the 1980s

9.1 From the *Environmental Shift* to the Ecological Turn

On March 19, 1976, the parliament of Hungary discussed a planned law on the protection of the natural environment. Many of the most influential party members and functionaries of the Hungarian Socialist Workers' Party (HSWP) took part in the debate. The presence of Jenő Fock (former Chairman of the Council of ministers), György Aczél (controlled culture and the arts in state-socialist Hungary), and Béla Biszku (Secretary of the Central Committee of the HSWP) signified the importance of the matter. The parliamentary debate shed light on the large degree of the *environmental shift* in Hungarian politics, because contributions stressed the pivotal importance of environmental protection and state environmentalism. MP István Fodorné in her speech called for a complete ecological turn: "Environmental protection shall be every citizen's human quality." Dr. József Schnitzler, University Professor and the Director of the University Hospital in the city of Debrecen claimed that "Environmental protection became a central question in our country, its part of our politics building socialism."[1] This parliamentary debate

V. Pál, *Technology and the Environment in State-Socialist Hungary*,
DOI 10.1007/978-3-319-63832-4_9

signaled that the environmental shift initiated and fueled by the state has reached its peak point in Hungary in the latter half of the 1970s. National trends of the escalating environmental shift were especially visible in the urbanized and industrialized parts of the country, such as the urban area of Miskolc and the industrialized Borsod Basin. Evidence from individual cases highlight the role of state environmental propaganda and state environmental mobilization in raising environmental consciousness in the entire society. For example, waste water treatment practices of the Borsod Chemical Combine (BVK) were publicized in a little over a hundred reports, written interviews and radio programs between 1972 and 1989. Ninety two of these reports were published in regional and national dailies and magazines. The focus of the news followed the change in environmental awareness, and the focal analysis of the news described the changing environmental attitudes between 1972 and 1989 at BVK.[2] Articles published on the wastewater treatment conditions at BVK covered (1) Technological, (2) Legal (3) Outreach/Public Relations, (4) and Environmental Political aspects. Throughout the period, newspaper articles focusing on environmentally related technological knowledge dominated discussions (46 out of 92).[3]

During the mid-1970s (1972–1977), the pivotal role of technology was more prevalent than throughout the entire 1972–1989 period. Favored topics changed from time to time, such as monitoring of a large UNDP project in 1972–1977 in the Sajó River Valley to install an automatic monitoring system along the Hungarian section of the river. Even so, between 1974 and 1978, the planned and ongoing works of the complex wastewater treatment plant was the favored topic of regional, national, and popular science articles.[4] When construction began in August 1975, regional media outlets had a designated and important role in the promotion process to educate the local population about its positive environmental impact. Reports were frequently published in local dailies. *Észak-Magyarország* and *Déli Hírlap* frequently, and national press and radio on occasion, published and broadcast reports on the progress of the construction process. From the point of view of journalistic accounts, the plant was an interesting, expensive and state-of-the-art environmental project with a very positive possible environmental impact for one of the most polluted regions in the country. The state socialist propaganda machine highlighted that this wastewater treatment plant incorporated very high caliber technology even by Western European standards, and was nationally unparalleled. Some of these press proceedings stated that it "*will discharge cleaner water than that taken in from the Sajó River.*" In fact, that statement was not an exaggeration, and the BVK wastewater treatment rather diluted the polluted Sajó after 1979.[5] State environmental propaganda worked and the marketing slogans stuck in local minds. Locals still remember the descriptions used in the environmental propaganda campaign. Project members take pride to be in the forefront of the state socialist fight against environmental pollution. Lajos Kárbin, vice-manager of BVK's waste treatment plant mentioned during an interview, that "*in the late 1970s, I was proud to be able to work on the BVK wastewater treatment plant. I knew it was a 'cutting edge' and 'state-of-the-art' facility. And it had been continuously improved since the late 1970s.*"[6]

Even though technologically minded reportage was the key component of regional news coverage over the BVK wastewater treatment plant between 1972 and 1977, this was very different from the Stalinist-style reports which prevailed when discussing massive industrial achievements between 1949 and 1956. Bigger was no longer necessarily better. Media coverage focused on the high-tech features, effectiveness of imported Western environmental technology and the sophistication of environmental protection know-how invested in project. Extensive project elements, which would have been on the front page of regional newspapers in the Stalinist 1950s, remained unreported. For example, in 1975–1977 large river regulation works were carried out on a section of the Sajó River, which included a 19-hectare earthwork and sedimentation project, the scope of the project and adjacent massive soil works remained largely unreported. Furthermore, upon completion of the wastewater treatment project, media reports paid little attention to the massive size of the BVK plant; instead, they stressed the effectiveness and environmental friendliness of that project and how rapidly pollution fines at BVK decreased.[7] The incorporation of advanced Western European and Japanese environmental technology was an important symbol of both the economic development and the success of the state socialist regime's environmental protection measures. In state socialist propaganda environmental protection was elevated to a new level. It now shared the main stage along with problems of politics and economics.

As construction was nearing completion in 1977, the number of reports which covered environmental themes increased. Superlatives and exaggerations were frequent. The new wastewater facility was a "*prestigious and complex investment*," and "*one of the trailblazers*" of such production plants in Hungary. Even before it was constructed it had evolved into "an example to be followed by other industrial plants."[8] Journalists' fantasy knew few limits. The plant joined the elite nationwide club of "modern, up-to-date" environmental investments. Optimistic articles discussed the bright future of the previously "dead Sajó River." Contemporary journalists contemplated if the trailblazing BVK would be followed by a series of similar treatment units, potentially bringing about significant change in Borsod environmental conditions.[9] Journalists also acknowledged that outstanding economic efforts were behind the environmental success of BVK because the effective wastewater treatment unit was a result "of the unprecedentedly high share of environmental protection bill." The cost totaled 1 billion Ft out of the 11.3 billion PVC III development budget.[10]

By the time it was constructed, the BVK wastewater treatment plant grew to be a symbol of environmentally conscious state socialist economic planning on a regional scale. It also symbolized the definite economic turn of the Hungarian political elite toward Western capitalist markets by the late 1970s. However, this project also highlighted the constraints of end-of-pipe technologies. With a large degree of investment, success could be achieved only up to a certain level. Instead of solving the pollution problem in real terms, end-of-pipe technologies reduced pollution components and externalized the water pollution problem by converting polluted water to sludge and solid waste. Optimistic journalists and local engineers showed little interest at first about what would happen to the growing volume of sediment.[11]

BVK creatively used the positive media reception for public relation purposes. Management aimed to underline that the company was not a passive subject of central development policies, but that it was an active driver, a facilitator in the planning process of the wastewater treatment unit. BVK emphasized that the saline water lagoons were partly the brainchild of engineers at its Department of Environment. Company public relations often reiterated that its Department of Environment engineers actively took part in the planning process. For example, BVK worked jointly on the biological treatment phase with the Alkaloida Company between 1972 and 1977.[12]

It was important for the management of BVK to improve its public image after 1970, and to overcome the negative environmental impression the company projected throughout the 1960s. When the wastewater treatment unit was in full swing, test results showed it operating with outstanding efficiency compared to regional equivalents. BVK used this success to represent the company as a whole as an environmentally conscious firm. The goal of this process was to prove that the company's attitude toward the environment had improved tremendously since the 1960s. By the end of the 1970s, BVK successfully overcame negative environmental labeling and was able to represent itself as an environmentally conscious company with one of the best environmental records in the Borsod Basin area.[13]

The "BVK story" had significant importance for the central authorities in Hungary. The relatively high degree of environmental awareness and the gigantic sums invested in environmental protection at BVK provided evidence for the central authorities that the state socialist regime was addressing pressing environmental concerns. It also provided a positive example, a path to be followed; because the population well remembered that BVK's wastewater discharge situation was critical at the end of the 1960s and changed dramatically by the end of the 1970s: "*There was a period of time, for example, when BVK paid over 20 million Ft in wastewater discharge fines during one year, but for the last few years the fine has been only a few thousand forints.*"[14]

BVK, however, was an exception to the rule and general environmental conditions of industrial wastewater treatment in Hungary were lagging behind the improved conditions at BVK. On May 8, 1980 in an interview on National Radio's Kossuth Station, a representative of the OVF talked about with reporter Dezső Pintér and was asked "why domestic industrial plants do not clean (waste) waters adequately?"[15] According to the OVF representative, the allocation of central development funds was inadequate to provide effective wastewater treatment. It was phenomenal that BVK received nearly 10% of its project development budget for environmental investments. According to the OVF official, this was the exception and not the norm. Moreover, it was assumed that BVK's investment was a milestone, and that in the future, Hungarian industry would make several similar large and effective investments. He reminded listeners that the Fifth Five-Year Plan designated 25 billion Ft for water-related environmental investments both in industry and in municipalities. In theory, that would cover the cost of 25 new wastewater treatment plants similar to the one at BVK. The OVF was selected by the Government to control the planning and implementation process of these new facilities and to decide which projects should be given priority: "Those investments should be started and constructed which have a visible impact on the total population."[16]

BVK's wastewater treatment plant was a success story employed for environmental propaganda purposes to cover the stressful environmental conditions nationally. In 1980, the National Environmental Protection Requirement Concept (*Országos Környezetvédelmi Koncepció és Követelményrendszer*) was under preparation. An effective wastewater treatment plant and the presence of a Department of Environment at BVK provided an opportunity for the national environmental administration to prove corporate attitudes towards their environmental impact can be changed tremendously.[17] Dr György Gonda, Under Secretary of the government, and Director of the National Environmental Protection Agency (*Országos Környezet és Természetvédelmi Hatóság*, OKTH, established in October 1977), assumed that complying with ever stricter international environmental limits was the priority for Hungarian environmental protection in the future. Dr. Gonda, explained in his foreword to the *National Environmental Concept* that Hungary needed to follow the recommendations formulated at the 1980 conference of the United Nations European Economic Commission (UN EEC). Gonda fostered an "immediate change" in environmental matters in Hungary. He recommended that in the future, environmental concerns should be represented at all levels of decision-making in Hungary. Gonda cited the positive example of

BVK as one of the first environmentally responsible decisions, and it was literary "extorted" by the factory. Gonda believed that environmental protection was not necessarily a financial question, since with only the 8–10% extra funding for any future industrial investment budget, secure and responsible wastewater treatment technologies could be built.[18]

In conclusion, when the three-phase wastewater treatment plant was adequately functioning in the early 1980, BVK's major environmental headaches were over. The company emerged as a positive example reducing the quantity of its wastewater and significantly improving the quality of discharged wastewater into the Sajó River. During the wastewater treatment process, and especially during the biological treatment process, large amounts of solid waste and active sludge remained. The wastewater treatment unit did significantly decrease the environmental impact of BVK, but did not solve it miraculously. Much of the waste that had been discharged into the Sajó was transferred to the sediment sludge of the biological wastewater treatment unit. During the coming years, BVK aimed to find solutions to dispose of and recycle its new type of solid waste.

9.2 The Ecological Turn

During the second half of the 1970s, a growing number of projects and media reports focusing on outreach and environmental information to the wider public appeared. These types of accounts included new forms of expressing environmental concerns, such as stories about voluntary environmental actions. Environmental programs were also facilitated by state youth organizations, for example, the Young Communists' Association (*Kommunista Ifjúsági Szövetség*, KISZ).[19] Environmental events became the norm nationally, with concentration in industrialized regions, such as the Borsod Basin. In April 1975, the 3rd and 24th troop of the Kazincbarcika KISZ organized an environmental exhibition at the Radnóti Miklós Cultural Center in Kazincbarcika. The exhibition addressed the deteriorating state of global environmental conditions and aimed to inform citizens about the environmental protection issues at Borsodi industrial plants, e.g., the BVK. This exhibition stressed the predicted positive environmental impact of the complex wastewater treatment facility.[20] Sections of this exhibition included "*Environmental Pollution and Environmental Protection*," "*The Changes of Sources and Quantity of Pollution*," "*From Production Equipment to Waste Recycling*," "*Waste Water Treatment at BVK I and II*," "*The Complex Wastewater Treatment Methods at the New PVC Factory*" and "*Surface Water Quality in Hungary*."[21]

This first KISZ environmental exhibition in Kazincbarcika was followed by a number of similar voluntary actions and exhibitions aimed at raising the awareness of the local community concerning the relationship between industrial pollution and environmental protection under state socialism. KISZ specifically targeted youth and young adults with its environmental exhibitions and subsequent environmental information and education sessions. According to KISZ documents, the 1975 exhibition targeted the "*under 30*" age group because they were more open to new influences. In addition, according to KISZ, young adults represented over 50% of the total BVK workforce 1975.[22] Environmental education activities by KISZ and the company leadership in the 1970s were complemented with popular environmental propaganda pamphlets distributed among workers. The aim of these short compilations was to educate workers about proper work behavior to eliminate leakage of hazardous waste and to minimize the impact of environmental hazards caused by negligence at work.[23] The *Environmental Protection at Work* (Munkahelyi Környezetvédelem) pamphlet stressed the importance of reaction time in the event of a hazardous wastewater leak. The brochure emphasized that workers "should immediately contact the foremen and KISZ leaders" within the factory.[24]

Environmental awareness was further enforced when a team of Volunteer Environmental Guards (*Önkéntes Környezeti Őrök*) was established at BVK by the local and county committees of the Patriotic Popular Front (*Hazafias Népfront,* HNF).[25] The HNF was a collection of state-sponsored popular and cultural associations in Hungary between 1954 and 1990. When the HNF included environmental information in its curriculum on industrial pollution, environmental protection reached a very large proportion of society. HNF

Environmental Guards volunteered to educate people about the hazards of environmental pollution and also pledged to maintain an environmentally friendly lifestyle to show a positive example to others.

A growing number of conferences were held on wastewater cleaning issues in Borsod. In 1976, the Third Waste Water Cleaning Conference was held in the village of Aggtelek, and frequent reports appeared in regional media about the event. At the Aggtelek conference, scientific discourse on the construction of BVK's new wastewater treatment was the main focus. Also, various methods of waste recycling at BVK were discussed, such as the utilization of ammonium-rich wastewater in agricultural production and the extraction of salt from saline wastewater.

Exhibitions, Environmental Guards, and conferences were all initiated by departments of the state to educate citizens about the natural environmental and raised their environmental awareness. State-orchestrated environmental activities reached its peak point over the 1970s and over time the initiation of the environmental discourse slipped out of central control. The reason for the emergence of the independent, grass-roots environmental discourse was outstanding success of central propaganda to promote the *environmental shift*. By the early 1980s, much of Hungarian society was "brainwashed" by the state's environmental protection propaganda. Environmental protection and environmentalism grew to be a core value of the Hungarian society. Just like participants of the 1976 parliamentary debate over environmental protection envisioned. In fact, the success of the environmental propaganda excelled far the success of technological environmental protection in municipalities and industrial plants.

In 1983 the Mass Communications Research Center (Tömegkommunkációs Kutatóközpont) in Budapest and the Institute of Socio-Economic Problems at the Academy of Sciences of the USSR (Институт социально-экономических проблем АН СССР) conducted an empirical sociological survey on ecological consciousness and behavior of the population of Hungary and the USSR. These pub lic opinion surveys were conducted with nonidentical methods, hence they were not be compared—unfortunately. Intended users these opinion surveys were scientists and decision-makers, and results were not be released for the public. At least not immediately. Imre Dobossy and

László Kulcsár research project leaders at the Mass Communications Research Center made their original 1983 report available for public in April 1988.[26] Dobossy and Kulcsár reasoned the relevance of public release of their five-year-old data and analysis that environmental consciousness reached to such a prime role in public discourse, that their old research project would explain the origins of the *ecological turn* that unfolded in Hungary by the late 1980s.

In their sociological survey Dobossy and Kulcsár's team tested whether ecological consciousness was an existing phenomenon and how ecological consciousness could be measured in a public opinion survey. Hungarian researchers applied theory developed by Marju Lauristin and Peeter Vihalemm, Estonian social scientists.[27] In their theory Lauristin and Vihalemm applied the theories of the interpretation-paradigm school of social psychology. According to authors experiences represent "challenges," which eventually trigger "responses," which may appear on a very diverse scale. Dobossy and Kulcsár interpreted the diverse spectrum of responses to ecological experiences as "ecological consciousness."[28] They believed that the "methods" respondents approached ecological problems would be typical what did they think about the reasons, threats, consequences, and solutions of ecological problems. To quantify and analyze the diverse responses to Dobossy and Kulcsár used the parameters developed by Lauristin and Vihalemm. One of their main goals was to measure ecological responses regardless of respondents' sociological status by how did respondents perceived ecological problems (for example, those who live in the center of Budapest or those who spend much of their leisure time in the nature with hiking, fishing, or hunting.)[29] When Dobossy and Kulcsár measured reasons for ecological problems with 15 possible factors. Respondents needed to choose three of these factors, which they thought were the most important. As result of their method, the most likely and most unlikely factors were a result of consensus: respondents thought that these were the most important and less important factor according to respondents (Fig. 9.1).

In 1983 the majority of respondents blamed human negligence for ecological problems. Beyond human factor claims in the among the top five reasons of ecological degradation: industrial production and agriculture, lack of and deficiency of end-of-pipe technology, and inefficiency of environmental bylaws and laws were listed. Respondents stressed

Reason	Respondents saying YES (%)
Human negligence	61
Industrial production and agriculture	37
Irresponsible youth	27
Lack of and deficiency of end-of-pipe technology	23
Inefficiency of environmental bylaws and laws	22
Negligence of company leaders	18
Comfort love of people	17
Extinction of old, traditional environmental practices	17
Underdevelopment of human sense of beauty and taste	13
Economic problems	12
Cold War (listed as international tensions)	12
Rapid urbanization	10
Government policies	6
Media is not paying enough attention to	4
Inadequate scientific knowledge	3

Fig. 9.1 Reasons of Ecological Problems Imre Dobossy and László Kulcsár, Az ökológiai tudat és viselkedés társadalmi tényezői. 1983. HU OSA TK-420-2-2-2-35-B8796 7

the importance of insufficient legal environment and technological background to control environmental problems. Dobossy and Kulcsár underlined that respondents stressing the legal and technological framework factors actually realized the contradiction between the legal system and the environmental protection technology that has been pointed out in this work as well. According to Dobossy and Lukács, environmental fines punished environmental wrongdoing but did not achieve their actual goals effectively: to facilitate new environmental protection investments. Some of the actual reasons of environmental problems in Hungary in the early 1980s: rapid urbanization, Cold War embargo, and the country's economic problems were listed as the least important factors triggering ecological issues. Respondent's had an analytic and clear image of environmental issues in Hungary in 1983, however, they did not and could not see the underlying reasons, since they did not access the primary sources historians have been using to recover ecological conditions in the 1980s. All in all, one needs to admit that based on Dobossy's and Lukács' ecological survey, Hungarians had a clear and well-defined image of their environmental conditions in 1983.

In the second phase of the survey, the research team examined the perception of future environmental destruction. Awareness of ecological problems was very high in the society, and 80% of respondents assumed that environmental issues cause significant problems in Hungary. Respondents were asked to forecast of possible future environmental destruction factors from two different perspectives: how likely these ecological events may occur, and when they unfold how harmful their impact would be (Fig. 9.2).[30]

According to the survey respondents used their awareness of Hungary's pressing environmental problems of the early 1980s, and by using contemporary trends predicted possible future environmental scenarios. Most pressing environmental issues of the early 1980s: the pollution of lakes and rivers, noise pollution in cities, and the deterioration of air quality were predicted to become even worse over time. Environmental phenomena not visible in the early 1980s, such as the extinction of natural healing techniques and climate change were selected as of marginal importance. In most of the other ecological problems, respondents had various diverse opinions, and did not share a consensus as with the most likely and least likely events of ecological destructions. According to the research team, this was the result of a wide array of everyday environmental experiences in the society. Respondents replied based on their social status and their involvement of environmental issues or closeness to ecological problems.[31] Oppositional perspectives to ecological problems, however, were less likely to be influenced by the social status of the respondent—according to the research group: *"We consider this an important research outcome, that the fracture between fractions was influenced primarily by the environmental relations of people, social-demographic status was only of secondary importance."*[32]

Type of pollution	Very likely (%)	Quite likely (%)
Pollution of lakes and rivers	44	37
Noise pollution in cities	47	34
Deterioration of air quality	32	47
The growing volume of street litter	28	39
Reduction of trees and green spaces	30	32
Extinction of rare animals and plant species.	26	35
Accumulation of household trash	27	33
Accumulation of hazardous and toxic industrial waste	26	32
The reduction of natural resources and raw materials	20	41
Destruction of landscapes	19	36
Deterioration of drinking water	17	30
Public health problems related to environmental destruction	16	34
Deterioration of agricultural lands	19	28
Deterioration of historical landmarks	14	25
Deterioration of foodstuff quality	13	23
Decreasing opportunities to enjoy nature	10	23
Shrinking area of woodlands	25	35
Extinction of natural healing methods	10	20
Climate change	11	20

Fig. 9.2 How likely ecological problems will occur in the future? Imre Dobossy and László Kulcsár, Az ökológiai tudat és viselkedés társadalmi tényezői. 1983. HU OSA TK-420-2-2-2-35-B8796 12–13

Questions	Respondents (%)
Individual sense of responsibility has to be increased	40
Better and more effective pollution abatement technologies	38
Stricter environmental legislation	31
Stricter enforcement of environmental legislation	29
Environmental friendly production practices	28
Stricter enforcement of public health regulations	24
Development of the sense of beauty	23
Larger state environmental protection budget	16
More financial sources devoted to environmental protection related scientific research	14
More effective international cooperation	13
Environmental protection mass movement	10
Increased financial interest of workers in environmental protection practices	9
More environmental protection areas and parks	8
More information and a more critical attitude over environmental protection in media	8

Fig. 9.3 Possible Solutions for Ecological Problems Imre Dobossy and László Kulcsár, Az ökológiai tudat és viselkedés társadalmi tényezői. 1983. HU OSA TK-420-2-2-2-35-B8796 25–26

In the last part of the survey, the research group investigated possible social and economic responses which could solve pressing ecological problems and their negative consequences. In this section, researchers emphasized that they did not seek for adequate and scientifically proven responses—which in many cases were not even available at the time, rather, they were seeking to find out attitudes and favored solutions of respondents to pressing environmental problems (Fig. 9.3).[33]

According to the research group, opinions were scattered and none of the responses gained a predominant position. This may have indicated uncertainty and lack of concrete ideas to tackle environmental problems. Senior respondents stressed the role of human responsibility and the role of a stricter environmental policy. Male respondents stressed the role of environment policy and pollution abatement technology.[34] On the lower end of the scale, more consensus was visible as less than 15% of respondents assumed that not enough funds were directed to environmental protection-related scientific research and that international cooperation was not effective enough with Comecon and Western countries. A small fragment of respondents, 10 or less per cent called for strengthened environmental mass movement, workers' involvement in environmental protection activities, more environmental protection areas and more attention to environmental issues by the media. Results, in this closing part of the survey indicated that respondents' acknowledged the virtues of the state induced *environmental shift*, but were somewhat, although not entirely dissatisfied with environmental protection technology applied and environmental policy instruments and their overall enforcement.

9.3 Mass Environmentalism and the End of Communism

Numerous scholarly accounts have already analyzed the high level of politicization of the environment in Hungary in late 1980. Several of these accounts were included in the Introductory chapter. In the 1980s activism and protests were closely related to the international legal debate over the infamous Gabčikovo-Nagymaros barrage system, built on the Danube River between the Slovak and Hungarian capitals Bratislava and Budapest. In the 1980s, the construction of the dam led to highly politicized environmental discourse. For the first time in the history of East-Central Europe, an environmental issue became a challenge to the local and central political culture and led to a change of existing power relations. The environmental protests supplied the opposition an opportunity to challenge the political and economic structure of the state-socialist system. The project became the focus of public debate in both Hungary and Slovakia. References to the project became a daily feature in newspapers and political debates.[35] For most Hungarians, Nagymaros became a symbol of socialism and of political

Fig. 9.4 Nagymaros Dam construction site, Danube Bend, 1989. *Photo* FORTEPAN / UVATERV

oppression. Via the politicization of Nagymaros it became obvious that the central government had lost power as well as legitimacy to control discourse over environmental issues. The dam project raised strong emotions among its proponents as well as its opponents. Most opponents to the projected dam—Budapest intellectuals and local residents—argued that the construction of the dam was a megalomaniac socialist idea, inspired by the construction of large river engineering projects in the Soviet Union. The barrage system was perceived economically unrealistic and unnecessary in a post-industrial era with declining heavy industry and cheaper sources of electrical energy (Fig. 9.4).

However, the idea of regulating the Danube between Bratislava and Budapest was originally not the idea of the communists. Ideology behind the project was springing up from the postwar era, when Hungarian democratic leaders were inspired by American river regulation projects, most notably the Tennessee Valley Administration Project (TVA). In 1946, Ferenc Nagy, Hungary's last democratically elected prime minister until the collapse of communism, visited the TVA to learn about its adoptability for Hungarian circumstances. PM Nagy was mesmerized by the TVA and expressed his enthusiasm in an interview: "*The result is compelling – said the prime minister – it is no wonder that it attracts visitors from all over the world.*"[36] Nagy explained his feelings with more detail in his 1948 memoirs: "*We visited the Fontana dam,* where water fell on giant turbines from 500 feet above. This wonderful creation by humankind presented us with an amazing spectacle. I was amazed at this creation by a country that focuses on the well-*being of its citizens and did not, again and again, suffer the devastations of war.*"[37] For Nagy the TVA represented a comprehensive social project and he was convinced that with the aide of modern technology, chemists, engineers and agronomist the economic and social problems of East-Central Europe, similarly to the Tennessee River region would be solved. Electricity would become available to local farmers at a reasonable price. With more energy available, farmers would acquire and operate more machinery, and thus make larger profits. Local industries would flourish and the standard of living would rise rapidly. Nagy was forced to resign in 1947 to make the way for communists in Hungary. The idea of the barrage system, however, was not abandoned. Only the technology would be now acquired from the USSR. Negotiations between Czechoslovakia and Hungary began in 1951. On December 7, 1958, governmental committees agreed on the multipurpose utilization of the River Danube between Bratislava and Budapest. On April 20, 1963, the preliminary design work was completed, and the committees reached an agreement on the joint project's basic features. The bilateral project committee accepted the Czechoslovakian initiative, and on June 30, 1967, the governments agreed on the terms of the project.[38] According to that timetable, the work would begin four years later and be completed within eight years.[39] The plan was accepted by the Ministerial Council of Hungary (Minisztertanács) on November 30, 1975 and by the National Plan Committee of Hungary (Állami Tervbizottság) on March 16, 1977.[40] A bilateral contract was signed on September 16, 1977. On October 1, 1981, however, the State Plan Committee of Hungary temporarily halted construction.

Without the *environmental shift* promoted by the state-socialist regime in the 1970s–1980s opposition against the

Gabčikovo-Nagymaros barrage system should have been significantly weaker. The state nurtured environmentalism which at last turned against it in the form of an opposition against the barrage system project. Under public pressure, on 21 June, 1983, the National Environmental Council of Hungary (Országos Környezet- és Természetvédelmi Tanács) decided to carry out a comprehensive environmental impact study on the barrage system. Governmental agencies, and other bodies involved with the construction of the dam, also took part in that investigation. The Ministerial Council debated the impact study in August 15, 1985. In 1986, the government ordered a full environmental impact plan.[41] This impact study recommended additional technological fixes, such as the installation of a monitor system, to prevent further environmental degradation. To prevent sewage discharges into the reservoirs, wastewater treatment plants would be constructed in the major towns along the Danube River and her tributaries.[42] A number of scientists expressed critical views toward this environmental impact study. Members of an "ad hoc" committee of the Hungarian Academy considered the project anachronistic and requested to stop the construction of the project. In 1988, the committee argued that the barrage system was based on an unrealistic macroeconomic budget analysis and the continuation of the project would endanger Hungary's fragile and stagnating economy. According to the committee's statement, the barrage system was not only economically but environmentally unrealistic (Fig. 9.5).

By 1988–1989 the Hungarian nation was united against the Nagymaros dam project. A series of protests were organized by the Danube Circle (Duna Kör) and hundreds of thousands engaged in political protest. On 13 May, 1989 the government ordered the construction to be abandoned. This was seen as the victory of the people's will over monolithic communism. Similarly to the 300 or so residents of District 78, who protected their trees with a tooth around in the 1982 satirical television series, millions of Hungarians protected their beloved Danube Bend and Visegrád-Nagymaros cultural-natural landscape with success. Its telling how little connection has been made between the high level of environmental consciousness, fierce environmental activism of Hungarians, and the state-sponsored environmental

Fig. 9.5 Protest against the Nagymaros Dam, Danube Bend, 1989. *Photo* FORTEPAN / TM

propaganda of earlier decades. Without doubt, for contemporaries, journalists, scholars the environmental protests against the Gabčikovo-Nagymaros barrage system would spring up from civic courage and from thirst for democratic institutions. Surely, these factors played important roles in the organization of the environmental movement in Hungary in the 1980s. So as the decades-long environmental protection propaganda orchestrated the state.

Notes

1. István Fodorné: "Váljék minden állampolgár emberi tuljadonságává a környezetvédelem." Dr József Schnitzler: "Hazánkban a környezetvédelem központi kérdéssé vált, része embercentrikus, szocializmust építő politikánknak. "*Népújság,* March 20, 1976.
2. *Déli Hírlap* and *Észak-Magyarország* between 1972 and 1989.
3. Ibid.
4. Ibid.

5. "(...) szennyvíztisztító mű elkészülte után a kombinát tisztább vizet ad vissza a Sajóba, mint amilyet onnan kivesz." (...) after the completion of the waste water treatment plant it (the waste water treatment plant) will discharge cleaner waste water to the River Sajó, than the water it (the plant) had been taken in)."
"A BVK szennyvíztisztító üzeme (The Waste Water Treatment Unit of the BVK)," *Déli Hírlap*, May 24, 1975.
6. Interview with Lajos Kárbin, Kazincbarcika, Hungary, November 14, 2007.
7. "BVK Szennyvízkezelése (Waste Water Treatment of BVK)," *Magyar Nemzet*, August 1975.
"A BVK környezetvédelmi helyzetéről (About BVK and its Environmental Protection Situation)," *Borsod Rádió*, October 30, 1975.
"A BVK és a környezetvédelem (BVK and Environmental protection)," *Észak-Magyarország*, January 21, 1976,
"A BVK szennyvítisztítótelepéről (About the Waste Water Treatment Unit of the BVK)," *Déli Hírlap*, May 24, 1976.
"Környezetvédelem a Kazincbarcikai BVK-ban (Environmental Protection in the BVK in Kazincbarcika)," *Észak-Magyarország*, December 23, 1977.
8. Ibid.
9. Ibid.
10. "Környezet és Gazdaságosság (The Environment and Efficiency in Economics)," *Déli Hírlap*, March 3, 1978.
11. *Déli Hírlap* and *Észak-Magyarország* between 1972 and 1989.
12. Ibid.
13. "Szennyvízkezelés és a BVK (Waste Water Treatment and the BVK)," *Észak-Magyarország*, August 16, 1978.
14. "Volt olyan időszak pl., amikor a BVK egy év alatt 20MFt-nál több szennyvízbírságot fiztetett, néhány éve azonban már csak pár ezer forintot." "Környezet és Gazdaságosság (The Environment and Economy)," *Déli Hírlap*, March 3, 1978.
15. "Mi az oka, hogy a hazai üzemek nem tisztítják megfelelően a vizet?" "180 Perc (The 180 min Show)," *Kossuth Rádió*, May 8, 1980.
16. „Olyan beruházásokat kell megkezdeni, illetve kivitelezni, amelyek hatása az egész lakosság körében közvetlenül érzékelhető."
"180 Perc (The 180 Minute Show)," *Kossuth Rádió*, May 8, 1980.
17. „ Az *Országos Környezetvédelmi Koncepció és Követelményrendszer (The* National Environmental Protection Requirement Concept)," Észak-Magyarország, May 11, 1980.

18. "Interjú Dr Gonda Györggyel (An Interview with Dr György Gonda)," *Magyar Nemzet*, July 6, 1980.
19. "Környezetvédelmi napok Kazincbarcikán (Environmental Days in Kazincbarcika)," *Észak-Magyarország*, April 16, 1975.
20. Ibid.
21. Ibid.
22. Ibid.
23. "Munkahelyi környezetvédelem (Environmental Protection at Work)," *Észak-Magyarország*, January 24, 1975.
24. Ibid.
25. "Önkéntes Környezeti Őrök (Volunteer Environmental Guards)," *Népszava*, April 24, 1975.
26. Imre Dobossy and László Kulcsár, Az ökológiai tudat és viselkedés társadalmi tényezői. 1983. OSA420 1–2
27. Marju Lauristin and Peeter Vihalemm, Paradigmatikus tartalomelemzés, elméleti megközelítés és módszertani problémák.
28. Imre Dobossy and László Kulcsár, Az ökológiai tudat és viselkedés társadalmi tényezői. 1983. HU OSA TK-420-2-2-2-35-B8796. 4.
29. Ibid., 5.
30. Ibid., 11–12.
31. Ibid., 14–15.
32. "Fontosnak eredménynek tartjuk, hogy ez a törésvonal elsősorban az embereknek a környezetükhöz való viszonya mentén húzódik, és csak másodlagos szerepe van a társadalmi-demográfiai státusznak." Ibid., 15.
33. Ibid., 25.
34. Ibid., 26.
35. Fitzmaurice, John. 1996. *Damming the Danube. Gabčikovo and the Post-Communist Politics in Europe*. Boulder, Colorado: Westview Press. 94–95.
36. Miért látogatták meg Nagy Ferencék a Tennessee völgyét? Egy szociálisan átgondolt folyamszabályozás amely példát mutat a világ valamennyi népének. 1946 [Why did Nagy Ferenc and others visit the valley the Tennesee River Valley. A socially well-planned river regulation showing positive example for all nations on the globe]. Új Magyarország 25. June (3) 7.
37. Nagy, Ferenc. 1990. Küzdelem a vasfüggyöny mögött [A struggle behind the Iron Curtain] Vol.1. Budapest-Európa-História. 305. (The

quoted excerpt is the author's translation of the original Hungarian text written in 1947.

38. Magyar-Csehszlovák Gazdasági és Műszaki-Tudományos Együttműködési Vegyesbizottság.
39. *Országos Vízügyi Hivatal, Tájékoztató a közös magyar-csehszlovák dunai vízerőműrendszer beruházás előkészítéséről.* 1972. [National Water Agency, Information on the preliminary planning of the joint Hungarian-Czechoslovakian barrage system on the River Danube], Budapest: OVH.
40. No. 3540/1975, No. 5011/1977
41. *Előterjesztés az Állami Tervbizottság részére a Bős (Gabčikovo)-Nagymarosi Vízlépcsőrendszer nagyberuházás módosított beruházási javaslatáról és műszaki-ökológiai-ökonómiai összefüggéseinek értékeléséről. (Tervezet)* [Initiative for the National Plan Committee on the Gabči kovo- Nagymaros Barrage System's modified investments strategies and their technological, ecological and economic impacts]. 1986 Budapest.
42. Besides a number of villages and small towns, some of the region's larger urban centers would be affected. For example, Győr, Komárom, Esztergom, Tatabánya, and Oroszlány.

10

Epilogue

In 2007, the Socialist Party-led administration ordered plans to enlarge the Museum of Fine Arts located in the City Park (Városliget or Liget) in Budapest. Városliget is a 1.2 sq km UNESCO World Heritage Site, one of the first city parks in the world. The enlargement project was reasoned by soaring visitor numbers which were hovering around 500,000 annually. Due to increased interest in the Museum of Fine Arts long lines became a regular sight in front of the old museum building.[1] In 2010 the right wing/populist Fidesz-KDNP Party won national and municipal elections in Hungary. The new government canceled the enlargement project of the Museum of Fine Arts in early 2011. Géza Szőcs, Under-secretary of Culture announced a new 3.7 billion Ft (12 million euros) Museum Quarter project on 56-osok tere, a few hundred metres from Museum of Fine Arts.[2] During the course of 2011 and 2012 newer ideas were included in the original, relatively modest concept. Finally, the enlargement of the Museum of Fine Arts, evolved into a monster art district project plan, with several, mega-construction sites within Budapest's City Park. The list of museums and attractions to be constructed or refurbished in within the Liget continued to change and seemed to grow ever longer. The 1397/2013. (VII. 2.) Governmental

V. Pál, *Technology and the Environment in State-Socialist Hungary*,
DOI 10.1007/978-3-319-63832-4_10

Order on the "comprehensive utilization" of the city park marked a turning point, and made apparent that the Orbán administration would aim to reconstruction the entire city park by planting megastructures and attracting more visitors to the park. Between 2011 and 2015 project budget grew from 3.7 billion Ft (12 million euros) to 150 billion forints (490 million euros).

One of the chief actors in the new project is László Baán, director of Museum of Fine Arts and Hungarian National Gallery. After August 2012 Baán became the commissioner of the new "Liget Projekt." He has close ties to the government of Hungary and the shadow advisers behind the government. Baán was part of a scandal in 2016, when several valuable artworks were lent to Árpád Habony, one of the unofficial advisers of PM Orbán.[3] Baán fiercefully defends the transformation of the entire city park, and believes that the project should be finalized by 2020.[4]

In 2013 members of the architecture and landscape designer community have already criticized the proposed plan. Critics pointed out that the city park has already very high ratio of built-up areas, which will be doubled as a result of the new mega-project. Architects referred to the 253/1997. (XII. 20.) governmental order that points out that urban park areas should not have more than 3% built up ratio.[5] The City Park had 5.7% built up areas in 2013 and this already high level was estimated to climb up to 12–13% by 2020, when the mega-project is finalized.[6] Sándor Bardóczi and Imre Pákozdi criticized that new buildings were to be 20–40 meters tall, taller than 10-storey housing units. In their view, such gigantic structures would not fit into the city park.[7] They also pointed out that similar cultural developments in Europe have been constructed in urban rust belts since decades ago, and recommended the Orbán administration to follow these European trends and use Budapest's massive rust belt for the development of this cultural megaproject. Criticism of the professional community was not taken into account and the government opened the design tender megastructures in February 2014.

The first civic demonstration took place in the city park on June 13, 2014.[8] Sporadic civic activism grew into a Gezi Park style occupy movement when in March 2016 a group of activists fiercely occupied demolition sites in the Városliget and aimed to stop the construction project. During 2016 conflicts between the protesters and police/security forces became regular. Riot police and private security forces with ties in the shadow economy were employed against peaceful protester at several occasions. It seems, however, that the Liget issue is not able to reach out to a large proportion of society and not going to evolve into a second Gabčikovo-Nagymaros. Rather this environmental movement will be channelized into a broader framework of protest against Orbán's Putin style hybrid democracy.

One of the most important reasons why the Liget movement managed to gain only niche audience is that in recent decades environmentalism and environmental questions were not among the most pressing issues of Hungarian society. Aging population, emigration, brain drain, the crisis of the education, and health care sectors received significantly more attention than Budapest's foul air problems and the impact of climate change within Hungary. Environmental consciousness levels of contemporary Hungarians may score much lower in the research framework of Dobossy's and Kulcsár's than respondents' in 1983.

This book expressed that between the 1960s–1980s, Hungarian environmental attitudes changed considerably. Such a change was effectively nurtured, facilitated and propagated by the state. Public concern over pollution rose and local environmental debates were mostly confined to local media platforms in the 1960s. As a result of societal changes and government sponsored environmentalist propaganda, environmental concerns grew significantly in Hungarian society by the mid-1970s. Communist social and youth organizations incorporated environmental protection into their agenda. Government organizations, factories, and municipalities organized a growing number of public events with an environmental theme. Public concern over the environment orchestrated by the state socialist regime was an earlier overlooked, but extremely important component of the ecological turn in the late 1980s.

Notes

1. Fővárosi Blog (Capital Blog), *Fájdalmas tágulás (Painful Enlargement)*, http://fovarosi.blog.hu/2010/04/07/szepmuveszeti_bovit (accessed July 31, 2017).
2. Fővárosi Blog (Capital Blog), *A Városliget beépítésének sztorija: a kezdetek (History of Construction in the City Park: The Beginnings)*, http://fovarosi.blog.hu/2016/04/20/a_varosliget_beepitesenek_sztorija_a_kezdetek (accessed July 31, 2017).
3. Átlátszó.hu, *A Szépművészeti Múzeum tíz értékes antik festményt kölcsönzött ki a Szerb utca 9-be (Museum of Fine Arts Loaned 10 Antique Paintings to Hang in Szerb Str. 9)*, https://atlatszo.hu/2016/02/09/a-szepmuveszeti-muzeum-tiz-ertekes-antik-festmenytkolcsonzott-ki-a-szerb-utca-9-be/ (accessed July 31, 2017).
4. Index.hu, *A kormány továbbra is számít Baán Lászlóra és Ókovács Szilveszterre (L. Baán's and Sz. Ókovács' Services are Countinously Needed by the Government)*, http://index.hu/belfold/2012/07/28/a_kormany_tovabbra_is_szamit_baan_laszlora_es_okovacs_szilveszterre/ (accessed July 31, 2017).
5. 253/1997. (XII. 20.) Korm. rendelet az országos településrendezési és építési követelményekről (253/1997. (XII. 20.) Governmental Order, National Urban Planning and Construction Requirements), https://net.jogtar.hu/jr/gen/hjegy_doc.cgi?docid=99700253.KOR (accessed July 31, 2017).
6. Építészfórum.hu, *Liget Budapest* +, http://epiteszforum.hu/liget-budapest1 (accessed July 31, 2017).
7. Fővárosi Blog (Capital Blog), http://indafoto.hu/fovarosiblog/image/23983604-2eb3853b (accessed July 31, 2017).
8. Átlátszó.hu, *Ezután már bármit meg lehet tenni a Városligettel - civilek tiltakoztak a beépítési tervek ellen (From Now on They Do As They Please in the City Park - Protest Against the City Park Construction Project)*, https://vimeo.com/98185125 (accessed July 31, 2017).

Bibliography

Archival Sources

Borsod-Abaúj-Zemplén Megyei Levéltár, Mezőcsát Fióklevéltár (Borsod-Abaúj-Zemplén County Archives Mezőcsát Branch Archives) XXIX. 113. Miskolci Vízművek Iratai. 33–42/b boxes.

Duna Múzeum, Magyar Környezetvédelmi- és Vízügyi Múzeum, Irattár, (Danube Museum, Hungarian Environmental- and Water Museum, Archives, Esztergom) environmental activist documentation, Uncatalogued documentation.

Ecological Institute Foundation Library, Miskolc, environmental activist documentation. Uncatalogued.

Hungarian National Archives, Minutes of the Hungarian Socialist Workers' Party's Central Committee, 288.f.

Környezetvédelmi és Vízügyi Levéltár (Environmental and Water Archives) VI. 9. Miskolci Kulturmérnöki Hivatal Vizikönyvek 1867–1971 (Miskolc „Culture" Engineering Office „Waterlogs"), 291, 296, 303, 304, boxes.

Open Society Archives, Budapest, Hungary, HU OSA TK-420.

V. Pál, *Technology and the Environment in State-Socialist Hungary*,
DOI 10.1007/978-3-319-63832-4

Legal Documents

1871 évi XXXVII. törvénycikk a gömöri iparvasutak hálózatának kiépitéséről (Act. XXXVII in 1871 on the Construction of the Network of the Gömör Industrial Railways) Enacted in Budapest, Hungary.

1874 évi VIII. törvénycikk a métermérték behozataláról, (Act VIII/1874 on the Implementation of Metric Standard). Enacted in Budapest, Hungary.

1885 évi XXIII. törvénycikk a vizjogról (Act. XXIII. in 1885 on Water Rights) Enacted in Budapest, Hungary.

1949 évi XXV. törvény A Magyar Népköztársaság első ötéves népgazdasági tervéről, az 1950. január 1-től az 1954. december 31-ig terjedő időszakra. (Act XXV/1949 on the First Five Year Plan of the People"s Republic of Hungary from January 1, 1950 to December 31, 1954.) Enacted in Budapest, Hungary.

1958 évi II. törvény az 1958–1960. évi hároméves népgazdaságfejlesztési terv irányelveiről (Act. II. in 1958 on on the guidelines of the 1958–1960 three year people's-economy development plan.) Enacted in Budapest, Hungary.

1961 évi II. törvény a Magyar Népköztársaság második ötéves népgazdaságfejlesztési tervéről az 1961. január 1-jétől 1965. december 31-ig terjedő időszakra (Act. II in 1961 on the Second Five Year Plan of the People's Republic (effective) for the period from January 1, 1961 to December 31, 1965) Enacted in Budapest, Hungary.

1060/53 (IX.30) Kormány Határozat (1060/53 (IX.30) Order of the Council of Ministers), 30 September, 1953, Budapest, Hungary.

4354/1955 (VII.18.) Kormány Határozat (4354/1955 (VII.18) Order of the Council of Ministers), 18 July, 1955, Budapest, Hungary.

5/1966 (I.23) korm.sz.rendelet. (Governmental order).

28/1967 (IX.3) korm.sz.rendelet (Governmental order).

40/1969 (XI.25) korm.sz.rendelet (Governmental Order). Enacted on November 25, 1969 in Budapest, Hungary.

Magyar Dolgozók Pártja, Gazdasági Bizottság (Hungarian Workers' Party, Economic Committee), 126/1952 Határozat, 1952.03.20. (Decision No. 126/1952 on March 20, 1952).

Magyar Dolgozók Pártja, Gazdasági Bizottság (Hungarian Workers' Party, Economic Committee), 319/1952 Határozat, 1952.08.07. (Decision No. 319/1952 on August 7, 1952).

Magyar Dolgozók Pártja, Gazdasági Bizottság (Hungarian Workers' Party, Economic Committee), 540703/2/1952 Határozat, 1954.07.09. (Decision No. 540703/2/1952 on July 9, 1952).

Newspapers and Periodicals

Borsod Műszaki Élet 1956–1980.
Borsodi Szemle 1968.
Déli Hírlap, 1969–1980.
Észak-Magyarország, 1949–1980.
Felvidéki Népszava 1946

Books and Articles

"BVK Szennyvízkezelése (Waste Water Treatment of BVK)," *Magyar Nemzet*, August 1975.

"Interjú Dr Gonda Györggyel (An Interview with Dr György Gonda)," *Magyar Nemzet*, July 6, 1980.

"Önkéntes Környezeti Őrök (Volunteer Environmental Guards)," *Népszava*, April 24, 1975.

A Diósgyőri M. Kir. Vas- és Aczélgyár története 1765–1910 (The History of the Royal Hungarian Diósgyőr Iron- and Steel Factory 1765–1910). Miskolc, 1910.

Aldcroft, Derek. *The European Economy 1914–2000.* London-New York: Routledge, 2001.

Anders, George. "Soviet Bloc Bus Builder Hits Bumpy Road in U.S.," *The Wall Street Journal*, March 28, 1984, Eastern Edition, 1.

Armengaud, Andre. "Population in Europe 1700–1914," In *The Fontana Economic History of Europe. Volume 3. Part 1.* by Carlo M. Cipolla. 22–76. London: Fontana/Collins, 1973.

Bayly, A. Christopher. The Birth of the Modern World, 1780–1914. Oxford: Blackwell, 2004.

Berend, T. Iván, and Ránki, György. *Studies on Central and Eastern Europe in the Twentieth Century, Regional Crises and the Case of Hungary.* Aldershot, Hampshire: Ashgate, 2002.

Berend, T. Iván, and Ránki, György. *The Hungarian Economy in the Twentieth Century*. London: Croom Helm, 1985.

Berend, T. Iván. *A szocialista gazdaság fejlődése Magyarországon (The development of socialist economy in Hungary)*. Budapest: Akadémiai Kiadó, 1974.

Berend, T. Iván. *An Economic History of Twentieth-Century Europe*. Cambridge: Cambridge University Press, 2006.

Berend, T. Iván. *Central and Eastern Europe 1944–1993. Detour from the periphery to the periphery.* Cambridge: Cambridge University Press, 1996.

Berend, T. Ivan. *Decades of Crisis: Central and Eastern Europe Before World War II*. Berkeley: University of California Press, 1998.
Berend, T. Ivan. *From the Soviet Bloc to the European Union: The Economic and Social Transformation of Central and Eastern Europe Since 1973*. Cambridge: Cambridge University Press, 2009.
Berend, T. Iván. *Gazdaságpolitika az első ötéves terv megindításakor 1948–1950 (Economic Policy at the beginning of the First Three Year Plan 1948–1950)*. Budapest: Közgazdasági és Jogi Könyvkiadó, 1964.
Berend, T. Iván. *History Derailed, Central and Eastern Europe in the long nineteenth century*. Berkeley: University of California Press, 2003.
Berend, T. Iván. *The Hungarian Economic Reforms 1953–1988*. Cambrdige: Cambridge University Press, 1990.
Berghahn, Volker. "Demographic Growth, Industrialization and Social Change." In *19th century Germany. Politics, Culture and Society 1780–1918*, edited by John Breuilly, XXX. London: Arnold, 2001.
Blackbourn, David. *Fontana History of Germany, 1780–1918: the Long Nineteenth Century*. London: Fontana, 1997.
Blackbourn, David. *The Conquest of Nature, Water, Landscape, and the Making of Modern Germany*. New York-London: W.W. Norton, 2007.
Boonstra, J. Wiebrem. "The Social Dynamics of Degrowth." *Environmental Values* 22, No. 1 (2013): 171–189.
Borhi, László. *Hungary in the Cold War: 1945–1956*. Budapest-New York: Central European University Press, 2004.
Bori, R. Douglas. "Foreword." In *Pollution Abatement Strategies in Central and Eastern Europe*, edited by Michael A. Toman, I-IX. Washington D.C.: Resources for the Future, 1994.
BorsodChem Rt. Környezeti állapota. Tényfelmérő és állapotrögzítő tanulmány (BorsodChem Rt State of the Environment. Assessment Study of Facts and Conditions). Kazincbarcika: BorsodChem Rt, 1993.
Boyd, James, *Water Pollution Taxes: A Good Idea Doomed to Failure?, Discussion Paper 03–20*. Washington D. C.: Resources for the Future, 2003.
Brain, Stephen, *The Song of the Forest: Russian Forestry and Stalinist Environmentalism, 1905–1953*. Pittsburgh: University of Pittsburgh Press, 2011.
Braun, Hans-Joachim. *The German Economy in the Twentieth Century*. London-New York: Routledge, 1990.
Broadberry, Stephen, and O'Rourke, Kevin eds. *The Cambridge Economic History of Modern Europe*. Cambridge: Cambridge University Press, 2010.

Brüggemeier, Franz-Josef, and Rommelspacher, Thomas. *Blauer Himmel über der Ruhr: Geschichte der Umwelt im Rurhgebiet, 1840–1990.* Essen: Klartext, 1992.

Chaney, Sandra. *Nature of the Miracle Years, Conservation in West Germany 1945–75.* New York-Oxford: Berghahn Books, 2012.

Cioc, Mark. *The Rhine: an eco-biography, 1815*–2000. Seattle: University of Washington Press, 2002.

Cipolla, M. Carlo, ed. *The Fontana Economic History of Europe, Volume 6. Contemporary Economies, Part 1.* London: Collins-Fontana, 1976.

Cipolla, M. Carlo. *The Fontana Economic History of Europe, Volume 6. Contemporary Economies.* London: Collins-Fontana, 1976.

Clapp, W. Brian. *An Environmental History of Britain since the Industrial Revolution.* London-New York: Longman, 1994.

Cornelius, S. Deborah. *Hungary in World War II. Caught in the Cauldron.* New York: Fordham University Press, 2011.

Coumel, Laurent, "A Failed Environmental Turn? Khrushchev's Thaw and Nature Protection in Soviet Russia." *The Soviet and Post-Soviet Review*, 40, No. 2 (2013), 167–189.

Cronon, William. *Nature's Metropolis: Chicago and the Great West.* New York: W. W. Norton, 1991.

Davies, W. Robert. *Soviet Economic Development from Lenin to Khruschev.* Cambridge: Cambridge University Press, 1998.

Demaria, Federico, Schneider, François, Sekulova, Filka, Martinet-Alier, Joan. "What is Degrowth? From an Activist Slogan to a Social Movement." *Environmental Values* 22, No. 1 (2013): 191–215.

Dennis, Mike, *The Rise and Fall of the German Democratic Republic 1945–1990.* Longman: London-New York, 2000.

Disco, Cornelis. "Accepting Father Rhine? Technological Fixes, Vigilance, and Transnational Lobbies as „European" Strategies of Dutch Municipal Water Supplies 1900–1975." *Environment and History* 13, No. 4 (2007): 381–411.

Dominick, H. Raymond III. *The Environmental Movement in Germany, Prophets and Pioneers, 1871*–1971. Bloomington and Indianapolis: Indiana University Press, 1992.

Dominick, Raymond, "Capitalism, Communism and Environmental protection, Lessons from the Germany experience." *Environmetal History* 3, No. 3 (1998): 311–332.

Eichengreen, Barry. *The European Economy Since 1945: Co-ordinated Capitalism and Beyond.* Princeton: Princeton University Press, 2007.

Einaudi, Mario. “Nationalization of Industry in Western Europe: Recent Literature and Debates.” *The American Political Science Review* 44, No. 1 (1950): 177–191.

Einaudi, Mario. “Nationalization of Industry in Western Europe: Recent Literature and Debates.” In: *The American Political Science Review* 44, No. 1 (1950): 177–191.

Enyedi, György and Szirmai, Viktória. “Environmental Movements and Civil Society in Hungary.” In *Environment and Society in Eastern Europe,* edited by Andrew Tickle and Ian Welsh, XXX. Harlow: Longman, 1998.

Evans, J. W. Robert, *Austria, Hungary and the Habsburgs, Essays on Central Europe, c. 1863–1867.* Oxford: Oxford University Press, 2006.

Federman, Stan, "Settlement due on bus defects," *The Oregonian,* 13 February 1986, A17.

Federman, Stan, "Tri-Met sues over articulated bus defects," *The Oregonian,* 5 November 1981, B5.

Federman,Stan, "Tri-Met readies bendable buses," *The Oregonian,* 30 November 1981, B1.

Feinstein, H. Charles. “Capital accumulation and the industrial revolution.” In: *The Economic History of Britain since 1700,* edited by Roderick Floud and Donald McCloskey. XXX. Cambrdige: Cambridge University Press, 1981.

Feshback, Murray, and Friendly, Alfred Jr. *Ecocide in the USSR, Health and Nature Under Siege.* New York: BasicBooks, 1992.

Foreman-Peck, James, “Industry and industrial organisation in the inter-war years.” In *Economic History of Britain since 1700. Volume 2. 1860-1939.* edited by Roderick Floud and Donald McCloskey, 386–414. Cambrdige: Cambridge University Press, 1994.

Fotopoulos, Takis. *Towards Inclusive Democracy, The Crisis of the Growth Economy and the Need for a New Liberatory Project.* London:Cassell, 1997.

Foucault, Michel. *The Archeology of Knowledge.* London-New York: Routledge, 2002.

French, F. Hilary. *Green Revolutions: Environmental Reconstruction in Eastern Europe and the Soviet Union, Worldwatch Papers 99.* Washington D.C.: Worldwatch Institute, 1990.

Fresh Water pollution control in Europe. Council of Europe, 1966.

Frisnyák Dr., Sándor, *Kazincbarcika földrajza (Geography of Kazincbarcika).* Kazincbarcika Város Tanácsa (City Council Kazincbarcika): Kazincbarcika, 1979.

Germuska, Pál "Failed Eastern integration and a partly successful opening up to the West: the economic re-orientation of Hungary during the 1970s" *European Review of History* 21, No. 2 (2014): 271–291.

Germuska, Pál. *Indusztria bűvöletében (Mesmerized by Industry).* Budapest: 1956-os Intézet, 2004.

Gille, Zsuzsa, *From the Cult of Waste to the Trash Heap of History, The Politics of Waste in Socialist and Postsocialist Hungary*. Bloomington and Indianapolis: Indiana University Press, 2007.

Goldman, I. Marshall. *The Spils of Progress: Environmental Pollution in the Soviet Union*. Cambridge: MIT Press, 1972.

Harvey, David. *A Companion to Marx's Capital.* London: Verso, 2010.

Hector, Donald Charles, Christensen, Carleton Bruin, and Petrie, Jim. "Sustainability and Sustainable Development: Philosophical Distinctions and Practical Implications." *Environmental Values* 23, No. 1 (2014): 7–28.

Held, Joseph. *Dictionary of East European History since 1945*. London: Mansell, 1994.

Hobsbawm, Eric J., Industry and Empire, An Economic History of Britain since 1750, Weidenfeld and Nicolson: London, 1969. (Sixth impression: 1989).

Hobsbawm, J. Eric. *Industry and Empire. An Economic History of Britain since 1750.* London: Weidenfeld and Nicolson, 1989.

Hoensch, K. Jörg. *A history of modern Hungary*. London and New York: Longman, 1996.

Hoitsy, György, Losonci, Csaba, Nagy, Dezső, and Németh, Csaba. *Nehézfém szennyezések vizsgálata a Sajó-völgyben (Heavy metal pollution in the valley of the Sajó River).* Miskolc: Zöld Akció Egyesület, 1995.

Ioris, A. R. Antonio. "The Positioned Construction of Water Values: Pluralism, Positionality and Praxis." *Environmental Values* 21, No. 1 (2012): 143–162.

Jancar, Barbara, *Environmental Management in the Soviet Union and Yugoslavia. Structure and Regulation in Federal Communist* States. Durham: Duke University Press, 1987.

Josephson, Paul et al., *An Environmental History of Russia*. Cambridge: Cambridge University Press, 2013.

Katus, László. "A Gazdasági fejlődés politikai feltételei (The Political Preconditions of Economic Development)." In *Magyarország története 1848–1890 (A History of Hungary 1848–1890),* edited by László Katus, 933-1038. Budapest: Akadémiai Kiadó, 1979.

Kenez, Peter. *Hungary from the Nazis to the Soviets. The Establishment of the communist Regime in Hungary, 1944–1948.* Cambridge: Cambridge University Press, 2006.

Kirschbaum, J. Stanislav. *A History of Slovakia, The Struggle for Survival.* London: Macmillan, 1995.

Kneese, V. Allen, and Bower, T. Blair. *Managing Water Quality, Economics, Technology, Institutions.* Washington D.C: Resources for the Future and the John Hopkins University Press, 1985.

Korbel, Joseph, *Twentieth century Czechoslovakia. The Meanings of Its History*, New York: Columbia University Press, 1977.

Kornai, Janos, *The State Socialist System, The Political Economy of Communism.* Princeton: Princeton University Press, 1992.

Kovel, Joel. *The Enemy of Nature. The End of Capitalism or the End of the World.* London-New York: Zed Books, 2007.

Krejčí, Jaroslav and Machonin, Pavel, *Czechoslovakia, 1918–92. A laboratory for Social Change.* London: Macmillan, 1996.

Laakkonen, Simo, Pál, Viktor, Tucker, Richard "The Cold War and environmental history: complementary fields" *Cold War History,* No. 4 (2016): 1–18.

Latouche, Serge. *Farewell to Growth.* Cambridge: Polity, 2009.

Latour, Bruno. *Reassembling the Social: An Actor-Network-Theory.* Oxford-New York: Oxford University Press, 2005.

Lekan, M. Thomas. *Imagining the Nation in Nature: Landscape Preservation and Germany Identity, 1885–1945.* Cambridge: Harvard University Press, 2004.

Liszewski, Stanisław. "The Origins and Stages of Development of Industrial Łódź Urban Region." In: *A Comparative Study of Łódź and Manchester. Geographies of European Cities in Transition*, edited by XXX, XXX. Łódź: University of Łódź, 1997.

Maddison, Angus. *The world economy: a millenial perspective.* Paris: OECD, 2001.

Magyar Statisztikai Zsebkönyv 1984 (*Hungarian Statistical Pocketbook 1984*). Budapest: Statisztikai Kiadó Vállalat, 1985.

Makarewicz, Henryk and Pental, Wiktor, *802 procent normy (802 per cent of the norm).* Kraków: Fundacja Imago Mundi, Without Year.

Małowist, Marian. "East and West Europe in the 13th–16th centuries. Confrontation of social and economic structures." In: *Eastern Europe and World Development 13th–18th centuries. Collection of Essays of Marian Małowist*, edited by Jean Batou and Henryk Szlajfer, 215–227. Leiden-Boston: Brill, 2009.

Mamatey, S. Victor. "The development of Czechoslovak Democracy, 1918–1920." In: *A History of the Czechoslovak Republic 1918–1948.* edited by Victor. S. Mamatey and Radomír Luža, XXX. Princeton: Princeton University Press, 1973.

Manser, Roger. *Failed transitions. The Eastern European Economy and Environment Since the Fall of Communism.* New York: The New Press, 1993.

McCauley, Martin, *The German Democratic Republic since 1945. Studies in Russia and East Europe.* Basingstroke- London: Macmillan, 1983.

McNeill, John Robert. *Something New Under the Sun: An Environmental History of the Twentieth-Century World.* New York: W. W. Norton, 2000.

Meadows, H. Donella et al. eds. *The Limits to Growth : a Report for the Club of Rome's Project on the Predicament of Mankind.* New York: Universe Books, 1972.

Melosi, V. Martin. *The Sanitary City: Urban Infrastructure in America from Colonial Times to Present.* Baltimore: John Hopkins University Press, 2000.

Michal, M. Jan. *Central Planning in Czechoslovakia, Organization for Growth in a Mature Economy.* Stanford: Stanford University Press, 1960.

Mokyr, Joel, *The Enlightened Economy, An Economic History of Britain, 1700–1850,* New Haven: Yale University Press, 2009.

Molnár, Miklós, *A Concise History of Hungary,* Cambridge: Cambridge University Press, 2001.

Mong, Attila *Kádár Hitele. A Magyar Államadósság Története 1956–1990 (Kádár's Credit. The History of Hungary's State Debt 1956–1990).* Budapest: Libri, 2012.

Montias, John Michael. *Central Planning in Poland.* New Haven: Yale University Press.

Morgan, O. Kenneth, *The people's peace, British history, 1945–1989,* Oxford: Oxford University Press, 1995.

Morse, L. Anita. "The Cost of Purity: Use of the Effluent Charge in Water Quality control and Management." *Valparaiso University Law Review* 7, No. 2 (1973): 169–189.

Mosley, Stephen. *The Chimney of the World. A history of Smoke Pollution in Victorian and Edwardian* Manchester. London-New York: Routledge, 2008.

Myant, Matin. *The Czechoslovak Economy in 1948 1988, The battle for economic reform.* Cambridge: Cambridge University Press, 1989.

Nigel Swain, *Hungary. The Rise and Fall of Feasible Socialism.* London-New York: Verso, 1992.

Ormos, Mária. *Padovától-Trianonig (From Padua to Trianon) 1918–1920.* Budapest: Kossuth Könyvkiadó, 1983.

Papp, Attila. *Ismerkedjünk Kazincbarcikával (Introduction to Kazincbarcika).* Kazincbarcika: Kazincbarcikai Városi Könyvtár, 1974.
Pál, Viktor. *Crave for Growth: The Environmental History of Water in the Borsod Basin, Hungary, 1945–1980.* Doctoral Dissertation. University of Tampere, 2015.
Pavlínek, Petr, and Pickles, John. *Environmental Transitions, Transformation and ecological defense in Central and Eastern Europe.* London-New York: Routledge, 2000.
Péch, Antal. *Jelentése a selmeczi és diósgyőri kerületben és Rézbánya vidékén létező állami bányák és kohók állapotáról (His report on the condition of mines and furnaces in the Selmecz, Diósgyőr and Rézbánya areas).* Budapest: Magyar Királyi Állami Nyomda, 1873.
Péter, Sándor. "New Directions in Environmental Management in Hungary." In *Environmental Action in Eastern Europe. Responses to Crisis,* edited by Barbara Jancar-Webster, 28–41. London: Amonk, 1993.
Pittaway, Mark, "Workers in Hungary." In: *Power and the People, A Social History of Central European Politics, 1945–56.* edited by Eleonore Breuning, Jill Lewis and Gareth Pritchard. Manchester-New York: Manchester University Press, 2005.
Postan, M. Michael, *An Economic History of Western Europe 1945–1964,* London: Methuen & Co, 1967.
Prazmowska, Anita. *Poland: A Modern History.* London-New York: I.B. Tauris, 2010.
Prinz, Friedrich. *Geschichte Böhmens, 1848–1948.* Hamburg: Langen Müller, 1988.
Pryde, Philip R. *Environmental management in the Soviet Union.* Cambridge: Cambridge University Press, 1991.
Rainer, M. János. *Bevezetés a Kádárizmusba (Introduction to Kádárism).* 1956–os Intézet-L'Harmattan: Budapest, 2011.
Renz, F. W. "Goals and management of the Ruhr Reservoir System Since the Beginning of Our Century" *Scientific, Procedures Applied to the Planning, Design and Management of Water, Resources Systems. Proceedings of the Hamburg Symposium of IAHS, August 1983,* 637–647. Hamburg: IAHSPubi, 1983.
Romsics, Ignác. *Hungary in the Twentieth century.* Budapest: Corvina-Osiris, 1999.

Rudolp, Karl-Ulrich, and Block, Thomas. *The German Water Sector, Policies and Experiences.* Bonn: Federal Ministry for the Environment, Nature Conservation and Nuclear Safety, 2001.

Sándor, Péter. "New Directions in Environmental Management in Hungary." In *Environmental Action in Eastern Europe. Responses to Crisis,* edited by Barbara Jancar-Webster. XXX. London: Amonk, 1993.

Schreurs, A. Miranda. *Environmental Politics in Japan, Germany, and the United States,* Cambridge: Cambridge University Press, 2003.

Shapiro, Judith. *Mao's War Against Nature: Politics and the Environment in Revolutionary China.* Cambridge: Cambridge University Press, 2001.

Sheail, John. *An Environmental history of twentieth-century Britain.* Basingstroke: Palgrave, 2002.

Singleton, Fred, ed. *Environmental Misuse in the Soviet Union.* Westport: Praeger Publishers, 1976.

Snajdr, Edward. *Nature Protests: The End of Ecology in Slovakia.*Seattle: Washington University Press, 2008, 22–48.

Stark, Tamás, *Magyarország második világháborús emberveszteségе (Hungary"s losses of human lives during World War II).* Budapest: MTA Történettudományi Intézete, 1989.

Szitkey, László. "Szennyízcsatornázásunk helyzete 1958. év végén (National Waste Water Drainage at the End of 1958)." *Vízügyi Közlemények* 41, No.3 (1959):XXX.

Tájékoztatás az iparág és a tagvállalatok környezetvédelméről (Information about the Environmental Protection of the [Chemical] Industry and its Member Companies). Budapest: Magyar Vegyipari Egyesülés: Budapest, 1978.

Teichova, Alice. "Industry." In: *The Economic History of Eastern Europe, 1919–1975. Vol. 1. Economic Structure and Performance between the Two Wars,* edited by Michael C. Kaser and Edward.A. Radice, 222–323. Oxford: Clarendon Press, 1985.

Thorsheim, Peter. *Inventing Pollution. Coal, Smoke, and Culture in Britain since 1800.* Athens: Ohio University Press, 2006.

Tipton, B Frank, and Aldrich, Robert, *An Economic and Social History of Europe, 1890–1939.* Basingstroke-London: Macmillan, 1987.

Tomka, Béla, *A magyarországi pénzintézetek rövid története (A Short History of Financial Institutions in Hungary) 1836–1947.* Budapest: Aula, 2000.

Tomlinson, R. Brian, "The British Economy and the Empire, 1900–1939." In *A Companion to Early Twentieth Century Britain,* edited by Chris Wrigley, 198–211. Oxford: Blackwell Publishing, 2003.

Tóth, Péter. *A Borsod szénbányászat a kapitalizmus korában, 1849–1945 (The History of Borsod Coal Mines in the Capitalist Era, 1849–1945)*. Miskolc: Borsod Szénbányák; (Szolnok) Nagyalföldi Kőolaj- és Földgáztermelő Vállalat, 1986.

Turnbull, Mildred. *Soviet Environmental Policies and Practices*. Sadbury: Dartmouth, 1991.

Uekötter, Frank. "Polycentrism in Full Swing, Air Pollution Control in Nazi Germany." In: *How Green were the Nazis?, Nature, Environment and Nation in the Third Reich*, edited by Franz-Joseph Brüggemeier, Mark Cioc, and Thomas Zeller, 101–128. Athens: Ohio University Press, 2005.

Uekötter, Frank. *Naturschutz im Aufbruch: eine Geschichte des Naturschutzes in Nordrhein-Westfalen 1945–1980*. Frankfurt-New York: Campus, 2004.

Uekötter, Frank. *The Age of Smoke, Environmental Policy in Germany and the United States, 1880–1970*. Pittsburgh: University of Pittsburgh Press, 2009.

Ungváry, Krisztián, *Budapest ostroma (The Siege of Budapest)*. Corvina: Budapest: Corvina, 2005.

Vincze Oszkár, "Miskolc Vízellátása." *Borsod Szemle* 12, No 3. (1968): 97–99.

Vincze, Oszkár. "A miskolci vízmű (Miskolc Waterworks)." *Vízgazdálkodás* 5, No. 5 (1965): 140–144.

Vörös, Károly. "Magyarország Gazdasági Központja (An Economic Center of Hungary)." In *Budapest története a Márciusi Forradalomtól az Őszirózsás Forradalomig (A History of Budapest from the Revolution of March (1848) to the Revolution of Roses (1918))*, edited by Károly Vörös, 325–377. Budapest: Akadémiai Kiadó, 1978.

Webb, Adrian, *The Longman Companion to Germany since 1945*, London-New York: Longman, 1998.

Weiner, Douglas R. *A Little Corner of Freedom: Russian Nature Protection from Stalin to Gorbachev*: University of California Press: Berkeley and London, 1999.

White, Richard. *The Organic Machine*. New York: Hill and Wang, 1995.

Wrigley, Chris. "The Impact of the World War I." In *A Companion to Early Twentieth Century Britain,* edited by Chris Wrigley, 502–516. Oxford: Blackwell Publishing, 2003.

Yin, K. Robert. *Case Study Research, Design and* Methods. Thousand Oaks-London-New Delhi: Sage Publications, 2002.

Young, John, and Kent, John, *International Relations Since 1945. A Global History*. Oxford University Press, 2004.

ZumBrunnen, Craig. "Water Pollution in the Black and Azov Seas." In *Environmental Misuse in the Soviet Union*, edited by Fred Singleton, 33–59. Westport: Praeger Publishers, 1976.

Websites

Agency for Toxic Substances and Disease Registry's Website. http://www.atsdr.cdc.gov/substances/toxsubstance.asp?toxid=27, (accessed July on 14, 2013).

Átlátszó.hu, (accessed on July 31, 2017).

Cornell University Law School, Legal Information Institute website.http://www.law.cornell.edu/cfr/text/40/401.15 *(accessed on June 19, 2013)*.

Építészfórum.hu, (accessed on July 31, 2017).

Északmagyarországi Regionális Vízművek Rt. Company Website. http://www.ervrt.hu/cgi-bin/index.php?hlid=10, (accessed on August 20, 2013).

Fázold, Ádám. "Környezetvédelem alakulása Borsod megyében különös tekintettel a vízminőségvédelemre (The history of Environmental Protection in Borsod County with special notice on water quality control)," *Proceedings of the XXIXth Annual Conference of the Hungarian Hydrology Association, Eger 2011*. http://www.hidrologia.hu/vandorgyules/29/dolgozatok/fazold_adam.html, (accessed on August 20, 2013).

Fővárosi Blog (Capital City Blog). http://www.fovarosi.blog.hu, (accessed on July 31, 2017).

Gerencsér, Árpád. "A magyar vízgazdálkodás fejlődése 1945 és 1990 között (The Development of Water Management in Hungary between 1945 and 1990)." *A Magyar Hidrológiai Társaság XXX. Vándorgyűlésének dolgozatai (Proceedings of the 30th Annual Conference of the Hungarian Society for Hydrology 2012)*. http://www.hidrologia.hu/vandorgyules/30/dolgozatok/dolgozatok.html, *(accessed on August 20, 2013)*.

Index.hu, (accessed on July 31, 2017).

Kielder Hydro Site website at RWE website. http://www.rwe.com/web/cms/en/312572/rwe-innogy/sites/hydroelectric-power-station/united-kingdom/sites-in-operation/kielder/, *(Accessed July 8, 2013)*.

Manfred Pütz, "Monitoring Industrial Emissions: A successful instrument for environmental enforcement," *Third International Conference on Environmental Enforcement: Proceedings Volume 1, 1994 Oaxaca, Mexico at the National Service Center for Environmental Publications (NSCEP) Website* http://nepis.epa.gov/Exe/ZyNET.exe/300R94002.HTM?ZyActionD=ZyD

ocument&Client=EPA&Index=1995%20Thru%201999%7C1976%20 Thru%201980%7C2006%20Thru%202010%7C1991%20 Thru%201994%7CHardcopy%20Publications%7C2000%20 Thru%202005%7C1986%20Thru%201990%7C2011%20 Thru%202015%7C1981%20Thru%201985%7CPrior%20to%20 1976&Docs=&Query=Oaxaca%20&Time=&EndTime=&SearchMethod=2&TocRestrict=n&Toc=&TocEntry=&QField=&QFieldYear=&QFieldMonth=&QFieldDay=&UseQField=&IntQFieldOp=0&ExtQFieldOp=0&XmlQuery=&File=D%3A%5CZYFILES%5CINDEX%20 DATA%5CNSCEP%5CELECTRONIC%5C00000002%5C300R94002. HTM&User=ANONYMOUS&Password=anonymous&SortMethod=-%7Ch&MaximumDocuments=15&FuzzyDegree=0&ImageQuality=r85g16/r85g16/x150y150g16/i500&Display=hpfr&DefSeekPage=x&SearchBack=ZyActionL&Back=ZyActionS&BackDesc=Results%20page&MaximumPages=1&ZyEntry=1&SeekPage=x, (accessed July 22, 2014).

Office of Waste Water Management, Environmental Protection Agency (EPA) Website. http://www.epa.gov/npdes/pubs/101pape.pdf, (accessed on June 16, 2013).

Rába Company Website. http://www.raba.hu/cegtortenet.html, (accessed on September 18, 2013).

Rába-Steiger 250. http://trakesz.gportal.hu/gindex.php?pg=11460994&PHPSESSID=41daa3408ba705c71ff1bdea625fd98d, *(accessed on September 18, 2013).*

United Nations, Report of the World Commission on Environment and Development: Our Common Future. http://www.un-documents.net/our-common-future.pdf, (accessed May 21, 2014).

Broadcasts

"180 Perc (The 180 Minute Show)," *Kossuth Rádió*, May 8, 1980.

"A BVK környezetvédelmi helyzetéről (About BVK and its Environmental Protection Situation)," *Borsod Rádió*, October 30, 1975.

253/1997. (XII. 20.) Governmental Order.

Index

V. Pál, *Technology and the Environment in State-Socialist Hungary*,
DOI 10.1007/978-3-319-63832-4

D

E